Embodied Idolatry

Embodied Idolatry

A Critique of Christian Nationalism

Kyle Edward Haden

LEXINGTON BOOKS
Lanham • Boulder • New York • London

Published by Lexington Books
An imprint of The Rowman & Littlefield Publishing Group, Inc.
4501 Forbes Boulevard, Suite 200, Lanham, Maryland 20706
www.rowman.com

6 Tinworth Street, London SE11 5AL

Copyright © 2020 by The Rowman & Littlefield Publishing Group, Inc.

All rights reserved. No part of this book may be reproduced in any form or by any electronic or mechanical means, including information storage and retrieval systems, without written permission from the publisher, except by a reviewer who may quote passages in a review.

British Library Cataloguing in Publication Information Available

Library of Congress Control Number: 2019956985

ISBN: 978-1-7936-1109-3 (cloth : alk. paper)
ISBN: 978-1-7936-1110-9 (electronic)
ISBN: 978-1-7936-1111-6 (pbk. : alk. paper)

For Krijn Pansters.

Friendship is more precious than gold.

Contents

Acknowledgments ix
Introduction 1

1 Embodied Habitus 11
2 Emotions, Feelings, and Desires 31
3 Identity Needs and Mimetic Desire 53
4 Ideology, Beliefs, and Social/Group Influence 73
5 Jesus' Summons to Hospitality and Table Fellowship 93
6 Nationalism as Idolatry 117

Conclusion: Healing Our Embodied Idolatry 139
Bibliography 153
Index 159
About the Author 163

Acknowledgments

I want to express my deepest gratitude to Fr. James Alison who offered needed encouragement and suggestions. His own works have been deeply inspirational to me for several years. I want to offer a big thanks to my friend Dr. Krijn Pansters who read through various incarnations of this text, offering insights and encouragement. I want to thank Br. Robert Lentz, OFM, for editing the text, saving me from much grammatical embarrassment. Any mistakes are my own. Thanks to Michael Gibson, editor at Lexington Books for giving my project a chance, and to Mikayla Mislak for her editorial assistance.

Introduction

"*Who do you think you are?*" How does one respond to such a question? Well, it depends on the context in which it is asked. When you just read that line did you automatically recall an occasion when you were in a conflict with someone and they angrily asked you this? Do you recall your initial response? No, not your verbal rejoinder, but your initial physical response. Did it cause you to *feel* defensive, angry, nervous, anxious, or . . .? What if the question was asked in the context of a psychology class? Now, instead of the question being delivered in a confrontational manner, your response may be one of reflection, causing you to ponder who you are as a human being. What is it that makes you—you? In this context you might now be experiencing feelings that give rise to thoughts of wonder or confusion. Despite the context surrounding the question, feelings arise giving shape to both thought, as well as strategies for action. In the first case, where you are being angrily confronted, your emotions may give rise to thoughts on how best to respond—angrily, apologetically, and so on. In the second case your feelings may lead you to begin thinking about the various aspects of what it means to be human. Because you want to be able to have some grasp on who you really are, you might be motivated to seek answers from sources like books, articles, friends (in conversation), and so forth. In both cases, you were motivated to act due to the feelings arising from the question and its context.

Emotions play a profound role in the formation of thoughts. For example, anger can tend to form thoughts about an individual which tend toward the negative. As one comes to settle on thoughts about a person, one begins to strategize behavior accordingly. This may take the form of avoidance, gossip (denigrating the person behind their back), or acts of vengeance. Being angry at someone is fairly common, and we all react in some fashion within a set of standard reactions. But when it comes to how we decide to respond to our feelings we tend to make our choices from both conscious and unconscious sources. And how unconscious sources affect our choice of response can be complex and a bit mysterious, because we simply aren't fully cognizant of the influences present underneath conscious awareness. They just seem naturally a part of the feelings informing our responses.

Now, what if the original question was asked in the context of a theology course, or a Bible study? A professor, teaching a course on Christian theology, after discussing St. Paul's metaphors concerning the identity of Jesus followers, wants you to express who, as a Christian, you think you are. In all three contexts—confrontational, psychological, and now theological—we are dealing with issues of identity. Who am I? How do I identify myself? What affect does my sense of identity have on my way of being in the world? And, in the context of Christian identity, first, what does it mean to identify as a Christian, and second, how does this inform my actions and reactions in the world? A possible initial reaction may be to turn to the sources informing Christian identity, that is, the Bible, Church teaching, liturgy, and so on. All well and good. But there are a number of things that complicate our attempt to answer the question of Christian identity.

We each live amongst a variety of cultural and social forces impressing themselves upon our lives, informing and shaping our values, convictions, principles, emotions, beliefs, and thoughts. While our conscious mind gives us a similitude of inner unity, that is, a center point from which we navigate the many currents of culture we swim in, the reality is that many of these currents are contradictory, and even antithetical to each other. And yet, somehow, we balance these contradictions. But in most cases, we do this unconsciously, being unaware of the contradictions. This in turn gives rise to living lives of dissonance. Our identities become an amalgam of worldviews, ideologies shaping our interpretations about the nature of reality. In much of our conscious lives we don't recognize that among these competing ideologies lie conflicting values.

Embodied Idolatry: A Critique of Christian Nationalism is an attempt to do a couple of things regarding the question 'who do you think you are'. First, I am concerned with attempting to give a coherent response to what informs a Christian identity. As any identity must be examined contextually, that is, in its social and cultural locale, this work is focused specifically on American (USA) Christians. Thus, one must be able to recognize the differentiation between those specifically Christian elements informing a sense of self and the myriad social and cultural elements that are antithetical to a Christian identity. Because we are embodied social creatures, where we live, both in time and space, profoundly informs how we shape our sense of identity, a sense of self. Being a citizen of the United States, and a professed Christian, I have come to recognize a dissonance between my understanding of the gospel and aspects of American Christian practice; specifically, the assimilation by many American (specifically the United States) Christians of the ideology of nationalism.[1] So, along with attempting to give a response to the question of Christian identity, I will attempt to explicate the complex formation of identity.

In this study I draw from several disciplines; sociology, social psychology, neuropsychology, philosophy, anthropology, theology, and spirituality. Using multiple disciplines is not an easy thing. It requires a working knowledge of several disciplines. In some cases, the author will have a better facility with some disciplines than others. In my case, my background is in the disciplines of history and theology. Thus, in my explication of those disciplines that I have a working knowledge, but not expertise, I have relied upon many experts in the various disciplines. I have chosen to make this a multidisciplinary study because of the complex reality that is the human person. No one discipline can capture the complexity that is the human person. In fact, I have had to neglect a number of disciplines because, first, I simply do not have the intellectual capacity for those disciplines, and second, even if I did have the capacity, to add them into the mix would make this a multivolume work that would take a lifetime to write. It is important to note that due to my use of these many disciplines, I realize that for some readers I have either attempted to do too much or too little. While I accept that one or both may be the case, my hope is that I will inspire other scholars to fill out my deficiencies. If I inspire just a few to pursue such an endeavor I believe I will have accomplished something useful.

The primary argument that I make in this book is this; *many US American Christians have assimilated into their identity ideologies that are antithetical to the teachings of Jesus the Christ. I maintain that appropriating identities that contravene, what I believe is a (as best as I can discern from my examination of the gospels) true Christian identity ultimately leads to idolatry.* I focus on the United States because of its unique history, a history that blends nationalist ideology with racial and religious issues. Many Christian nationalists tend toward attitudes of White supremacy, whether explicitly or implicitly.

Because many Christians are typically unaware of the dissonance of competing identities, I utilize a variety of theories that I believe help to shed light on the complex formation of self-identity. I see two in particular, one sociological, the other anthropological, as helpful and complimentary. From the discipline of sociology, I draw from the French sociologist Pierre Bourdieu, specifically his theory of *habitus*. I discuss his theory in chapter one. From the field of anthropology, I use the theory of mimetic desire as explicated by the French American writer René Girard, which I discuss in chapter three. My intuition that each theory complements the other is based on the recognition that Bourdieu offers, in my opinion, an excellent analysis of the role society and culture play in the formation of one's *habitus*, that is, one's total sense of self, both one's inner sense of self-identity (how society and culture is embodied and shapes a total vision of life), as well as one's practice, or way of presenting oneself in one's social landscape. Where Girard compliments Bourdieu is with regard to the mechanisms by which society and culture are transferred and replicated in the individual. Because of the nature of humanity identities are formed through the structures of social relations. We have, I maintain, *identity needs* as social creatures. This in turn affects the nature of human desire. Girard's theory helps to explain how individuals go about fulfilling these identity needs. Along with my examination of these two theories, I examine the profound affect that being an embodied creature has on the formation of identity as it relates to motivations and actions. That is, how one's identity shapes one's actions and reactions toward others informing attitudes of inclusion and exclusion.

As noted above, emotions and feelings give rise to and inform one's thinking, that is, emotions and feelings inform thoughts, concepts, and beliefs. I examine this dynamic in chapter two. I examine the nature of emotions, moods, feelings, desires, and beliefs, and how each inform thoughts, concepts, ideologies, and actions. Because we are social creatures, we are profoundly influenced by society and culture in the formation not only of our desires and emotions, but the means by which we make sense of the world as well. Interpretations about the nature of life and society gives form to a variety of ideologies, that is, concepts about the nature of reality. These various ideologies in turn are sedimented into the emotional structures of our embodied consciousness. Because we all maintain ideologies informing our worldviews, chapter four examines the nature of ideology, as well as the influence that social groups have on the reinforcement of ideologies in individual consciousness. Because ideologies play a significant role in helping to articulate and shape identity, I maintain that many ideologies, from a Christian theological perspective, are by nature idolatrous. Nationalism is one such ideology.

A Christian identity is necessarily informed by the Christian tradition, first and foremost as found in the Scriptures. In chapter five I focus on, and give priority to, the life, teachings, actions, and emotions of Jesus as found in the Gospels. My methodology is to examine not merely the events in Jesus' life as they are narrated in the gospels, but to highlight the intentions, motivations, and the emotions that informed Jesus' words and actions within the cultural, social, economic, political, and religious context in which he lived. My endeavor is to examine Jesus' own habitus. Since Christians profess Jesus Christ as the concrete and definitive manifestation of the will of God in human flesh, it is imperative for Christians to examine the true nature of the divine habitus in human form. In imitating Christ, one's own habitus is formed and transformed by the one who came to do the Father's will. As my primary interlocutors in this study are professed Christians, I am not particularly concerned with the intricacies of theological differences that have shaped distinctions in ortho*dox* hermeneutics among the different branches of the Christian family. I am much more concerned with Christian praxis; thus, I focus on how the life, teachings, and intentions of Jesus challenge Christian ortho*praxis*. By focusing on the historical Jesus' praxis, I have left aside other texts from the New Testament that do not focus on the narrative of Jesus' actions. Instead, I concentrate solely on the gospels—the synoptic gospels specifically.

In chapter six I examine the ideology of nationalism. While the field of study on this topic is broad, with a plethora of scholarly books and articles on the topic, my primary focus is to examine nationalism as it relates to identity formation. I argue that nationalism is at its core antithetical to the teachings of Christ, forming identities that put one's loyalty and commitment toward the nation at odds with one's Christian commitments. As a source for fulfilling identity needs, as discussed in chapter three, I argue that the ideology of nationalism is by its nature idolatrous.

The majority of this book is descriptive, examining and describing social, cultural, psychological, and ideological influences in the formation of one's identity, as well as some of the mechanisms by which one's identity is formed. In the conclusion, my focus will be both descriptive as well as prescriptive. While many studies have been fruitful in illuminating the threat of idolatrous ideologies to Christian practice, the prescriptive means of dealing with deeply embodied beliefs, informing and forming emotions that give a sense of veracity to ideological idolatrous constructs, tends to be relegated to works on spirituality, or spiritual psychology. This book is a critique of idolatrous ideologies, in this case nationalism. Thus, I feel it necessary to offer a possible schema by which the Christian is able to seek transformation from embodied dispositions that have taken root in the emotional structures of one's consciousness, leading to beliefs and practices that I maintain are idolatrous. In this effort I will rely upon the works of the late Benedictine theologian, Dom Sebastian Moore, and the Trappist Benedictine monk Thomas Keating, OCSO. Both Moore's and Keating's works have the advantage of being a wonderful synthesis of traditional Christian spiritual thought and practice and contemporary psychological studies.

The use of the term idolatry in the title is provocative and meant to be so. My use of the term is informed by my understanding of the nature of the divine. Christians proclaim belief in one God in three persons, Father, Son, and Holy Spirit. Most Christians would grimace at and dispute any accusation of idolatry, because they do not have "other" gods in their explicit belief system for whom they knowingly give worship and professed allegiance. My understanding of the divine consists of the following. God is Creator of all that is, and all that is not God is dependent for its existence on God. As David Bentley Hart states, "all things that exist receive their being continuously from him, who is the infinite wellspring of all that is, in whom . . . all things live and move and have their being." It is God "whose creative act is an eternal gift of being to the whole of space and time, sustaining all things in existence in every moment."[2] God created all things in the light of God's love, that is, God loves God's creation, and desires for creation to flourish. God is concerned about creation, thus is involved with creation. While God transcends creation, God is also immanent in creation. God has desired each of us into being. Yet, in coming to full self-consciousness without an immediate experience of God's loving presence, we experience a sense of separation from God and others. This forms within us a quest for fullness. We experience a restlessness, agitated by a sense of lack. In Augustine's terms, our restlessness, our sense of lack, incompleteness, and search for fullness and happiness can only finally be found in the fullness of God's infinite love. This is because our heart's desire for fullness is boundless and can never be satisfied by limited goods. Because we have been created in the image of God, the *imago Dei*, our nature reflects the nature of the divine. To understand human nature, one must have some insight into the nature of the divine. As Richard Lints puts it, "[a]s a divine being who writes and speaks, this same God constitutes his creation in such a fashion that his categories of understanding are built into that creation. Put succinctly, we are the way we are because God is the way he is," but at the same time "we are the way we are because we are not God." [3]

Because God is love, and love requires relationality—love needs to have someone or something to share itself with—we humans, participating in the nature of God as an *imago Dei*, are by nature relational, and our happiness is dependent upon loving relationships. At the same time, because of our creatureliness we are limited, finite creatures who cannot self-create the means for our fullness and happiness. Putting these dynamics together, our boundless need for infinite love along with the limitations of human knowledge, as well as our tendency toward distorted and misguided desires, there develops a natural tendency to look for the satisfaction of an infinite need in finite objects. Because an infinite need can never be fully satisfied by the finite, there arises a sense of alienation and isolation from reality—from the whole. This in turn compels us to seek connection through the finite offerings given to us in our social and cultural landscapes. But many of these offerings themselves arise from the human experience of alienation and isolation. Thus, the perpetuation of limited goods acting in the place of the infinite intensifies our frustrations over our experience of lack. By recognizing our lack, we are able to admit that the finite objects sought to attain fullness and happiness are limited. Blindness to our misdirected search for fullness and happiness easily lends itself to an attempted acquisition of power and control in order to obtain and secure the finite and limited objects of desire. These objects become the perceived ends for the attainment of one's longing, restless pursuit for fullness and happiness. As ends, they become sacred. These objects are then elevated to the status of gods, whose obeyance and devotion requires the supplicant to be formed in the divine image—in this case, a divinity fashioned in the image of its devotee. These small gods tend toward exclusive membership. Only a certain elect can join. Unlike the one true God, whose all-embracing love knows no exclusion, the jealousy of these false gods results in suspicion and exclusion. The jealousy of the one true God is not comparable to these false gods. It is not the result of a desire for exclusivity or a matter of divine narcissism. Rather, it is grounded in a love so deep that, like any lover, God desires the beloved to share in the infinite love that the beloved truly desires and seeks. The divine lover is distraught over the suffering of the beloved who has lost his/her way. God finds each human being desirable, bringing each into existence from this desire. Due to the fact that this truth is not experienced in the process of coming to self-consciousness, the beloved is misguided and led to fulfill the craving for the experience of desirability by serpentine promises that ultimately lead to alienation and isolation. This is the very opposite of the beloved's true eschatological *telos*.

The idols by which one's fullness and happiness is sought not only lead to frustration, alienation and isolation; attachment to these idols has dire consequences for human society and the natural world. Lurking behind all wars, human violence, attitudes and practices of exclusion, and the myriad crimes humans perpetrate on each other, lie the many idols shaping visions of fullness and happiness. Idols destroy the inner world as well as the outer. They must be called out for what they are. Christians must recognize these idols and rid themselves of their devotion to these illusions.

What I attempt in this book is to examine human nature from a variety of angles, using a variety of academic disciplines. I am interested in what makes us tick, what shapes our motivations, what makes us, us. It is an attempt to understand how we form our identity, and how our sense of self informs our Christian practice. I attempt to offer Christians tools in order to gain a greater sense of self-knowledge, which hopefully will compel a desire for a deeper conformity to the image of God in Christ.

What I do not do in this book is offer a political philosophy or theology. While I do believe Christians should be involved in the political processes of the state, I am more interested in examining the motivations behind political practice. I am of the conviction that our true loyalty lies with the kingdom of God, or, in Augustine's phrase, the city of God. This does not mean that I am advocating a form of quietism, a call to separate oneself from the world, as some fundamentalists do. I am actually calling for a much more vigorous engagement with the world, and the political process. But I believe that undergirding every Christian's political motivations must be the will of God as manifested in the life and teachings of Jesus. This requires deep self-reflection on the part of Christians as to the motivating influences in his or her political objectives. I believe as members of the body of Christ we have been commissioned to be a leaven of Christ's peace, healing, and reconciliation in the world. As Church, we must confront our own complicity in practices that have done harm to this mission.

For Christians, the Church is not an institution of human construction. While the structures and polity of the various denominations are matters of human conceptions, constructs, and history, the ontological nature of the Church is grounded in its relationship with the triune God, who bonds the members of the ecclesia through the power and indwelling of the Holy Spirit, received in baptism, and nourished by the Eucharist, the body and blood of Christ. As the body of Christ, the Church participates in the saving work of Christ in the world. Vatican II's document on the Church, *Lumen Gentium*, describes the Church in the following way:

> The mystery of the holy Church is manifest in its very foundation. The Lord Jesus set it on its course by preaching the Good News, that is, the coming of the Kingdom of God, which, for centuries, had been promised in the Scriptures: "The time is fulfilled, and the kingdom of God is at hand." In the word, in the works, and in the presence of Christ, this kingdom was clearly open to the view of men. (LG 1: 5)[4]

The Church's mission is to proclaim the Kingdom of God, as taught and lived by Jesus in his historical reality. The proclamation of the Kingdom is both a call for personal transformation as well as a call to proclaim and witness to the good news within history, to bring about a transformation of structures that have given rise to systems of injustice, violence, greed, and domination. The Church is a sacrament of God's mercy, compassion, forgiveness, and nonviolence. It is a beacon of God's hospitality and inclusion, especially for those who have been marginalized due to the use of power as domination and exclusion. The Christian's overarching loyalties, his/her dominant identity, is to be found and formed in Christ, leading to a profound imitation of and conformity to Christ. Kenan Osborne writes,

> The fundamental relationship of the church's very nature is its relationship to Jesus and through Jesus to God. A renewed theology of church must begin with these two fundamental relationships: namely, a relationship to the human Jesus and a relationship to the presence of God in the human Jesus.... With this centrality on Jesus ... the community called church is to reflect Jesus if the community truly wants to be church. Spiritually, it is our centering on Jesus that makes us truly Christian.[5]

Any other dominant loyalty or sense of identity, grounded in a temporality pursued as one's end, is idolatrous. Temporal ends are dead ends. Ideologies that inform loyalties and identities that contravene and contradict the teachings of Jesus are such dead ends. One such ideology is nationalism. I maintain that Christian nationalism, and prevalent in American (USA) society, White Christian nationalism, is an oxymoron that has become a motivating influence for many Christians, in attitudes and actions, especially in the denigration and marginalization of those deemed "other."

A word about who I intend by the designation "Christian." I preface this by noting my own denominational affiliation. My earliest formation in the Christian tradition was in a variety of Christian communions. Baptized in the American Baptist church, I was later confirmed in the United Methodist church. Before formally entering into communion with the Roman Catholic church, I attended for some years various charismatic, nondenominational, churches. For the last three decades I have been a practicing Catholic, and an ordained priest, thus my worldview has been profoundly shaped by the Catholic tradition, which is reflected in this text. Nevertheless, I have in mind in this book all the varieties of US Christians who claim Jesus as their Lord. It has been my experience in teaching theology, as well as pastoring various parishes in different parts of the United States, that most US Christians have little to no theological training or knowledge. Christian Smith has demonstrated this in his excellent sociological studies. Many Christians among the various denominations would find it difficult to explain the theological differences between the different traditions. A type of generic set of Christian beliefs can be found among many congregants in both Protestant and Catholic churches. Thus, I intend by the use of the term "Christian," members of all the various Christian denominations. Knowing that the predominant readers of this text will be academics and possibly educated clergy, my hope is that this study can offer tools from the various disciplines I utilize in this text for engaging students or interested congregants and parishioners.

NOTES

1. While this study can be applied to numerous ideologies conflicting with Christian teaching, I have chosen nationalism because of its ubiquitous and destructive presence in the modern world. I have also chosen to focus on nationalism because at the time of this writing it has become an important issue in American culture, causing a destructive divisiveness, not only among Americans in general, but also among American Christians.
2. David Bentley Hart, *The Experience of God: Being, Consciousness, Bliss* (New Haven: Yale University Press, 2013), 30, 36.
3. Richard Lints, *Identity and Idolatry: The Image of God and Its inversion* (Downers Grove: InterVarsity Press, 2015), 21.
4. http://www.vatican.va/archive/hist_councils/ii_vatican_council/documents/vat-ii_const_19641121_lumen-gentium_en.html (Accessed 5–10–2019).
5. Kenan Osborne, OFM, *A Theology of the Church for the Third Millennium* (Leiden: Brill, 2009), 383, 393.

Chapter One

Embodied Habitus

Imagine you're watching TV and on comes a program about religion. It turns out to be a debate between an atheist and a Christian. You are a Christian so naturally you are siding with the Christian apologist. The problem is, you don't have a great deal of background in theology, philosophy, or science, so some of the arguments go over your head. At times it seems that the atheist is making seemingly logical points, and you feel yourself getting a bit agitated, and you want the Christian to come back with plausible rejoinders. Then, the atheist makes a nasty statement about the Virgin Mary, that she had an extramarital affair and then lied in order not to receive punishment from her community or lose her betrothal to Joseph. Now you're just plain mad. Your heart rate rises, you can feel your blood pressure go up. Your mind begins to produce some rather uncharitable thoughts about the atheist. Your body is responding to the clash between your beliefs and opposing beliefs in a powerful way. While you will be aware of aspects of your emotional state, your focus will be drawn to your thoughts, not recognizing the impact that your bodily emotional state has on the formation of these thoughts. This is not the first time that you have reacted when someone said something that threatened your cherished beliefs. You have, probably without realizing it, formed dispositions around your worldviews that influence how your body manifests its inner psychological states. If you think about it, you will notice that there is an intimate relationship between your mental states and your emotional, feeling states. This is because of the fact that you are an embodied creature.

EMBODIMENT

What it means to be embodied has been an issue in philosophy and theology from time immemorial. What this has meant to various thinkers has changed according to philosophical and theological perspectives and hypotheses, and in contemporary times, sociological and psychological theories. But there is a seemingly natural tendency among everyday experiences to sense a dichotomy, a separate existence between our bodies and our mental faculties. Of course, we recognize the impact of the body on our cognitive functions, but we often fail to see the profound role the body plays in the formation and sustaining of our affective actions and reactions in our social interactions. For example, as I write this, I am aware of my embodied reality because my back is a little sore. When I feel this and other bodily pains, my consciousness becomes attentive to the feelings of discomfort. My bodily pain presses upon my consciousness. I focus on the discomfort, and I have various thoughts appresented with this physical awareness. My consciousness is not merely responding to a bodily discomfort, as though that is all that is operating. It is also triggering a complexity of unconscious items constructed in my mind giving rise to emotions that are informed by a lifetime of experience. As Peter Berger and Thomas Luckmann state, "[o]nly a small part of the totality of human experience is retained in consciousness. The experiences that are so retained become sedimented, that is, they congeal in recollection as recognizable and memorable entities."[1] So then, while there is actual physical distress, the discomfort brings to the surface of my mind various thoughts that have structured my outlook toward the world. From the simple wish that my back didn't hurt arises the thought that I am getting old. While this may seem rather mundane, within the context of my social and cultural space it takes on a much more intricate and complex meaning. For example, while *feeling* old because of my bodily pains, the *idea* around "being old" is fraught with judgments of identity. Sitting in the university library where I work, I can see out of the corner of my eyes young people walking across campus. Comparatively speaking I am old, *in their eyes*. Behind this comparative judgment lies an unconscious—present moment excepted—cultural force, influence, belief, and/or philosophy that youth is a good and better state than being old, whether that means middle-age or ready for the nursing home. This belief is found prominently in media and commercial forms. We in the West are a youth-oriented culture. It's sexy, desirable to be young. We exercise and color our hair to maintain at least the appearance of youth. (The hair on my head has yet to turn white, and I am accused of coloring it. I have and do not!). If I have allowed myself to buy into this cultural belief, then I may begin to feel nostalgia for my youth, or begin to resent their youth, or feel somewhat irrelevant, or feel a bit of shame around my middle-aged paunch. In other words, as an embodied creature I have engendered the multiple influences impressed upon me by my social and cultural landscape, thus making judgments about my identity, worth, and well-being. Now, not all of this will be clear in my conscious awareness. It will most likely manifest in feelings of discomfort, agitation, shame, anxiety, and so on. But I will most likely not put a great deal of reflection on the social and cultural influences that have informed the structures, or created the concepts, shaping my tacit beliefs. This formation, in many cases, happens through my acquiescence to the various cultural beliefs and practices I have been presented over time. It will probably just seem like a natural conclusion to me that youth is better and more desirable than middle or old age. *It feels true.* But is it?

From a small bodily pain arises a plethora of appresented thoughts and feelings. How I experience my back pain seems on the surface a simple reality. But in fact, my consciousness of said pain is, as stated above, supremely complexified by the uncountable cultural influences shaping it throughout my life. Much of this cultural influence is unconscious and unreflected upon. It simply is present like the air I am breathing and remains unacknowledged until someone or something draws my attention to it. And these unreflected ideas and beliefs have a *feeling* of truth about them. On numerous occasions I have said to myself things like "I wish I was young again," or "getting old sucks," and so forth. On the surface, these sentiments will be unremarkable. But they may in fact obfuscate an unconscious acceptance of hegemonic cultural beliefs that aging lacks value, in the sense in which many ancient cultures understood this. That is, age and experience are necessary to a deeper knowledge about the meaning and purpose of life, eventuating, hopefully, in wisdom. In an age of functionality, knowledge is pursued and valued by many for its technological and economic utility, while pursuit of wisdom seems to be a time-wasting search for useless transcendentals that have no market value. John Henry Newman noted and contested this perspective in the nineteenth century. He argued against academics who took the view of John Locke who considered study of the humanities a waste of time and resources. Locke made the argument that

> men of quality and parts should suffer themselves to be so far mislead by custom and implicit faith. Reason, if consulted with, would advise, that their children's time should be spent in acquiring what might be *useful* to them, when they come to be men, rather than that their heads should be stuffed with a deal of trash, a great apart whereof then usually never do ('tis certain they never need to) think on again as long as they live; and so much of it as does stick by then they are only the worse for.[2]

There were—and are, though becoming rarer—cultures in which some *old* people were/are honored, sometimes venerated, because they had attained admiration for their wisdom. This wisdom was pursued to understand better how to attain and live a good and virtuous life. There are books in the Hebrew Scriptures which praise such wisdom. So, does this mean that some of the "truth" that I have unconsciously assumed unreflectively, that youth has more value than old age, is, in fact, simply a modern cultural phenomenon, a contemporary ideology or belief having no meaningful substance? *But it feels true.* And this feeling of truth informs my self-identity.

When I was a child it was the practice of my family to attend weekly Church services. It was my father's practice to dress formally when going to Church, and my siblings and I were expected to wear our "Sunday best." To this day it is a rare occasion when my father dresses casually when attending Church. In my teens, in the 1970s, I was taken by my mother to a charismatic/Pentecostal Church. One of the first things I noticed, besides the very different way people worshipped, was the style of clothing being worn by the congregants. Jeans and T-shirts were prevalent, as well as long hair on many of the men. This struck me as a bit strange, and maybe even a bit disrespectful. In time I became acclimated to this style, but my initial visceral reaction of concern was the result of years of believing and practicing a different style of clothing within the confines of what I thought of as sacred space. I had developed emotional concepts informing my dispositions, shaping how I experienced and interpreted differences of styles and tastes.

While I came to embrace this different style, accepting the idea that maybe God doesn't care what one wears in Church, it was different when I experienced a very dissimilar, and for me, alien form of worship. Having been raised in various Protestant denominations, I was explicitly warned to beware of Catholics. The first time I had an experience of the Mass I was a pre-teen and found the service strange. In my teens I had been formed to believe that Protestantism had freed Christians from the idolatry of Catholicism and works righteousness. In high school I met and began dating a Catholic girl. I had concerns about her salvation, but my feelings for her overrode whatever prejudices I carried with me (lust may have played a part also). Nevertheless, I was quite uncomfortable when attending Mass with her. I even felt like it might be a sin to do so, a betrayal of my Protestant beliefs. While sitting in Mass, I found myself physically distressed. I had embodied the doctrinal and ideological misgivings and distrust of Catholicism instilled in me by years of anti-Catholic sermons. I even had a bit of fear when it came to Catholic priests. I believed them to be peddlers of a false religion. On one occasion during freshman year of college I nervously confronted the university Catholic chaplain, trying to convince him of his misguided religious beliefs. My disposition toward Catholicism, and most Catholics, was confrontational, grounded in what I now believe to be misunderstandings about what Catholicism teaches and professes. The social and cultural milieu in which I had grown up with had shaped my religious disposition. Even as I began to move toward the Catholic Church (a long story), I had to struggle against several negative reactions I found in myself. While I was convinced intellectually that Catholicism was a legitimate Church, my feelings and dispositions had to be reeducated and transformed.

Now imagine the countless ways each of us have been formed by the many different social and cultural forces shaping our feelings, especially with issues concerning cultural and social mores, conventions, and taboos. As a Caucasian, I have experienced, not realizing in many cases, the privileges that come with being White in American culture. My worldview and my emotional reactions to social space have disposed me to feel much safer than many of my African American, Latino/a, and Asian fellow citizens. When I hear the anxiety and anger voiced from members of these ethnic groups, I have to rely on empathy to feel their distress. It simply is not my experience. I have not embodied a sense of exclusion simply because of the pigmentation of my skin. I don't typically feel my skin color in most of my social encounters. I don't think twice about my security in situations that a black, Asian, or Latino/a might find dangerous, like being pulled over by a White cop. On the other hand, what if I have incorporated cultural beliefs claiming that Whiteness is superior? If I have taken this ideology for granted, having it reinforced by my social compatriots, my feelings and dispositions would match these beliefs. Very possibly, when confronted by the contrary belief that all people, regardless of ethnicity or race, are equal in dignity, as taught in most enlightened Christian social teachings, how will I deal with these apparent contradictory worldviews? It is especially difficult for many White Americans, including White Christians, to confront an ideology that is socially beneficial, as it offers the advantages and promises of cultural, economic, and symbolic capital/power. I discuss this in chapter six, in terms of the relationship between White Christian supremacy and American (USA) conceptions of nationalism.

The power of culture plays a significant role, not only in our conscious awareness, but even in our bodies, that is, our embodied dispositions. Our sedimented experiences shape our emotional responses, and through habitually acting and reacting in the same or similar fashion to similar types of experiences, form durable feelings and dispositions.

DUALISM

Dualism, the idea that the mind or spirit is superior to the body, while the body is somehow a hindrance to spiritual development, has played an influential role in Christian theology. Much of this was inherited through various philosophical schools of thought like Platonism and Stoicism. Modern theological and philosophical thinking has attempted to overcome this dualism. For example, the philosopher Maurice Merleau-Ponty, from a phenomenological approach, collapsed the body-mind divide arguing, the "body is a 'setting in relation to the world,' and consciousness is the body projecting itself into the world."[3] For Merleau-Ponty objects are not prior to perception;

rather, our perceptions end in objects. What he is getting at is that an individual's recognition of an object is the result of reflective thinking, which cannot take place prior to perception. "[O]n the level of perception we have no objects, we are simply in the world."[4] Perception does not begin with the object, it begins in the body—the body in the world:

> . . . consciousness projects itself into a physical world and has a body, as it projects itself into a cultural world and has its habits: because it cannot be consciousness without playing upon significances given either in the absolute past of nature or in its own personal past, and because any form of lived experience tends toward a certain generality whether that of our habits or that of our bodily functions. . . . It is as false to place ourselves in society as an object among other objects, as it is to place society within ourselves as an object of thought, and in both cases the mistake lies in treating the social as an object. We must return to the social with which we are in contact by the mere fact of existing, and which we carry about inseparably with us before any objectification.[5]

What constitutes cultural objects, for Merleau-Ponty, depends on intentionality. The determination that a large rock is an obstacle follows from the intention to surmount it. The act of climbing over the rock is determined by the physiological structure of one's body—for humans, upright with two legs and two hands. Cultural constructs and embodiment shape each other. Baseball, as an analogy, has the rule that umpires determine the strike zone, and whether a pitch is a strike or not is not determined until the umpire declares that it is one or the other. And while the determination of the umpire

> tells us about an act of bestowing cultural meaning . . . it presupposes something about the cultural fact that the pitches are already there *to be called*. It presupposes objectification of a particular space of the body between the knees and shoulder (the strike zone) in conjunction with a particular way of moving the arms from the shoulders (swinging the bat). It is the process of this objectification to which Merleau-Ponty draws our attention.[6]

The perceiving body takes into itself the objects of perception and through intentionality projects consciousness into the world. The structure of the perceiving body intricately informs the shape of the intentions. Thus, selfhood is an intricate and complex matrix and location of consciousness, fashioned by the natural design of the body.

HABITUS

Merleau-Ponty is interested in examining the process of perception of objects to objectification, emphasizing the "objective conditions of possibility of social life," that is, the *"opus operatum"* of social life. The French sociologist, Pierre Bourdieu, has the goal of analyzing the *"modus operandi* of social life." One of his means of doing this is through an explication of a person's or group's *habitus*. For Bourdieu, habitus is the "principle generating and unifying all practices."[7] Practices here means actions taken by an agent, the individual. Actions are the result of the coalescence and generation of "inseparably cognitive and evaluative structures" which organize and order an individual's worldviews "in accordance with the objective structures of a determinant state of the social life."[8] That is, the individual has been structured, or formed, by the many different social institutions he/she lives within. This is a formation of the whole person; emotions, feelings, ideas, and beliefs. Acting together, the emotional and cognitive form judgments. The formation of judgments includes feeling states. This is like our Christian friend at the beginning of the chapter. He *felt* anger over a contrary religious, or nonreligious, viewpoint. Habitus is the term for the whole of our feeling-cognitive constructs shaping our actions and reactions to, and judgments about, our social environments. Bourdieu writes that habitus is

> nothing other than the *socially informed body*, with its tastes and distastes, its compulsions and repulsions, with, in a word, all its *senses*, that is to say, not only the traditional five senses—which never escape the structuring action of social determinisms—but also the sense of necessity and the sense of duty, the sense of direction and the sense of the sacred, tactical sense and the sense of responsibility, business sense and the sense of propriety, the sense of humor and the sense of absurdity, moral sense and the sense of practicality, and so on. (emphasis in original) [9]

While the objective conditions of our experiences of culture influence our feelings and dispositions—I will speak more about dispositions below—they are not the only conditions of our cultural and social space that shape our embodied actions and reactions. James M. Ostrow notes that our "'objective conditions' are interpreted in so far as they have effect on the subjective material that is capable of showing itself in the observed situation—for instance, values, and, in sociology, systems of values, attitudes, displays of emotion, and, of course, purely physical behavior."[10] What is left out are those experiences that are not "directly visible to the observer, or, indeed, to the conscious subject." In other words, there are unconscious forces that, regardless of their hiddenness, give context to those objects that are observable. The idea that our attitudes, values, beliefs, and so on, are "either logically constructed by a recurring kind of a valuation of conditions, or that they are somehow magically 'internalized' beforehand in the same forms in which they find expression, is on both accounts to miss that human beings are rooted to the world in ways deeper than the appearances and expressions of situated experience."[11]

Culture offers us guidance for living in social space, both through the "objective conditions" we encounter, as well as the interpretive frameworks "underlying" the "realm of experience." These interpretations can be subtle, shaping more our emotions and intuitions than our cognitive conscious awareness. We must learn to navigate our unique social landscapes by imitating the already present givens within the social and cultural space in which we find ourselves. We unconsciously, in many cases, "embody a sense of objective reality which lodges us within it according to its temporal rhythms and spatial organization. Hence, when we reflect on things, we are conscious of what has already been given to us within the original world of sense."[12]

Because we are social creatures, we have a profound need of fitting in, being connected to others (see chapter three). The more we have a sense of connectedness to significant others, be they individuals or groups, the deeper is our sense of well-being. In fact, social bonding is an imperative for human development, necessary for biological, psychological, and spiritual well-being. We have evolved as social creatures, which challenges prevailing Western beliefs in autonomous individualism, so prevalent in American culture.[13] Because we have a natural desire for a sense of well-being, we tend to acclimate ourselves to the cultural matrix which influences our actions and reactions to the world. We embody much of this cultural matrix, creating a naturalness to our feelings about our visions and concepts about the nature and meaning of life. The way the world is experienced by us, shaping a sense of familiarity, "by which we are predisposed to certain ways of perception and conduct," is profoundly influenced by the pregivens in our cultural milieu. When "we take thought" of something it is of something that is "already self-evident for us." If this was not the case the result would be a constant state of chaos, and we would be continually disoriented. It is because of the pregivens of culture, along with the facility of reflexivity, that we can have a sense of self beyond that of other animals. "It is by virtue of the fact that human beings figure into the world that it is possible for them to figure it out."[14]

Because of the need not to have to constantly relearn, in every moment, how to navigate our social and cultural landscape our brain, in its constant activity of predicting outcomes for the myriad stimuli received through the senses (see chapter two), habituate typical responses based on previous experiences. This knowledge through experience acts something like an internal GPS. We don't have to be cognizant of every minutia of cultural and social practice. It becomes bodily, that is, emotionally, attitudinally, and dispositionally habituated. It is this habituation that is both a saving grace, allowing us to attain greater knowledge without reinventing the wheel at every step, as well as a profound problem. The problem resides in the fact that we many times acclimate ourselves to social and cultural practices, concepts, and ideologies which are destructive to social harmony, to the common good, such as the acceptance of bigotries and prejudices that marginalize certain "others," those who do not fit within the defined margins of inclusion. These feelings that form dispositions of exclusion can *feel* natural.

Pierre Bourdieu's concept of *habitus* is not the easiest of theories to grasp by non-specialists in the field of sociology. In fact, the works of Bourdieu themselves can be rather daunting for both the neophyte and the expert. Kate Cregan notes this about Bourdieu's work, stating that aspects of it are "by and large, some of the most impenetrably written social theory of the late-twentieth century."[15] At the same time, once an individual gets hold of Bourdieu's thinking, one finds that his "theorisations also provide some of the most useful demystifying tools of the socio-political realm—with relevance not only across all academic disciplines but also in everyday life. Once comprehended, they are remarkably simple tools at that."[16] Among the array of Bourdieu scholarship, the concept of habitus has been interpreted from a variety of angles, for various purposes, be they issues concerning education, class, or economy. While much of this I found intriguing, my goal is to attempt to explain and utilize his theory of habitus as it relates to the main thesis in this book; that is, how many Christians in the West, and specifically the United States of America, have interpreted and embodied ideologies and dispositions that are contrary to the gospel teachings of Jesus and his preaching of the kingdom of God.

Cregan demonstrates, in my opinion, the usefulness of Bourdieu's theory for analyzing the social processes by which individuals, and for my purposes, Christians, embody cultural concepts and ideologies shaping feelings and dispositions. Cregan's take on habitus sees it as the engendering of the "social, cultural and physical environment that we as social beings inhabit." It is through our habitus that we both know ourselves and how others identify us. Habitus is "complex, detailed and interpenetrating." Habitus incorporates "all the kinds of social connections, achievements, attainments and attachments one acquires from birth," whether this comes about "by formal or informal means."[17] The entirety of our social life plays into the formation of our sense of *self*. In fact, there is no sense of self divorced from the interrelationships between us and our social landscape. How we perceive ourselves as well as others can only make sense when we investigate the myriad social influences shaping our hermeneutic mental and emotional lenses. Bourdieu, in his book *In Other Words*, writes that "constructing the notion of habitus functioning on the practical level as categories of perception and assessment or as classificatory principles as well as the organizing principles of action meant constituting the social agent in his (*sic*) true role as the practical operator of the construction of objects."[18] By this he means that in the formation/structuring of a habitus, each is a participant whose volition is intimately involved in the construction of concepts that form judgments about the world. This means that we are not necessarily slaves to social and cultural forces.

DISPOSITIONS

The structuring of habitus is the project by which the individual has "society written into the body, into the biological individual."[19] As an individual embodies social and cultural practice he or she develops embodied *dispositions*, that is, he or she manifests attitudes, understandings, actions, and meanings about the world that have become consistent over time, reflected even in the movements of the body in social space. One's beliefs about the meaning of life are maintained day-to-day through habituated ways of incorporating society's mores, values, conventions, and tastes through embodied actions and reactions, shaping *durable* dispositions that become more and more concretized into a type of second nature. (This is not to suggest that meanings don't change. It is that as they become more and more concretized, they become more resistant to change.) For example, in my youth I was a competitive tennis player. This meant hours and hours of practice nearly every day for years. I had coaches to educate me in the best techniques. The purpose of the practice was to make my tennis strokes second nature, a type of automatic response in my body, acting and reacting to my opponent's shots without need for wasteful cognition causing me to waste time mentally calculating every move necessary in order to hit a winning shot. In fact, one's game was best if one did not engage in too much thought. (My generation of tennis players had a saying that when someone was playing quite well; "he/she is treeing out." This meant metaphorically that their minds were in the treetops, and their body was doing what it was trained to do.) The embodied knowledge of how to respond to an opponent's shots becomes natural, automatic. It is important to note that while my coaches gave verbal instruction, I learned a good deal through observing the coach's own techniques, as well as his approval and disapproval manifested in bodily expressions, moods, and attitudes. While I might improvise a strategy, a look of disapproval would be enough to end the enterprise. This means of observation of bodily expressions is analogous to various forms of social and cultural learning. Social and cultural education is not always discursive. It is accomplished many times through imitation of others' behavior and attitudinal dispositions.

Habitus, Paul Sweetman explains, "[i]n the broadest terms . . . refers to our overall orientation to our way of being in the world; our predisposed ways of thinking, acting and moving in and through the social environment that encompasses posture, demeanor, outlook, expectations and tastes."[20] Habitus not only affects our ways of thinking and acting, but also informs "both the smallest and largest of actions and gestures, habitus also encompasses bodily hexis; the way we walk, talk, sit, and blow our nose."[21] Cregan states that "[b]odily hexis or embodiment, is the political expression of all the factors that make up one's habitus—and embodied or embedded in our physical being. This occurs as they are played out in various fields of valued cultural knowledge or practice (education, sport, music, cooking, etc.)."[22] Habitus is also one's sense of identity (while changing over a lifetime, there is a feeling of consistency from day-to-day), one's views about life, how one automatically acts and reacts to various and sundry circumstances faced on a daily basis. How we feel and view the world, how we've shaped meaning about the nature of life and existence, takes on a *feeling of veracity*. This does not mean that our views, understanding, philosophy, beliefs, and so on, are *in fact* true; we nevertheless *feel* them to be true much of the time. And when we are presented with alternatives we have, in many cases, negative emotional reactions. We might not be "disposed" to accept an alternate view, understanding, philosophy, and/or interpretation because of the profound embeddedness of our beliefs, embodied in our overall sense of self.

Bourdieu further defines the concept of habitus as a "structured and structuring structure."[23] The structuring of the individual agent is formed through the various social institutions he or she encounters and engenders in his or her life. These institutions consist of things like family, educational institutions, sports teams, occupations, political party affiliation, Church membership, national identity, and so forth. Karl Maton notes that the use of the word *structure* by Bourdieu is significant because it implies "that it is systematically ordered rather than random or unpatterned. This "structure" comprises a system of dispositions which generate perceptions, appreciations and practice."[24] Bourdieu, in *Outline of a Theory of Practice*, notes disposition

> expresses first the result of an organizing action, with a meaning close to that of words such as structure; it also designates a way of being, a habitual state (especially of the body) and, in particular, a predisposition, tendency, propensity or inclination.[25]

Maton notes that Bourdieu is not claiming that individuals are simply "automatons acting out the implications of our upbringings. Rather, practices are the result of what he calls 'an obscure and double relation' or 'an unconscious relationship' between a habitus and a field."[26] We are agents who participate in the construction of our habitus, as stated above. We participate in the formation of our habitus from the pregiven of our natural human nature with the resources of our social-cultural landscape.

FIELD

For Bourdieu, a *field* indicates a social arena that an agent encounters and acts in. Bourdieu's use of the term *field* is analogous to the playing of a game; for example, baseball. Baseball, like all games, has set rules and regulations, along with required tools—resources required if an individual wants to participate. (For example, one must have economic resources to enter the *field/game* of higher education.) To play the game the participant must both learn the rules, and must acquiesce to obeying the rules, for the most part, to be accepted on the field of play. In the playing of the game, those who excel, both by mastering the rules, and possibly stretching them—without going beyond acceptable red lines—acquire what Bourdieu refers to as *cultural capital*. In each field of play, whether it be art, literature, business or education, there is a relational dynamic, "an obscure and double relation" or "an unconscious relationship" between a habitus and the field. The participant must choose to play his or her part, learn the rules, embody those rules, which in turn shapes and structures his or her embodied dispositions in the field. At the same time, the agent is not free simply to change the rules of the game unilaterally. This would be the equivalent of opting out of the game. Changing or refusing to abide by the rules would more than likely cause the individual to be ostracized and marginalized, unless his or her social capital was so great that others could not, or would not want to, exclude him or her. We see this with the ultra-rich who seem to be able to play by different social and legal rules as opposed to the poor and subalterns of society.

While learning the rules, values, mores, conventions and taboos of a field of play requires volitional participation, this does not mean that the individual is always cognizant of the complex formations taking shape beneath the surface of consciousness. Dispositions influenced by feelings of rightness or wrongness, liking or disliking, acceptance or rejection, are not always immediately present to one's awareness. Let us take as an example the institution of the family. Each of our family experiences are unique, no doubt. The personalities that make up a family play a profound influence in the formation of the various members. But while the various relational dynamics between and among the family members may be unique, there are aspects of the family structure that share commonalties with other families within the same social and cultural landscape. Society has an important influence upon the structure of family life. In some cultures, patriarchy is dominant, influencing the formation of authority and gender roles. In some cultures, religious mores, conventions and taboos shape the "legitimate" structure of familial relations. Within these social and cultural structures, while each volitionally participates, the individual agent will not always be cognizant of the totality of the structuring that is taking place, shaping habitual dispositions. An eldest son will, in some patriarchal cultures, present himself with a demeanor that is socially constructed and accepted without realizing that his self-presentation has been socially defined and dictated through expressions of approval and disapproval, and not simply chosen as personal preference.

PRACTICE

Bourdieu understands habitus as fitting into his overall theory of *practice*. It is the engendering of social and cultural dispositions manifested in social fields. Bourdieu notes that it is not only individuals but groups and classes also who have a habitus. The group or class habitus acts as a homogenizing influence in social formation. It is the homogenizing influence on groups or classes that enables "practices to be objectively harmonized without any calculation or conscious reference to a norm and mutually adjusted in the absence of any direct interaction or . . . explicit coordination."[27] Norms, in many cases, are not explicitly or apodictically proclaimed, but are enforced and reinforced through social practice. For example, while the first amendment allows the freedom of speech, the act of shaming offensive speech, through ostracizing individuals, acts as an implicit form of social control. There may be no policy against such speech, but the unspoken social norm will act to contain the use of such speech.

Bourdieu understands practice as a dialectical relationship between the structures of one's social and cultural environment and the subjectivity of the agent. Dispositions are then formed and embodied in people, which in turn leads individuals to reproduce the structured environment, thus the *structuring* in the "structured and structuring structure." We can see this in the transference of civil life through the formative institutions of family and governmentally regulated and funded education. The goal is the formation of a well-adjusted and productive individual who will be an asset, and not a strain, to civil society. For the individual who succeeds at instilling the proper attitudes and dispositions as dictated by the structured environment there is the hope and promise of greater cultural capital. But there is never a perfect replication, or, in Bourdieu's term, reproduction, of the various structures, due to the volitional agency of individuals who may develop different tastes, inclinations, or worldviews. As long as these do not wander too far from the norm, they will most likely be accepted, though possibly discouraged. If they do wander beyond socially accepted boundaries, the individual may experience several negative reactions and consequences, such as marginalization, imprisonment, exile, and possible death. Social pressures help to maintain a certain homogeneity in individual practice with the idea of social stability, maintenance of the *status quo*. Many social boundaries are the result of historical contingencies. An important boundary in the United States has been the demarcation of ethnic and religious hegemony and subaltern status, developed over three centuries. It has formed among the majority attitudes of White and Christian supremacy, which in turn has acquired for White Christians a largess of cultural capital.

CULTURAL CAPITAL

Bourdieu defines *cultural capital* as "the sum of the resources, actual or virtual, that accrue to an individual or a group by virtue of possessing a durable network of more or less institutionalized relationships of mutual acquaintance and recognition."[28] Within social fields, *cultural capital* (power) is pursued as a means of social status, support, and security. John Lechte describes Bourdieu's concept of habitus, as it applies to the theory of practice, as the expression of dispositions "in social space." Social space is synonymous with a social field. Lechte writes that the various positions in a social field form

> a system of relations based on stakes (power) that are meaningful and desired by those occupying the positions in social space. Habitus is a kind of expression of the (unconscious) investment social actors have in the power stakes implied. Habitus is a kind of grammar of actions which serves to differentiate one class (e.g. the dominant) from another (e.g. dominated) in the social field.[29]

As an example of this, I will imitate two types of walk for my students. I will state that one represents that of a gang member in the Bronx, and the other of a Wall Street investor. By my gait they easily recognize who walks like a gang member and who walks like an investor. This also applies to numerous other indicators of class and status, including tastes and styles. In each social field, practice within that field is reflected partially by different gaits. Other forms of practice would include types of dress, use of language (slang, technical), types of acts of obeisance to social betters, and so on.

Power is for Bourdieu foundational to his theory of practice. Craig Calhoun notes that, for Bourdieu, "power is always *used*, if sometimes unconsciously."[30] Within a social field the desire to attain cultural capital is the struggle to gain greater levels of position/status/place within the field. For example, in the world of academia one observes this struggle in the pursuit, by some, to gain prestige through either the production of well-reviewed articles and books, and/or popularity among students. With the increase in prestige comes the possibility for economic gain—money from book sales, higher salary—or more prestigious appointments to better regarded institutions. This in turn can bring about a movement up the ladder of class status, which in turn can bring many social and economic benefits, like living in a better neighborhood, sending children to better schools, and so forth.

One of the criticisms of Bourdieu's theory is that he seemed "on the whole to have little of interest to say about specific issues of identity (the concrete negotiations of the self in relation to social relations), despite having provided a whole range of sociological enquiries, from education to aesthetics."[31] It is this negotiations of the self in relation to social relations that I believe is complimented by the mimetic theories of René Girard. I will discuss this more fully in chapter three.

David Swartz notes that while "[h]abitus results from early socialization experiences in which external structures are internalized,"[32] individuals can either reinforce these early formed dispositions or can develop new one's based on motivating factors, as described by Bourdieu's concepts of capital and field. Habitus generates "an infinite number of behaviors from a limited number of principles."[33] An individual will incorporate the rules of society throughout life by means of socialization, as well as "social trajectory." The rules are few, but they have the power to "determine a representational matrix as well as a matrix of action."[34] That is, habitus, through socialization schemes for social action, "produce practices as well as schemes of classification that allow the perception and appreciation of practices. The agent perceives, understands, evaluates, adapts, and acts in a situation according to his or her habitus."[35] Mathieu Hilgers describes the workings of habitus as an "analogical transfer of schemes."[36] That is, past experiences act as means of making sense of new situations. These past experiences act as structuring mechanisms, transposing dispositions, thus giving "meaning to new experiences and situations, and contribute to the more or less congruent adjustment of practice to objective rules and structures."[37] It is this analogical schema that creates for the individual a creative way of seeing the present situation with a sense of newness, though relying on past experiences to navigate new territories. "This sense is produced by the immanent law of habitus that makes the agent adjust, un-adjust, and readjust his or her practices to be compatible with objective reality as it appears subjectively."[38] While past experiences shape and color present situations, the individual is not trapped into replicating past actions and reactions. Past experiences are guides to navigate situations that have a feeling of commonality to the present. People have agency and can choose a different way of acting as they assess the uniqueness of the present situation. Thus, free will is integral to the formation of habitus.

FREE WILL

From a Catholic theological anthropological perspective, one of the great gifts that God has given to humans is the gift of freedom. In the Franciscan theological tradition, this freedom is grounded in the very nature of God, who is absolute freedom, in whose image we have been created. This freedom is the gift of each person's *haecceity*, a formal gift of uniqueness despite each individual's participation in the commonalities (*natura communis*—common nature) that bind individuals to a common human nature. I am not you, by means of my haecceity, my unique *thisness*. The Orthodox theologian Vladimir Lossky attempted to capture this *something* that allows a sense in which the individual both shares in and is at the same time free from the common human nature. It is this something that allows a sense of personhood, distinct and free from that of other persons. He writes that "'person' signifies the irreducibility of man to his nature—'irreducibility' and not 'something irreducible' or 'something which makes man irreducible to his nature' precisely because it cannot be a question here of 'something' distinct from 'another nature' but of someone who is distinct from his own nature, of someone who goes beyond his nature while still containing it, who makes it exist as human nature by this overstepping of it."[39]

In our uniqueness we have a freedom that allows us to choose what social and cultural items we *will* and desire to incorporate into the construction of our personhood. The theological anthropology of *haecceity* as expounded in the writings of the medieval Franciscan scholastic John Duns Scotus is an optimistic view of human nature in which we are each created to be drawn to goodness and truth. As Scotus scholar Mary Beth Ingham writes, "[w]e are each drawn to walk a path that, at every moment, calls upon our 'yes' or 'no'. Our free choice is part of who we are, and who we are called to become."[40] This is not, however, a theological form of individualism. The beauty of being human, from a Franciscan perspective, is its relationality. Unlike Sartre, hell is not other people, but in fact a gift of graced communion that reflects the triune relational communion of Father, Son, and Holy Spirit. Our consciousness reflects this in its operations. Rowan Williams captures this, stating that

> Consciousness as we normally think about it has a relational dimension. I can't think without thinking of the other. I can't even think of my body, this zero point of orientation, without understanding that it's an object to another. . . . And this means that my consciousness is mobile, engaged, incomplete: because I can't construct the idea of any object without supposing a diversity of points of view, I know that my point of view is always partial, and to be conscious of myself is to be aware of myself as a node point in a web of information exchange, which corporately constructs the idea of objects, selves, persons. To be conscious is, primitively, to be able to find my way around a material environment without bumping into things.[41]

Scotian theological anthropology is teleological, as with many Catholic, Orthodox, and Protestant theological visions, offering us a glimpse of our project's trajectory. Scotus himself was not ignorant, or naïve, of the reality that human freedom has been greatly distorted and limited by sin. It is traditional Christian teaching that the human will has been distorted, corrupted by what Augustine calls concupiscence, a distorted will formed by distorted desires, leading each of us away from the good, true, and beautiful. St. Paul recognized this propensity to choose wrongly, having been weakened in our capacity to choose the good and the true because of sin (*see Romans 7: 13–24*). In more contemporary terms, one way we can look at this distortion is from a psychological perspective. The psychiatrist and spiritual writer, Gerald May, describes our loss of freedom of the will in terms of addiction. He writes

> For generations, psychologists thought that virtually all self-defeating behavior was caused by repression. I now come to believe that addiction is a separate and even more self-defeating force that abuses our freedom and makes us do things we really do not want to do. While repression stifles desire, addiction *attaches* desire, bonds and enslaves the energy of desire to certain specific behaviors, things, or people. The objects of attachment then become preoccupations and obsessions; they come to rule our lives.[42]

John Prendiville notes that St. Augustine recognized the role that habits play in our lives. "Augustine was . . . aware of the idea of habit as a second nature."[43] For Augustine, we have habituated our neglect to turn our gaze to God, addicted—to use the contemporary expression—to focus on ourselves with its distorted and misguided desires. While May is speaking about addictions as they are commonly understood, the abuse of drugs and alcohol, there is, I believe an analogue to the addictive bonds to certain social and cultural ideologies, values, mores and dispositions that are as destructive to human flourishing as toxic substances are to the body. Just as the overuse of certain intoxicants negatively affects health, so too do attachments and the consumption of negative concepts and ideologies harm and impede a Christian's journey toward goodness, truth, and love. For example, Catholic social teaching maintains that each person, regardless of gender, race, national identity, religion, and so on, has and can never lose dignity and worth. The racist has formed perspectives in which this is not true, and that there is a natural superiority grounded in racial makeup. The racist does not see the falsehood of such a position and would contest the idea that he or she was "addicted" to a false ideology that impedes his or her call to be conformed to the image of a loving God. Social and cultural influences play a profound role in forming the structures that present themselves as "goods." So then, a critical examination of the sources offered in social and cultural life is incumbent upon the Christian desiring to conform to the image and will of God.

The human project is dependent upon social and cultural supports. Individuals require resources to develop and flourish. Values are determined and embraced depending on how they are perceived to benefit development and flourishing. Social and cultural interests in the modern world compete for the attention of individuals. In the world of advertising, we see examples of promises that this or that product can deliver the comfort, status, well-being one desires. Celebrity culture enhances the desire for fame and recognition.

While one is free to pursue various avenues in life, for example, education, career, belief system, and so on, and shape aesthetic tastes, there is still the reality that the objects in the various social fields are pregivens, limiting the types of choices an individual can choose from. How one chooses a career, for example, is limited by such factors as: endowment—physical and mental, education, place, economic resources, ethnicity (depending on social and cultural prejudices), gender, and so forth. Other exterior influences shape how one makes one's choices: family influence, social and cultural mores and taboos. Social concepts of the meaning of success and failure, prestige, and status play significant influence in career and other life choices. Another important constraint upon choice is the deeply embedded structured dispositions acquired in early life. As an extreme example, there are those who were raised in situations of abuse, physical and/or psychological. Many years of abusive experience shaped by abusive behavior as normative can be very difficult to overcome emotionally. For some there is the good fortune of escaping these tragic environments, and learning that abusive behavior is not, and should never be considered normal. Despite this knowledge, the individual's disposition toward the world is profoundly shaped by these early experiences. While the individual may be able, through therapy, to alleviate some of the internal damage, there is still for many an abiding insecurity. The same can be seen when it comes to other contingencies. Ethnicity, gender, national identity, poverty and other social and cultural influences form attitudes and feelings unconsciously assimilated to one's dispositions toward the world. They shape deep and abiding interpretations about the meaning of life, forming worldviews that feel second nature.

The formation of dispositions shaped by the many social fields acquires the "production of action and most importantly for the production of mundane judgments (e.g., judgments of moral propriety or impropriety, of likelihood or unlikelihood, of certainty or uncertainty, or judgments of taste such as likes and dislikes)."[44] It is the formation and production of judgments that influence and reinforce behavior in social space. This formation takes place in the flow of relationships, making dispositional constructs *relational* in nature. To develop as a person is necessarily to be in relationships. The nature of these relationships is profoundly influential in the types of dispositions one acquires, especially when it comes to issues of power, values, and ideology. While Bourdieu offers, in my opinion, an excellent schema for understanding the interrelationship between individuals and social and cultural institutions, he does not spend much time with the actual mechanism of cultural transference, other than pointing to the various institutions producing cultural information. While he makes a nod toward imitation, which is limited to representational imitation, he does not explore its dynamics. Why does a particular field seem attractive while another does not? Why do I attempt to practice this cultural and social structure but not that one, especially in multicultural societies? This is where the mimetic theories of René Girard complements Bourdieu's sociological theory of habitus.

I have attempted to utilize those aspects of Bourdieu's theories I find helpful in aiding Christians to examine their own inner formation, and the social and cultural structures that influence that formation. His theory of habitus helps to understand the formation of one's embodied emotional and conceptual dispositions. The importance of self-knowledge is very much a part of the Christian journey to God. St. Augustine recognized this need centuries ago, writing "God, always the same, let me know myself, let me know Thee!"[45] The danger in lacking self-knowledge is the tendency of projecting one's distorted and misguided concepts and ideologies of the divine onto God, making God an image of one's own making. When we desire to make the will of God the guiding motivation for our actions and affections it is important to know which God we are following: either the God beyond our constructs whose unconditional love breaks into our world in the incarnation of Jesus, calling us to love beyond our cultural limitations; or the god shaped by our distorted and biased ideological constructs shaping how we use power—as a means of domination rather than acts of loving service. An important way of attaining greater self-knowledge is to reflect on the various influences shaping our values, attitudes, worldviews, and ideologies, each shaping our motivations and intentions, embodied, felt, and manifested in social space. I believe that René Girard's theories concerning the nature and function of desire is an important tool in order to attain greater self-knowledge. But before I turn to Girard's theory of mimetic desire, I want first to examine the nature of desire itself.

NOTES

1. Peter Berger and Thomas Luckmann, *The Social Construction of Reality: A Treatise in the Sociology of Knowledge* (New York: Penguin Books, 1966), 85.
2. Quoted in John Henry Cardinal Newman, *The Idea of a University* (London: Longmans, Green, and Co., 1891), 159.
3. Thomas J. Csordas, "Embodiment as a Paradigm for Anthropology," *Ethos* 18, no. 1 (1990), 8.
4. Ibid.
5. Maurice Merleau-Ponty, *Phenomenology of Perception* (London: Routledge and Kegan Paul, 1962), 137, 362; quoted in Thomas J. Csordas, "Embodiment as a Paradigm for Anthropology," 10.
6. Ibid.
7. Pierre Bourdieu, *Outline of a Theory of Practice* (Cambridge: Cambridge University Press, 1977), 124.
8. Ibid.
9. Ibid.
10. James M. Ostrow, "Review: Culture as a Fundamental Dimension of Experience: A Discussion of Pierre Bourdieu's Theory of Human Habitus," *Human Studies*, 4, no. 3 (1981): 279–281.
11. Ibid.

12. Ibid.
13. See Mary Clark, "Meaningful Social Bonding as a Universal Human Need," in *Conflict: Human Needs Theory*, ed. John W. Burton (New York: Palgrave Macmillan, 1990).
14. James M. Ostrow, "Review: Culture as a Fundamental Dimension of Experience: A Discussion of Pierre Bourdieu's Theory of Human Habitus," 279–281.
15. Kate Cregan, *The Sociology of the Body: Mapping the Abstraction of Embodiment* (London: SAGE Publications, 2006), 66.
16. Ibid.
17. Ibid.
18. Pierre Bourdieu, *In Other Words*, (Stanford: Stanford University Press, 1990), 13.
19. Ibid, 63.
20. Paul Sweetman, "Twenty-first century dis-ease? Habitual reflexivity or the reflexive habitus," *Sociological Review*, 51, no. 4 (2003): 532–533.
21. Ibid.
22. Kate Cregan, *The Sociology of the Body*, 67.
23. Ibid, 170.
24. Karl Maton, "Habitus," in *Pierre Bourdieu: Key Concepts*, ed. Michael Grenfell (Durham: Acumen Publishing Limited, 2008), 51.
25. Quoted in Ibid.
26. Ibid.
27. Pierre Bourdieu, *The Logic of Practice* (Stanford: Stanford University Press, 1990), 58–59.
28. Pierre Bourdieu and Loic Wacquant, *An Invitation to Reflexive Sociology* (Chicago: University of Chicago Press, 1992), 119.
29. John Lechte, *Contemporary Thinkers: From Structuralism to Post-Humanism*, 2nd Edition (New York: Routledge, 2008), 68.
30. Craig Calhoun, "Habitus, Field, and Capital: The Question of Historical Specificity," in *Bourdieu: Critical Perspective*, eds. Craig Calhoun, Edward LiPuma, Moishe Postone (Cambridge: Polity Press, 1993), 64.
31. Ibid, 100.
32. David Swartz, *Culture and Power: The Sociology of Pierre Bourdieu* (Chicago: The University of Chicago Press, 1997), 102–103.
33. Ibid.
34. Ibid.
35. Mathieu Hilgers, "Habitus, Freedom, and Reflexivity," *Theory & Psychology* 19, no. 6 (2009): 730–731.
36. Ibid, 734
37. Ibid, 731.
38. Ibid.
39. Vladimir Lossky, *In the Image and Likeness of God* (New York, St Vladimir's Seminary Press, 1974), p. 120, quoted in Rowan Williams, *Being Human: Bodies, Mind, Persons* (London: SPCK, 2018), Kindle.
40. Mary Beth Ingham, *Understanding John Duns Scotus: 'Of Reality the Rarest-Veined Unraveller'* (St. Bonaventure: Franciscan Institute Publications, 2017), 87.
41. Rowan Williams, *Being Human*.
42. Gerald G. May, *Addictions and Grace: Love and Spirituality in the Healing of Addictions* (New York: HarperCollins, 1988), 3.
43. John G. Prendiville, SJ, "The Development of the Idea of Habit in the Thought of Saint Augustine," *Traditio*, 28 (1972), 29.
44. Omar Lizardo, "Habitus," https://www3.nd.edu/~olizardo/papers/habitus-entry.pdf. (Accessed July 2, 2018).
45. *The Soliloquies of St. Augustine*, trans. Rose Elizabeth Cleveland (Boston: Little, Brown, and Company, 1910), 51.

Chapter Two

Emotions, Feelings, and Desires

Bourdieu, as I have attempted to demonstrate in chapter one, has offered an excellent analysis of, in sociological terms, the formation of one's habitus. Bourdieu demonstrated the power of culture in the formation of one's bodily hexis, one's habitus. This chapter is an attempt to articulate the mechanics of how one embodies one's social, cultural, and ideological fields. This includes the recognition of not only social, but psychological, and neurobiological influences as well. With this chapter it is my intention to bridge Bourdieu's theory of habitus and Girard's theory of mimetic desire by explicating the processes by which emotions and desires are constructed, as well as the impact that emotions and desires have in the formation of one's worldview. I attempt to explore how the body plays a part in the formation of one's habitus, with an emphasis on emotions and desires. In other words, what are the mechanics by which society and culture are embodied by individuals? My argument in this chapter is that, though much of the Western intellectual tradition has put a priority on the power of reason and rationality to inform and form human motivation and behavior, emotions and feelings have a much more central and profound effect on our rational judgments and deliberations. Jonathan Haidt uses the metaphor of elephant and rider, illustrating the influence unconscious material has on one's rational deliberations. He writes that *"the mind is divided, like a rider on an elephant, and the rider's job is to serve the elephant.* The rider is our conscious reasoning—the stream of words and images of which we are fully aware. The elephant is the other 99 percent of mental processes—the ones that occur outside of awareness but that actually govern most of our behavior."[1] A good deal of the 99 percent of what Haidt calls our mental processes outside of awareness is made up of emotional content formed in the matrix of social and cultural relationships. Our emotional feelings inform our reason, as well as our evaluations and motivations. Emotions and feelings also give us a greater insight into our identity. Emotions are the prime indicator of our actual value system, as well as a clue to our actual identity, beyond the many illusions we construct about ourselves. Sebastian Moore writes

> It is often said, 'You are what you do.' It is much truer to say, 'You are what you feel.' It is in feeling happy, or angry, or sad, or hopeful, in response to an event, that I touch base with myself. My *identity* lights up in one of these *feelings*. Who I am can become known to others, and to myself, far more accurately by how I feel than by the image I may form of myself.[2]

MAKING EMOTIONS

Imagine waking up one morning and you find yourself feeling a little under the weather. Despite this annoyance you still have to go to work. You happen to like your job, but this morning you really wish you could call in sick, but you don't want to waste your sick days. Besides, you are only feeling a little bit sick, probably something you ate last night, it will pass. You arrive at your workplace and you see the other employees you have gotten to know fairly well over the time that you have been employed there. For the most part you find them congenial. You have not gotten any worse, but you still feel a little lousy. Then Tammy comes over to ask you something and you notice that she makes you feel a little irritated, and you wish she would go back to her desk. You have not felt this before. Now you begin to think to yourself, Tammy is kind of annoying, why haven't I noticed this before. While you may be thinking that you have suddenly had an insight about Tammy, what you may not realize is that the physical discomfort you are feeling is affecting your reasoning. You have connected your emotional state of discomfort to a judgment about the character of another person who happens to land in your social space as you are having feelings of discomfort. This example is an attempt to demonstrate that emotional feelings have a profound effect on our rational judgments. In other words, reasoning does not create emotions. Our emotional feelings inform our reason. They are the impetus for action, whether that be the act of judgment or rational deliberation.

In her book, *How Emotions Are Made: The Secret Life of the Brain*, Lisa Feldman Barrett challenges the classic orthodox view of emotions as "a kind of brute reflex, very often at odds with our rationality."[3] This classic notion is the idea that "[w]e all have emotions built-in from birth. They are distinct, recognizable phenomena inside us. When something happens in the world, whether it's a gunshot or a flirtatious glance, our emotions come on quickly and automatically, as if someone has flipped a switch."[4] This has led to the futile search, according to Barrett, to find emotion's "fingerprints" in the brain. With a plethora of clinical and experimental evidence at her disposal, she argues that the neuroscientific evidence demonstrates that emotions are constructions that utilize multiple regions of the brain. Leaving aside the more technical discussion of neuronal brain functions, her evidence leads her to conclude the following. In her chapter "Emotions Are Constructed" Barrett asks the reader to look at an image that seems on first encounter to be random black markings. It looks like the random scribblings of a child. Then she directs the reader to look to a page near the end of the book and see above the same illustration a clear picture of a bee. Now, when one looks back at the original black-and-white illustration one sees the outline of a bee. What has happened in the brain to change a nondescript blob of black and white is the addition of information from the photograph of the bee. So then, "[y]our brain added stuff from the full photograph into its vast array of prior experiences and *constructed* the familiar object you now see in the blobs. Neurons in your visual cortex changed their firing to create lines that aren't present, linking the blobs into a shape that isn't physically there."[5] What this implies is that one's past experiences, whatever they may be, "give meaning to present sensations."[6] This process of construction is not visible to consciousness. So, when the original blob was suddenly changed after the combination of the photograph and past experiences of bees, there is a change in the firing of the brain's sensory neurons. Even though the blob lacks incoming sensory input to help decipher its meaning, with additional information, the blob automatically takes on a new meaning. From now on you will see the blob as a bee. This is called *simulation*.

Simulations are rooted in concepts that have been created in the brain through experiences of stimuli from both the exterior world and interior world of the individual. Inner stimuli, such as a stomachache, will appear to the brain in a general nondescript fashion, simply neuronal information, and only take on meaning based on what the brain tries to guess is happening in one's environment. For example, unease in the stomach can be interpreted by an individual as caused by anxiety, illness, anticipation, nervousness, and so on. It depends on the circumstances of the individual. "In every waking moment, you're faced with ambiguous, noisy information from your eyes, ears, nose, and other sensory organs. Your brain uses your past experiences to construct a hypothesis—the simulation—and compares it to the cacophony arriving from your senses. In this manner, simulation lets your brain impose meaning on the noise, selecting what's relevant in ignoring the rest."[7] As we experience life over time, our brains develop a variety of concepts in order to "guess the meaning of incoming sensory inputs."[8] Over time, when there is a regularity in interpretive meaning, the simulative act will impose meaning where the stimuli appear recognizable. However, when the stimuli do not match the concept's anticipated experience, there is a feeling of revulsion, shock, anger, sadness, disappointment, and so forth. For example, when a friend of mine took me to a German bistro when we were in high school, he suggested a sandwich I had never heard of. When I asked him what it was, he indicated it was the German version of the American hamburger—he was pranking me. After eating half the sandwich, which tasted ok, I asked him what the meat was. He told me that it was cows' tongue. I immediately spit out what was in my mouth, and I began to feel queasy. I couldn't get the "bad" taste out of my mouth for hours, no matter how many mints I chewed. I had obviously at some time in my past formed an aversion to cow tongue, imagining it as revolting. While I wasn't aware of the type of meat, I was fine, having a simulated concept that it was like regular beef, though I did notice a difference in texture. My knowledge of the actual type of meat with the addition of my concept of grossness had created a reaction of aversion and the emotion of disgust. The creation of meaning from exterior stimuli also takes place for internal sensations. "From an aching stomach, your brain constructs an instance of hunger, nausea, or mistrust."[9] An analogous simulation can be observed when listening to a political pundit on TV. One's simulative evaluation of the veracity of the pundit's perspective will be informed by one's formed value system. For example, if a TV pundit states a particular opinion on some issue of interest to you, how you react to the opinion will be influenced by whether the pundit is someone in your political camp or not. Because we have formed feelings around political ideologies, the sedimentation of simulative reactions influences our acceptance or rejection of another's position, not necessarily on the merits of the argument, but on the affiliation of the individual making the argument.

Barrett distinguishes between what she calls an *emotional concept* and an *instance of emotion*. An emotional concept consists of categories of the various types of emotions there are, for example, joy, fear, disgust, anxiety, and so on. An instance in which one experiences an internal or external stimulus, for example, a stomachache or ice cream, "your brain makes meaning" from your experience, "together with the sensations from the world around you, by constructing an instance of the concept."[10] This is an instance of emotion. In contradistinction with the classic view, Barrett maintains that "emotions are not reactions to the world." The formation of emotions is not passive. "From sensory input and past experience, your brain constructs meaning and prescribes action. . . . With concepts, your brain makes meaning of sensation, and sometimes that meaning is an emotion."[11] Thus, emotions are not the "inevitable consequences of your genes."[12] Barrett's theorizing on the construction of emotions is holistic, in that it incorporates elements from three directions: *social construction, psychological construction,* and *neuroconstruction*. "From social construction, it acknowledges the importance of culture and concepts. From psychological construction, it considers emotions to be constructed by core systems in the brain and body. And from neuroconstruction, it adopts the idea that experience wires the brain."[13] Barrett makes a strong case for the construction of emotions based on numerous clinical studies. These many studies demonstrate that feelings have affective influences on beliefs. Barrett demonstrates that when an experience develops concepts in the mind—such as associating seeing pink-colored ice cream with the belief that it is strawberry, a disposition developed through numerous and consistent experiences, it will come as a shock if the flavor is actually pink salmon. Emotions thus affect the development of concepts about the world, shaping a sense of regularity, consistency, and order to our environment. These concepts incorporate beliefs about the world, shaping the hermeneutical lenses we use to interpret the world, structuring meaning.

MOODS, EMOTIONAL FEELINGS AND BELIEFS

Gerald Clore and Karen Gaspar have summarized several studies on the affective influences on belief and have offered a series of hypotheses based on these findings. Affective feelings function as an important feedback for the individual, helping the individual to locate the stimuli from which a feeling or mood is constructed. They distinguish emotions and moods. "Affective influences on attention characterize emotions rather than moods."[14] Moods are object ambiguous, so explanations for a mood state will attribute the feeling to whatever object is in attentional space. Emotions usually have an immediate object or objects that help to guide them and tend to cause a narrowing of attention "to object-relevant information and emotion-relevant goals."[15] For example, I may be in a sour mood which affects my disposition. I will likely attribute it to some object or event that will give me the needed information for the emotional state I am in. I might blame the weather or having slept poorly. An emotion is directly constructed by an object or event; the agent does not have to seek possibilities and choose among various options for attribution. When an emotion of joy arises, I know that the cause is the fact that I passed the exam, or any other event that normally gives me the feeling of joy. I don't have to search for the object stimulating my emotion, it is immediately present to me. A mood is attributionally open. With a mood the object is not immediately present, and my attribution may be either correct or incorrect. But once I have attributed my mood to an object, Clore and Gaspar state, "[i]n this way, affective experience and attentional focus may form an intensity funnel, a positive feedback circuit in which extremity of emotion and intensity of belief might amplify each other through their effects on the mediating factor of attentional focus."[16] For example, once I have concluded that Tammy is annoying my attention to this fact will be reinforced every time I see her, unless I get different information that might change my feelings about Tammy. But I probably will feed information to myself every time I see her that she is annoying, creating a feedback circuit that will intensify my negative emotions about Tammy, and intensifying my belief that she is in fact an annoying human being. And, as Tammy becomes a scapegoat through an attribution of blame in correlation with my physical discomfort, so too will I tend to assign scapegoats for other emotional tensions or distress. Blaming another ethnic group may result from feelings of anxiety or distress arising from a perceived loss of status.

Moods and emotions will affect and have consequences on cognition which are "mediated by the subjective experience of affect (affective feelings)."[17] In other words, affective feelings have influence on how one thinks about a situation in which a mood or emotion is constructed. This in turn means that emotional stimuli will affect an individual's judgments. There is an immediacy to affective feelings. If the emotion is due to physical injury, the person easily locates on the body the injury in order to find relief. But affective feelings are not so easy to locate in the body because they are psychological. But they are immediate all the same. I immediately feel annoyed when I see Tammy, or fear, anxiety, insecurity, or anger when I encounter a member of a despised group, though I wouldn't say the feeling is located in one or another part of my body. "[T]his immediacy leads to the attribution of affect to whatever is in focus at the time."[18] Whether the affective feeling is positive or negative, the individual will seek to attribute the feeling to some object, which the attribution principle maintains that "the apparent meaning of an affective feeling depends in part on the object to which it is attributed."[19] In the act of attribution affective feelings influence beliefs "through attribution of affect to objects. Such attributions then allow affect to serve as a basis for new beliefs or as validation of prior beliefs about the object."[20] Sustained beliefs about an object will form affective dispositions, which can be felt regularly, or remain dormant until an object arises to bring the feeling to the individual's awareness. Now that I am convinced that Tammy is an annoying person, or non-Whites, or non-Christians are somehow inferior, I have formed a disposition toward her/them in my attempt to avoid her/them. When such a person is near my disposition and behavior will reflect my feelings and attitude toward him or her.

EXPERIENCES OF LACK

One of the ubiquitous experiences we each have is the experience of lack. This is appetitive, emotional, and spiritual. When I am hungry, I experience the lack of food, thus I am compelled by my feelings of hunger to procure sustenance. If I feel a lack of love, self-esteem, connectedness to others, and so on, I will most likely seek to fill this lack through positive human relationships. And if I feel a lack of spiritual vitality, I may seek various spiritual practices to give myself a deeper connection to the meaning and purpose of life. In each case, my choice of objects to fill the experienced lack will be sought and chosen based on social and cultural pregivens presented within my social and cultural landscape. James Ostrow states that

> [t]he forms in which the world is familiar to us, by which we are predisposed to certain ways of perception and conduct, are the 'pregiven' grounds of reflection. . . . If there was not this 'preliminary presence,' or this 'actual world' which precedes 'cognitive activity,' we would be in a constant chaotic state of the absurd, continuously disoriented.[21]

As we accustom ourselves to fulfilling our needs with social and cultural pregivens, we will tend to attribute this lack to the absence of typical objects we have become accustomed for satisfying these needs. We may also attribute this lack to outside forces. These outside forces may be the cause of my lack, and they may simply be distorted beliefs about the source of my lack. As we become habituated to particular beliefs around the nature and causes of feelings of lack, we will tend to form dispositions informed by these beliefs. For example, I may feel a lack of self-esteem in a particular situation, say in a faculty meeting where I'm not feeling the level of respect I believe I deserve. If I have typically attributed and formed beliefs that these feelings arise because of the actions of others, I might develop habitual ways of reacting, such as acting aloof, dismissive, or arrogant.

FEELING-AS-EVIDENCE HYPOTHESIS

Clore and Gaspar suggest that "beliefs are adjusted to be compatible with internal evidence in the form of feelings, just as they are adjusted to be compatible with external evidence from perceptual experience."[22] This leads to what they call *feeling-as-evidence hypothesis*.

> [T]he feelings-as-evidence hypothesis is that belief-consistent feelings may be experienced as confirmation of those beliefs. Evidence from the sensations of feeling may be treated like sensory evidence from the external environment, so that something both believed propositionally and also felt emotionally may seem especially valid. In this sense, we assert that feeling is believing.[23]

When it comes to the acquisition of and belief in certain ideologies, these becoming the hermeneutical lenses through which one understands/interprets "reality," beliefs about the causes and resolution for feelings of lack are determined through these lenses. For example, if I have been taught that White people are the dominant race, and I experience a perceived loss of status due to increasing numbers of minorities, I might attribute my feelings of lack of status to the machinations of those I deem a threat to White hegemony. I may then form dispositions of prejudice and confrontation toward those I deem as "other." So then, my habitus incorporates the habituated practices through which I satisfy my feelings of lack.

EMOTION CATEGORIZATION

This dispositional hermeneutic of blame can affect similar emotions of lack. Clore and Gaspar call this *emotion categorization*. This hypothesis claims that "similarity of emotional reactions promotes inclusion of different situations into a single belief structure."[24] For example, let us say that John Jones, a White, white-collar bureaucrat with a nine-to-five office job, with skills developed through strenuous years of college training and on-the-job experience, has been informed that he was being replaced due to new technological methods in his occupational field that require new skill sets. Having spent economic resources, putting in several years of college training, now outdated, John feels a sense of unfairness. When he attempts to update his skills to be able to regain his bureaucratic job, he is told that the institution was looking to hire more minorities and women. Again, he experiences a sense of unfairness. Because the two emotional responses have a commonality to them, John conflates them, and "the conflation of beliefs about these two domains also provide secondary gains."[25] He may associate his immediate situation with a belief that society has begun to denigrate the worth of White men. So, in order to fill a lack—the loss of prestige and status, for example—he may promote a type of White men's revolt against policies of affirmative action that he believes are complicit in the denigration of White men's cultural status. This will offer John a sense of valorization, increasing his sense of self-worth as he stands bravely against the forces of cultural degradation.

ATTENTION HYPOTHESIS

Just as a toothache will draw one's attention and retain it, so too does an emotional feeling have effect on attention. The stronger the emotional feeling, the greater the attention. The location of the problem tooth guides the individual to form beliefs about the right action to be taken in order to alleviate the pain. So, one chooses to make an appointment with the dentist, believing this the best course of action—rather than putting a string around the infected tooth, tying it to a doorknob and pulling the door sharply. Emotional feelings also draw the attention of the individual, but the resolution to its meaning is not always clear. When I see smoke, I draw the conclusion that there is most probably fire. But unlike exterior stimuli, emotional feelings are "internally generated." Just as a loud and sharp noise will gain one's attention immediately, so too, the greater "the magnitude of the affective feelings, the more completely they should command attention."[26] This leads Clore and

Gaspar to propose the *attention hypothesis*. This "concerns the role of the informational components of emotion (their object and the qualitative aspects of feeling) in attention."[27] What this means is that just as attention to the pain of a tooth signifies that there is decay or damage to the tooth, so too do emotional feelings "guide attention, not so much to themselves, but to what they signify."[28] The role of leaders, be they political or religious, can act to heighten attention to issues that increase individuals' emotions. If individuals have sedimented feelings about certain political, economic, class, or religious issues, leaders can highlight these issues as a means of gaining support for their agenda. This should indicate to the reflective Christian the presence of a value system that may be problematic to their Christian practice.

Clore and Gaspar argue that it is the conceptual beliefs about what the emotional feelings signify that "provide the steering for attentional processes."[29] For example, let's say that I feel anger as a reaction to an unjust act against me. While I feel the emotion of anger, I may be guided by my conceptual beliefs about justice, or vengeance, or forgiveness. If I feel love for someone, my conceptual beliefs will guide me as to what loving behavior should look like. Summarizing research by Niedenthal and Setterland, Clore and Gaspar state that after examination of "both concept-related and feeling-related information . . . they found that attention was drawn only to semantic or descriptive content of the emotion, and not merely to information of similar valence as the feeling."[30] Clore and Gaspar conclude that, in terms of the *attention hypothesis*,

> Once an emotion is experienced, the system no longer operates as a scientist carefully weighing the pros and cons of the belief implied by the emotion. Instead, the emotional person acts like a prosecutor or a defense lawyer seeking by any means to find evidence for the belief. Presumably, the experiential aspect of the emotion is itself responsible for this process of interrupting the flow, providing information, and, through associated beliefs, guiding attention.[31]

The greater the plausibility of the conceptual beliefs, the more consistent the person will be in interpreting the same and similar emotional feelings in similar situations. Conceptual beliefs that are ideologically informed will, like other habituated concepts, most likely result in actions and reactions consistent over time. For example, Jack Jackson grows up in a family and educational system that instilled in him a great love and pride for his country. He read about the many men and women who sacrificed their lives in defense of the freedoms the country offered. After graduating from high school, Jack chose to join the military, proudly wore the uniform, and happily sang the national anthem when the flag was raised. The national anthem he sang came to symbolize the pride and joy he felt about his country. Then, going to a football game he notices what he interprets as players disrespecting the anthem by refusing to stand when it is sung. Despite the protestation by the players that their act of nonconformity was not an act of disrespect to the anthem, but rather a protest against racial injustice, Jack was unable to accept this explanation. His emotional feelings informed and guided by his beliefs and conceptual convictions could not allow for another point of view, this despite the fact that the country he proudly served granted and supported such acts of free speech in the Constitution Jack claimed to defend. If a conceptual belief has been embodied through social influences that regards Whites and Christians as representations of true American identity (see chapter six), it is understandable when such individuals give assent to statements from Donald Trump, who declared that certain congresswomen of color should "go back to where they came from."

Following Clore and Gaspar's analysis, I want to highlight and briefly summarize four of twelve conclusions they draw from their study I have found most salient for my purposes. Those are

> (1) "The information principle. The feelings of emotion provide information about the appraisal of situations with respect to one's goals and concerns." (2) "The attribution principle. The information value, and hence the consequences of affect, depend on how the experience of affect is attributed." (3) "The feelings-as-evidence is that belief-consistent feelings may be experienced as confirmation of those beliefs." (4) "The attention hypothesis is that intensity of feeling activates attentional processes, which are then guided by accessible concepts or beliefs toward concept-relevant information."[32]

When an individual has an emotion, such as a response to bodily pain, one will find and appraise the information that the bodily feeling offers, such as a headache, and with that information strategize how to find resolution to the cause of the negative emotional experience. If the emotional feeling is psychologically based the information will not, in some cases, be clear. Thus, the individual will have to choose among a variety of possible candidates for attribution in order to understand the nature of the feeling. Once an attribution has been determined, the individual believes that in fact the cause of the feeling is due to the chosen attribution. Once one has attributed the object or event as the cause for the emotional feeling, the belief that this is the case will be confirmed and reinforced as it is experienced consistently over time. If I have the feeling of being loved and attribute that to my spouse, this will be confirmed and reinforced if experienced consistently. If I have an intense feeling of love from my spouse, I will heighten my attention on that feeling and be guided by the belief that in fact this feeling of love comes from the experience of my spouse's love. This in turn will lead me to be guided by beliefs and concepts that I attribute to the nature of this love, such as the wonderful qualities I believe my spouse embodies. As long as the conditions remain fairly consistent, my beliefs will remain consistent. A change in circumstances can cause a change in beliefs. If I find that my spouse is no longer offering me the type of loving feelings as before, my feelings of love may lessen or dissipate altogether. My positive views of her qualities may change to a more negative perception, and I might find my feelings becoming those of dislike, annoyance, and even hate. Feelings shape and engender beliefs. Together they motivate action. Motivations to act on perceived needs are, I believe, grounded in the anthropology of human *creatureliness*. This implies dependence. We have fundamental feelings of lack, while at the same time are driven to attain a sense of fullness, a sense of self's well-being in the world. The engine driving this search for fullness is based in our *ontological needs*. These ontological needs give rise to desires. Desires in conjunction with beliefs are the engine in human motivations for action.

DESIRE—APPETITIVE, INTRINSIC, INSTRUMENTAL

There is a good deal of scholarly work by moral philosophers and moral psychologists concerning the roots of human action and motivation. Since this is not a book focused on the many theories offered concerning the nature of motivation, I will limit my discussion to the theory I find most convincing. The dominant theory which I presently find most compelling is the *Humean Theory of Motivation*. What this entails, in its simplest formulation, is "action always originates with a desire that furnishes the actor with a goal; that desire, when paired with a belief about how best to pursue the goal, comprises a motive. It follows on this view that neither a desire nor a belief by itself is sufficient for having a motive."[33] There are three distinctions of desire I believe are important to highlight. These are *appetitive*, *intrinsic*, and *instrumental*. In terms of ontological needs (I examine these needs in chapter three), *appetitive desire* is analogous to appetites for food and drink. The body has appetitive needs that require fulfillment beyond conscious choice. Hunger and sex are grounded in our biological nature such that we are compelled by our bodies to attend to the physical feelings that arise from biological urges. While I can choose to ignore my hunger, and if my will is strong enough, I can starve myself to death, I cannot free myself from the physical effects of hunger by willpower or by reasoning. The same is true of sexual feelings that arise due to the biological disposition to procreate. While I won't die by denying sexual urges (as a celibate I can attest to this, though it can feel like dying sometimes) I cannot rid myself of sexual feelings, no matter how hard I try. Wayne Davis notes that the "objects of appetitive desires are" both "*appealing*" and are "*viewed with pleasure.*"[34] When I am hungry, and I see a slice of pizza I find it appealing, and I see it as an object of pleasure (thus my middle-aged paunch).

Some desires are "desires for states of affairs that are wanted for themselves."[35] For example, my choice to eat can be for the pleasure of satiation, a state that is wanted for itself. But it can also be a desire for the welfare of another. *Intrinsic desire* is not the type of desire that seeks a state of affair for its own sake exclusively. Tim Schroeder states that "[t]o desire something intrinsically is not to desire it exclusively for its own sake, but to desire it at least partially for its own sake."[36] Back to that pizza—while I may desire to eat the pizza because I desire the pleasure of the taste of pizza, I also eat it because I want to stop the pain in my stomach caused by hunger. Wanting to stop the pain is a desire I want for its own sake, while I could easily do this by eating brussel sprouts. I have never to my knowledge had an intrinsic desire for brussel sprouts though. At the same time, I desire the pizza partially for its own sake because I find it appealing and pleasurable.

Neil Sinhababu describes an *instrumental desire* as that "which makes new desires out of pre-existing desires and beliefs about the means to their satisfaction. . . . The initial desires from which instrumental-desire formation begins are called intrinsic desires."[37] So, if I am hungry, I have an appetitive desire. If I want to satisfy my hunger with pizza, I have an intrinsic desire. If I believe that I can best get a freshly made pizza with my favorite toppings by going to my favorite pizza joint, then my desiring to go to said shop is instrumental to my goal of fulfilling my appetitive and intrinsic desires. Sinhababu states that, "[a]ccording to the Desire-Belief Theory of Action, all action is motivated by desire combined with means-end beliefs."[38] So, if I desire that luscious slice of pizza, and I believe that by going to my favorite pizza joint will heighten the probability that I will have my desire satisfied, I can choose to drive to the pizza shop. I could also choose not to do this if I have a stronger desire-belief that cancels my desire for pizza. I might not have enough gas in the car, and I don't have enough money for both gas and pizza, and because I have a desire to get to work tomorrow, that desire being stronger than my desire for the pizza, I can make the choice not to act on my desire for pizza. I will just eat the canned tomato soup in the cabinet, but not the brussel sprouts!

Sinhababu lists five properties of desire, following from his argument that action is not possible without there first being a desire motivating action. (1) *The Motivation Aspect*. "Motivation is the disposition to act."[39] The combination of desire-belief encourages one to act in order to "promote desire satisfaction."[40] The reverse is also true. When one does not believe action will bring about satisfaction, motivation will decrease. While Sinhababu maintains that desire and not belief is "a motivational state,"[41] desire alone is not sufficient for action. Desire "must combine with a means-end belief."[42] Desire, as motivation, is geared toward obtaining a desired state, thus making obtaining such a state intentional. For example, if I desire to lose weight, and I know that making healthier food choices will help in attaining this goal, I may be motivated to make the necessary changes. The reverse is also true; not wanting to lose weight or having a greater desire not to suffer a diet, I will not be motivated to make the necessary changes in behavior. "Believed means and ends can be objects of positive or negative motivation which we intend to achieve or avoid, while desire only makes its content the object of positive motivation and intention."[43] My desire for sugary foods is based on a feeling of pleasure I know will come when I eat such foods. The stronger the desire, the greater the motivation. Desires themselves will not cause us to act if we don't have a sufficient belief that we can acquire the desired object. I may desire a slice of homemade chocolate cake, but if there are no ingredients in the cupboard, and I don't feel like going to the store, I will probably not act on my desire.

(2) *The Hedonic Aspect.* "Thoughts of desires' objects cause pleasure and displeasure."[44] When we desire something, we imagine acquiring it with a sense of pleasure and satisfaction, while not obtaining it brings about displeasure and frustration. This is not a legitimization for philosophical hedonism. While the hedonic aspect of desire is true for all thoughts or experiences of desire-belief satisfaction, it is not true that everyone is motivated by pleasure as the primary goal or end. While a mother finds pleasure in seeing her child succeed at something, this does not mean her desire-belief was motivated by her own pleasure, but rather for the good and success of her child. Sinhababu states that "[d]ifferent desires come with different hedonically charged emotions."[45] We experience such emotions as joy, delight, and so on, when we experience the acquisition of our desired object, while we may experience disappointment, frustration, anger, and so forth, when we don't. Sinhababu highlights Timothy Schroeder's two types of desire in terms of the hedonic aspect, which are structured by the focus of the desire. "[A]version sets one up for anxiety or relief; positive desire makes possible joy or disappointment."[46] If I desire not to receive a driving violation when the patrol car pulls me over, I will desire to avert my possible fate and feel relief if the officer lets me go with just a warning. If I desire the prime rib I see on the menu, I will feel joy if it tastes as good as I imagine, or disappointed if it doesn't. Sinhababu sums up the hedonic aspect, stating "[i]f asked for a conceptual analysis of desire, I'd say that it's a mental state that has Motivational and Hedonic Aspects, or something like them. For something to be a desire—whether the creature having it is human, nonhuman, real, or fictional—it must motivate action in combination with means-end beliefs and be connected by thoughts of its object to pleasure and displeasure."[47]

(3) *The Attentional Aspect.* "Desire directs attention toward things one associates with its object."[48] Sinhababu's attentional aspect has a correlation with Clore's and Gaspar's *attention hypothesis*, discussed above. When I feel anger arising from an experience of injustice, the feeling helps me—within the attentional aspect of desire—to discover what I am desiring; to be treated fairly, with dignity and worth, and so on. At the same time, Sinhababu points out that while "[d]esire's effects on pleasure and attention help us discover

what we desire . . . they leave lots of room for error."[49] I may want to spend time with Diarmaid because I desire the pleasure of his wit and charm. I may deny that wanting to socialize with him may increase my prestige with others, though it might. My principled convictions may believe the use of others for self-aggrandizement unethical. But I may still have an unconscious desire to gain status and prestige, so my pursuit of friendship may be unconsciously motivated for less than principled ends. In the hedonic aspect "positive desires and aversions direct attention differently. Positive desires direct more attention towards desired things . . . aversions direct more attention towards things we desire to avoid."[50] As our desire attends to the objects we want to acquire, attention itself "drives the reasoning that happens when desire makes us 'cast our view' on the causes and effects of its objects."[51] When my desire "casts its view" on the newly open position at the company I work for, I will begin to strategize and reason the best course of action in order to get the position. Thus, "the means-end belief and the desire attach themselves in instrumental reasoning to produce an instrumental desire." My initial desire for the position will create instrumental desires such as working longer hours, taking shorter breaks, studying up on the demands of the new position, and so forth, whatever it takes to the land the job.

(4) *Amplification Aspect.* "Vivid representations of desire's object amplify its motivational, hedonic, and attentional effects."[52] This means that the greater the vividness of the representations of desired objects, the greater the passion. When I was young, I was not the most motivated student. Basically, I was lazy. My parents and teachers tried to motivate me by telling me I needed to get good grades in order to get into college, in order to get a good job. I didn't find their arguments particularly persuasive at the time, because the future seemed so far away. Then, after high school, when I began working menial jobs, at times backbreaking, the vividness of my future became much clearer. My motivation to go to college and study harder was amplified. Hume writes, "Imagination and affections have close union together, and that nothing, which affects the former, can be entirely indifferent to the latter. Wherever our ideas of good or evil acquire a new vivacity, the passions become more violent; and keep pace with the imagination in all its variations."[53] If you have a calm passion about a particular object, it means that the object is simply not vivid in your imagination. While the amplification of vividness helps to "describe how vividness immediately affects desires," it does not describe "its overall effects after triggering other psychological processes."[54] I may look hungrily at a luscious piece of chocolate cake that my friend is eating in front of me, wishing passionately to have a piece myself. But my motivation for the cake may change when I see him spit it out because it has worms in it. Watching this vivid representation changes my belief about the pleasure of the cake, and my motivation to order a piece for myself changes accordingly. So then, "[t]he claim that vividness

amplifies desire is a *pro tanto* claim about immediate effects, not an all-things-considered claim about long-term effects."[55]

(5) *The Desire-Belief Theory of Reasoning.* "The final property of desire is that reasoning doesn't easily change it."[56] We all have a number of desires that militate against our rational beliefs. Issues around sexuality are typical concerns for many religious people. This includes issues like sexual orientation and romantic desires. While there are some religious people who believe homosexuality is a choice rather than something natural to individuals, the reality is that no matter how hard a homosexually oriented person tries to be heterosexual, no amount of desiring will change same sex attraction. Addictions also demonstrate the difficulty of changing desires, no matter how rational the choice to do so. Even with mundane beliefs, desires can be hard to change. I very much believe that my eating habits contribute to my high glycerides, and I believe my doctor when he tells me that cutting out some of the fatty and greasy foods I eat will help lower them, but I have yet conquered my desire for anything that is fried. Rather than reason creating desires, Sinhababu argues, "desire causes experiences which cause the beliefs. The Hedonic Aspect, the Attentional Aspect, and Amplification by Vividness together give desire a rich perceptual phenomenology . . . normative beliefs accompany desires because desire's phenomenology causes beliefs by broadly perceptual processes, not because beliefs cause desires."[57] My ontological, appetitive need to be connected to another gives rise to a desire to be desired by another. My natural desire to be desired draws my attention to the pleasure of another's desiring me, satisfying my need to connect with this other. In my relations with others, I am drawn to those I experience as pleasurable, who make me feel good, and avoid those who I experience as causing displeasure, or make me feel bad. When that which was experienced as pleasurable is representationally vivid, my desire for it is amplified. My experience of the appetitive desire to be desired creates an intrinsic desire, which then leads me to form beliefs based on the pleasantness/unpleasantness of the object I seek to fulfill both my appetitive and intrinsic desire. So then, "desire does far more than motivate action and drive reasoning in human beings. It also causes pleasure and directs attention, and these effects are amplified when its object is vivid."[58] The pleasurable and displeasurable experiences form beliefs, which in turn become evaluative: this is good, this is bad. This evaluative process takes on moral ramifications when dealing with issues of moral action. Because we are self-aware, knowing that many of our actions have moral import, desire plays a significant role in moral motivation. If the objects of our appetitive desires, informed by our identity needs, become ends in themselves, shaping our instrumental desires—our Christian practice—as the source and summit of our goal for happiness, then those objects, taking the place of God, become idols.

THE IMAGO DEI AND MORALITY

The Christian theological tradition claims the divine gifting to human nature the *imago Dei*. Johan De Tavernier objects to those evolutionary biologists who deny this. He argues that

> [c]oncluding from the creation of human persons in God's image that human beings differ in kind and not just degree from other animals seems to me no longer plausible. The imago Dei is not a disembodied notion. I prefer a starting position that takes for granted the biological nature of human beings. The embodied human being, as the imago Dei, has emerged in evolutionary history as a self-conscious being with the capacity of religious awareness and of taking up moral responsibility. An embodied belief in the imago Dei represents our disposition for the religious meaning that is embedded in our species-specific symbolic behavior.[59]

For some, the claim is that this belief is irreconcilable with the fact that evolution has programmed human nature, and that consciousness is simply an epiphenomenon that gives the illusion that we have a volitional mind.[60] Morality, this argument holds, simply developed through the machinations of natural selection and adaptation to changing environments. Tavernier states that the primatologist Frans de Waal captures this with the phrase "the 'veneer theory of morality,' by which he means that human morality must be seen as 'a cultural overlay, a thin veneer hiding an otherwise selfish and brutish nature.'"[61] Instead, Tavernier argues, consciousness—the self-reflexive mind—arises from the body. From a Christian theological perspective, this is a gift of beneficence from a loving God who, through the complexity of evolution, desires for humanity a relationship of mutuality with the divine self. This requires volition, a freedom of choice to enter such relationships. The why and how of mind arising from neuronal and biological nature is beyond my comprehension. And unlike many neuroscientists and philosophers of mind, I do not believe that we are just brains. Markus Gabriel calls this *neurocentrism*.[62] At the same time, how mind arises from our biological materiality is, again, beyond my comprehension. It is a mystery. Our finite minds can never fully comprehend the mind of the infinite—*my thoughts are above your thoughts* (Isaiah 55:9). While some neurocentrists may claim consciousness to be epiphenomenal, there is no scientific proof for this position. This is an ideological perspective with no empirical evidence. It is as much a faith stance as faith in a creator God.

INSTINCTS AND DESIRE

Henri-Jérôme Gagey notes that as human evolution progressed, the advent of reflexive consciousness effected the reduction of human instincts. In nonhuman animals, instincts are programmed to guide biological and social relations. With the diminishment of instinctual drives in human development, the enlargement of the neo-cortex and brain size made possible the rise of self-reflexive consciousness/mind. In doing so, "desire exceeds instinct and historicizes it. Humans accomplish in the realm of desire and works the needs that animals satisfy through the instinct toward certain behaviors for which they are programmed. Human beings desire what they need."[63] In turn, for humans, there is an attribution of "meaningfulness to their desires."[64] Desire is fundamental to social life. It is the engine for all human motivation and social bonding, and it takes on symbolic significance. This is because humans naturally seek the meaning behind both feelings of lack and meaning for action. As Gagey states, "[i]n one way or another, humans satisfy a drive that cannot be extinguished by merely satisfying fundamental physiological needs but that unceasingly seeks satisfaction in new objects. From this perspective, there is a rupture with animal nature. The desire always exceeds, quantitatively and qualitatively, the instinct for which it is a substitute."[65]

LACK AND ONTOLOGICAL NEEDS

In the nature of human desire are fundamental needs giving rise to desires that exceed merely biological satisfaction. The need for *meaning* profoundly affects our motivation in both inner psychological states and in the realm of social life. It is my contention that the need for meaning is ontologically appetitive in nature, analogous to biological appetites. We are meaning makers, searching for the good, the true, and the beautiful. We naturally desire objects we believe will fulfill our psycho-socio-spiritual needs. This quest is teleological. The French psychiatrist Jean-Michel Qughourlian describes desire as

> *psychological movement.* In psychology, there is no movement that is not desire, and there is no desire that is not movement. Every movement requires an *energy*, a "driving force." It also supposes a *finality*, that is, a *goal* toward which its trajectory can be oriented—some object, an idea or an ideal that can order it, attract it, give it definiteness. (emphasis in original)[66]

This teleological trajectory is grounded in a Christian theological conviction that we have, as Michele Saracino puts it, "a built-in desire to be with God and to be like God."[67] Because God is the fountain fullness of all that is good, true, and beautiful, we have a natural inclination for the source of the good, true, and beautiful. Saracino continues, "human beings are created with a gift from God, the spiritual adornment chosen by God, one that reflects God's goodness, generosity, and interest in others."[68] The evolutionary phylogeny of humans has been mysteriously and graciously, for a lack of a better word, encoded, (predestined?), to evolve to become self-conscious creatures endowed with the capacity for loving relationality. In one sense, our facility for entering into mutually loving relationships is deterministic, because we cannot but desire satisfaction for our ontological needs. At the same time the mystery of human freedom is not extinguished. We have the freedom to pursue our ontological identity needs (our ontological desires) in the diversity of intrinsic and instrumental desires presented as options from our sociocultural landscape. We are free to fulfill our call to loving relationality, or we can refuse. But in refusing, we in fact go against our very nature.

Philip Hefner describes humans as "thoroughly natural creatures," which is "to be genetically informed." We have in us "the legacy of our planet's evolving history of motivating behavior by preprogrammed messages, and that this legacy is of primordial significance for us." But we are also, at the same time, "creatures of culture." This means that we have the ability to "self-consciously assess the world we live in and construct frames of meaning that interpret and justify the decisions we make concerning our behavior in this world."[69] Both the biological and the psycho-spiritual natures we possess have fundamental needs that require adequate fulfillment in order for us to flourish in our psycho-spiritual and sociocultural selves. Lacking the fulfillment of these needs leads to numerous deleterious effects in both our inner world and our social world. Despite the fact that we have these needs, this does not mean that we have an inbuilt knowledge guiding our desires to the objects of satisfaction. Desire is nondirectional, that is, "there are no predetermined contents of desire."[70] There is no instinctual drive guiding one as to how to satisfy experiences of lack. We are driven to fulfill our desires but are dependent on others for guiding us in how to accomplish this. Desire is dependent on a belief that a particular object can both satisfy the experienced lack and can be attained. For this we are dependent on others. Hefner notes that "biocultural phenomenon by themselves do not tell how the structures are to be observed, nor how the functioning of the processes is to be carried out. The biocultural sciences, *qua* science, do not tell us to what goals the structures and processes should be directed, nor the limits or value of human intervention into the structures and processes."[71] While instincts guide animal behavior, in both the satisfaction of biological and social needs, humans have to be taught. This is where cultural and social relations enter.

Along with the need for meaning, humans have other fundamental psycho-socio-spiritual needs that inform a sense of self, and feelings of well-being. Each is grounded in the reality of lack, the nature of creatureliness. Jonah Wharff captures this when he writes:

> A feeling of incompleteness is part of the human condition. It is by comparison with others that we become aware of this feeling. We compare ourselves on the

basis of comfort or feelings of well-being. We compare our insides to others' outsides and discover a difference that is experienced as an insufficiency.[72]

While our needs arise from our evolutionary development, they are, I am convinced, drawing each of us to a transcendental fullness that is finally discovered in the fullness of the divine. Our hearts are restless until they rest in the fullness of the self-giving, fountain-fullness of God's eternal love; a love that desired us into being, creating us as naturally desirable. But coming to full self-reflexive consciousness without an experience of being fully desired by the divine, we experience a sense of separation, alienation, and an experience of a lack of fullness, a lack of being. It is my contention that our experience of a lack of fullness/being, our self-reflexive minds, and nondirectional fundamental desires are intrinsically tied to our freedom of will. While our natural biological state, including the nature of brain and neuronal functions, determines our biological and aspects of our psychological existence on the one hand, nondirectional desire on the other hand creates the possibility for choice, despite its limitations and obstacles. We are free to choose among the possible objects of promised satisfaction if we believe we can obtain them. This freedom, however, is not grounded in the illusion of self-autonomy, but in mimesis, as is natural for self-aware social creatures. Our true freedom lies in relationality. It is a freedom that allows us to transcend the boundaries of sociocultural myopathy, a myopathy that is susceptible to habituses of exclusion and marginalization. This vision of freedom is eschatological, a promise of liberty—a liberty promised by the Gospel; for where the Spirit of the Lord is there is liberty. As Rowan Williams states:

> Our human identity therefore becomes one in which we both acknowledge in prayer this dependence and respond to the gift that sets up not only our being but our renewed being in Christ; and in acknowledging that dependence we are empowered to 'do the work of God', to be 'in Christ', as St. Paul puts it. It's about an authority that emerges from yielding not to an alien will but to an affirming source—recognizing that we are here because there is an act that draws us into being and affirms our being. So we do not have to be our own origin; we do not have to try to be self-creators. There is a level of affirmation bringing us into, and holding us in existence, which we do not have to work for.[73]

We have been made to partake in the life of the eternal one, and we are called into that divine reality by love. We are free to accept this call and free to reject it. Rejection is a choice against real freedom, and bondage to the illusion of self-creation. This always leads to idolatry. Idolatry is always a dead-end. It ends up being a worship of the self, a dependent self that claims its self-created independence. This is a madness rampant in the human condition. And it all comes down to a matter of desire.

Each of the human identity needs, experienced sometimes consciously, though usually unconsciously, underlie appetitive psycho-spiritual desires that in turn rely upon the structures of society to inform their means of fulfillment. Most of the time we are unaware of the roots of our fundamental needs, and how they actively compel us to seek objects of satisfaction. How they manifest can be complex and subtle, many times evading rational reflection. In the next chapter I will discuss basic human identity needs from which desires arise. I will then discuss the means of social transference and the structuring of desires in individuals. I hope to demonstrate that the mimetic theory of desire as explicated by René Girard helps reveal the hidden dynamics of both human relationality, as well as social reproduction; especially in relation to the formation of social norms, mores, conventions, taboos, as well as the force for social bonding and social conflict.

NOTES

1. Jonathan Haidt, *The Righteous Mind: Why Good People Are Divided by Politics and Religion* (New York: Pantheon Books, 2012), Kindle.
2. Sebastian Moore, *Let This Mind Be in You: The Quest for Identity Through Oedipus and Christ* (Minneapolis: Winston Press, 1985), 17.
3. Lisa Feldman Barrett, *How Emotions Are Made: The Secret Life of the Brain* (New York: Houghton Mifflin Harcourt, 2017), xi.
4. Ibid, x.
5. Ibid, 26.
6. Ibid.
7. Ibid, 27.
8. Ibid, 28.
9. Ibid, 30.
10. Ibid.
11. Ibid, 31.
12. Ibid, 33.
13. Ibid. 35.
14. Gerald L. Clore and Karen Gaspar, "Feeling Is Believing: Some affective influences on belief," in *Emotions and Beliefs: How Feelings Influence Thoughts*, ed. Nico H. Frijda, Antony S.R. Manstead, and Sacha Bem (Cambridge: Cambridge University Press, 2000), 11.
15. Ibid.
16. Ibid, 12.
17. Ibid.
18. Ibid, 16.
19. Ibid, 17.
20. Ibid.
21. James Ostrow, "Culture as a Fundamental Dimension of Experience: A Discussion of Pierre Bourdieu's Theory of Human Habitus," 279.
22. Gerald L. Clore and Karen Gaspar, "Feeling Is Believing: Some affective influences on belief," in *Emotions and Beliefs*, 25.
23. Ibid.
24. Ibid, 28.
25. Ibid.

26. Ibid, 30.
27. Ibid.
28. Ibid, 31.
29. Ibid. 33.
30. Ibid.
31. Ibid.
32. Ibid, 39.
33. Elizabeth S. Radcliffe, "The Humean Theory of Motivation and Its Critics," in *A Companion to Hume*, ed. Elizabeth S. Radcliffe (Oxford: Blackwell Publishing, 2008), 477.
34. Wayne A. Davis, "The Two Senses of Desire," *Philosophical Studies: An International Journal for Philosophy in the Analytic Tradition*, 45, no. 2 (1984), 183.
35. Schroeder, Tim, "Desire," *The Stanford Encyclopedia of Philosophy* (Summer 2017 Edition), Edward N. Zalta (ed.), https://plato.stanford.edu/archives/sum2017/entries/desire/.
36. Ibid.
37. Neil Sinhababu, *Humean Nature: How Desire Explains Action, Thought, and Feeling* (Oxford: Oxford University Press, 2017), 3.
38. Ibid, 2.
39. Ibid, 23.
40. Ibid.
41. Ibid.
42. Ibid.
43. Ibid.
44. Ibid, 28.
45. Ibid, 32.
46. Quoted in Ibid.
47. Ibid.
48. Ibid, 33.
49. Ibid, 35.
50. Ibid.
51. Ibid.
52. Ibid, 36.
53. Quoted in Ibid, 37.
54. Ibid.
55. Ibid.
56. Ibid, 38.
57. Ibid, 41.
58. Ibid, 43–44.
59. Johan De Tavernier, "Personalism and the Natural Roots of Morality," in *Questioning the Human: Toward a Theological Anthropology for the Twenty-First Century*, ed. Lieve Boeve, Yves De Maeseneer, and Ellen Van Stichel (New York: Fordham University Press, 2014), 56.
60. For a very persuasive argument against this position see Markus Gabriel, *I am Not a Brain* (Cambridge: Polity Press, 2017). Gabriel writes, "Epiphenomenalism generally speaking is the thesis that mental states and processes as a whole have no causal effects on processes in the universe. Epiphenomenalists consider mental states to be pure concomitant features. Epiphenomenalism thus admittedly accepts that there are mental states and processes (at least). But it denies that they causally impact natural occurrences." Kindle.
61. Quoted in Johan De Tavernier, "Personalism and the Natural Roots of Morality," 48.
62. Markus Gabriel, *I Am Not a Brain: Philosophy of Mind for the 21st Century* (Medford: Polity Press, 2017).
63. Henri-Jérôme Gagey, "The Concept of Natural Law in the Postmodern Context," in *Questioning the Human: Toward a Theological Anthropology for the Twenty-First Century*, ed. Lieven Boeve, Yves De Maeseneer, and Ellen Van Stichel (New York: Fordham University Press, 2014), 35.
64. Ibid.
65. Ibid.

66. Jean-Michel Oughourlian, *The Genesis of Desire* (East Lansing: Michigan State University Press, 2010), 17.

67. Michele Saracino, *Christian Anthropology: An Introduction to the Human Person* (New York: Paulist Press, 2015), 30–31.

68. Ibid.

69. Philip Hefner, *The Human Factor: Evolution, Culture, and Religion* (Minneapolis: Fortress Press, 1993), 19–20.

70. Wilhelm Guggenberger, "Desire, Mimetic Theory, and Original Sin," in *Questioning the Human*, 167.

71. Ibid.

72. Jonah Wharff, "Bernard of Clairvaux and René Girard on Desire and Envy," *Cistercian Studies Quarterly*, 42, no. 2 (2007), 183.

73. Rowan Williams, *Being Human: Bodies, Mind, Persons*, Kindle.

Chapter Three

Identity Needs and Mimetic Desire

When I woke up this morning, I did not find myself suddenly overcome with anxiety and vertigo, wondering what in the blazes is my life all about. In fact, I did what I pretty much do most mornings. Once I got over the annoyance of having to get out of a comfortable bed, I went through my usual morning routines. While doing all these things thoughts about my day crept in, what I needed to attend to, what appointments I might have, what books and articles I needed to read in preparation for lectures, or for a research project. In all of this I did not consciously think to myself, why am I doing all this? What is it all for? Yes, I have asked those questions many times, but those were intentional moments that took place when whatever life I was living changed, became difficult, or boring. But for the most part I have many of my *why am I doing this, what meaning does this have for me,* questions pretty much in hand, or at least in a manageable state. That is not to say I don't have my moments of doubt. But I am, for the most part, happy with the meanings that I give to the why's of my life. I feel that for the most part my life has meaning. It has purpose. I have people in my life I love and who love me. I feel that in the important places of my life I am connected to others. These needs for meaning, belonging, and love are sufficiently met in my overall experiences. This has not always been the case, of course. There have been times when I did not experience satisfaction in my need for meaning, belonging, and love. It has been at those times that things were not so fun. It is in the more difficult times that serious questions about the meaning of life arise.

IDENTITY NEEDS

The need for meaning is fundamental to life. Oscar Nudler states that the need for meaning is of the utmost significance for human needs. Meaning shapes and orders our "worlds," that is, the different fields in which we dwell. Meanings make our worlds feel real, and what is most real to us draws our attention. Nudler notes William James' response to the question "*under what circumstances do we think things are real?*" His response: "it is our selective attention that makes different 'worlds,' or 'subworlds,' real for us: 'each world, *whilst it is attended to*, is real after its own fashion, only the reality lapses with the attention.'" (emphasis in original).[1] Our attention goes from one world to another, be that home, school, science, religion, games, myths, and so on. "However, one of these worlds is stronger, 'realer' than the other because it provides the foundation or substratum of them."[2] Meaning in these worlds give us a sense of order, it helps us to experience the feeling that our place in the world is purposeful. When we suffer from a lack of meaning we can experience anger, fear, anxiety, and alienation. Meaning is intimately connected to the conceptual constructs that have been formed in us about the world that allow us to navigate our way in it. Not all of these constructs are cognitive. Many reside in the sedimentation of our emotional feelings. As Nudler states, "a common characteristic of worlds . . . is the non-reflective, uncritical acceptance of the basic assumptions on which they lie."[3]

A ubiquitous underlying fear we all have is of possible impending chaos. This happens when the constructs of our worlds are found to be either illusions or changed by forces beyond our control. Our constructs of meaning are informed by the social structures in which we live in. Over time we embody these structures, they inform and structure our habitus. Paul Sites points out that when "socially constructed realities are threatened, anger occurs; indeed 'righteous anger' often occurs. Since people base their selves and interactions on these constructions, if these are threatened by others, the world and self-constructions no longer make sense and people become angry: meaning is lost."[4] For those who lose all sense of meaning and purpose there arise, tragically, thoughts of suicide. We have heard all too many times that someone has taken his or her life, finding it meaningless. Love is integral to meaning. Love is dependent on the acquisition of connectedness, with ourselves and others.

In *Motivation and Personality*, Abraham Maslow recognized that human motivation is linked to human needs. Each of our basic needs requires objects of satisfaction so that we may develop and flourish. These basic needs are well known; food, shelter, and safety/security. When an individual suffers lack, her attention is drawn to these needs and becomes her overwhelming concern. In fact, if I am suffering from hunger, for example, no matter how much I would like to give my attention to other things, my focus will constantly be pulled toward the empty feeling in my stomach, the lightness in my head, as well as the headache I get when I haven't eaten for some time. Once my basic needs have been sufficiently cared for, I will find there are other needs requiring attention. Maslow recognizes higher needs for human growth and development required to feel a sense of well-being. We need to feel a sense of belonging and a need for love. Obviously, both are connected, in that love is by its nature relational. Even when talking about self-love we are talking about the dynamics of inner psychic relationality, or a response to one's self-concepts. We use ordinary language like, 'I said to myself,' 'I hate/love myself,' and other multiple varieties of self-talk. In the mystery of the human mind we are able to be in relationship with ourselves. Love is a dynamic that flows between one and an "other." We need to experience love from an "other," such as our mother, father, siblings, and friends, in order to feel a sense of worth. We desire to be desired. This natural and innate need for love draws us toward the other, and desires reciprocity. When love is received and returned, the need for belonging is satisfied.

A sense of connectedness to others requires that an individual to be embedded in relations that are consistent, reliable, nourishing. Trust is a key ingredient. Shared values create a sense of commonality and belonging. It would be a rare thing to see a White supremacist and an African American feeling a sense of connectedness to each other. Our experience of connectedness shapes our worlds of meaning. This occurs because shared symbols are acquired in the dynamic flow of relational give and take. We each belong to a variety of relations, in Bourdieu's language, fields. Each of these fields has a set of signifiers, metaphors, and concepts shaping "worlds of meaning." "As people find meaning within their context, they transform a living environment into a world which everything around them has a meaningful place."[5] Over time we embody these signifiers, metaphors, and concepts, which become the hermeneutical lenses by which we make sense of things.

As a fundamental need, meaning requires the articulation of object satisfaction. That is, I need to be able to articulate to myself the means by which I find the ends that make my world meaningful. At the beginning of our lives, we are thrown into a pregiven familial structure. The family has an already made set of rules and conventions shaping relational dynamics. We are taught these rules discursively and through non-verbal modeling. We experience the pleasure of reward when we follow the rules, and we experience displeasure when we don't, through punishment and sanctions. Tacitly we are learning the rules that connect the different members of the family, forming dispositions that help us to maintain a balance between self-expression and group conformity. This is not always an easy balance to maintain. In the relational dynamics of forming bonds and a sense of connectedness, we shape a sense of familiarity to the ways of the world. This familiarity becomes a map helping to guide us in new experiences, a mix of the old with the new. Over time our familiar "worlds of meaning" become more and more settled, concretized. We would experience feelings of constant unbalance if there were too many adjustments. It is this structuring of familiarity that brings us both a sense of well-being and the possibility for conflict. "[D]eep-rooted conflicts . . . clash between completely different ways of perceiving reality."[6] This can be due to *internal* struggles, for example, I come to doubt familiar ways of viewing the world, and *external* when I clash with another worldview because of a difference in hermeneutics.

Our worlds of meaning incorporate what Nudler calls "metaphor dialogues." Different meaning worlds, having their own root metaphors, "can lead to conflicting interpretations of the same facts and to quite diverse kinds of planning and action courses."[7] Let us take for example the metaphoric phrase *the road to salvation*. For most Christians, the meaning of this phrase seems obvious. Jesus is the way to salvation. This concept shapes the meaning worlds of all committed Christians. The problem lies with the explanations engendered by this metaphor. Protestants, Catholics, and Orthodox, as well as the myriad heterodox sects, would have very different interpretations about what this entails. In fact, this phrase and its many interpretations have caused major schisms among these groups, sometimes violent schisms. Intrenchment in worlds of meaning creates a dynamic of *us* and *them*. *Their* worlds of meaning threaten *us* because *they* may attempt to dominate *us* by forcing on *us their* worlds of meaning. We must oppose them, convince them that they are wrong, even if this may lead to violence. In these cases, a sense of being connected to the orthodox group has a *feel* of rightness, and righteousness. This occurs even among non-religious groups, for example, Democrats and Republicans, Capitalists and Socialists.

A sense of meaning and connectedness aids us in developing a sense of control. When we are babies, we begin to experience that certain behaviors on our part create certain reactions by others. Some of these reactions are pleasurable, others unpleasant. Over time, with a desire for the pleasurable we learn to act in ways that we believe will affect/control the actions of others. "If an infant's behavior produces pleasant effects on others, they provide rewarding behavior in turn."[8] A part of this need to control is biological. We need others to take care of us since we cannot do it ourselves in the early years of our lives. At the same time, "as individuals attempt to control the physical world to gratify their biological needs, they attempt to control others, either alone or in coalition(s) to gratify needs related to the self."[9] This need is based on the fact that we require the other(s) to react to us in such a way that we are not under threat. This includes not only threats to our physical well-being, but also to our self-esteem. Sites references studies demonstrating that a person's sense of control of his or her environment has direct effect on feelings of self-esteem. The greater the sense of control, the greater the self-esteem, and vice versa.[10] "People thus attempt to control others based upon a certain concept of self which, it is hoped, will produce certain effects on others in terms of others' estimates of them and/or others' responses toward them."[11] We learn the rules and regulations of the field in order to gain social and cultural capital, that is, the power to control our environment, so that we stave off threats to our well-being, while increasing our self-esteem. This may include desires for status, prestige, and economic security. This is not necessarily something negative. We all want to be free from forces we find threatening. That is why we avoid bullies and choose companions who make us feel good about ourselves. The problem arises when our need for control becomes a desire to dominate. It is also problematic when our need for control leads us to adopt beliefs that require us to subjugate ourselves to another, that in turn denigrate our dignity. In effect we turn our needs satisfaction over to a tyrant. This is pathological. We abdicate our freedom by entering into unequal relationships that utilize power as dominance rather than service. We objectivize ourselves by becoming objects for the other's use. This type of relationship is dehumanizing. It is pathological. We see this manifested in political populism that borders on fascism, where individuals give their wills over to demagogues, violating their moral principles through a form of groupthink. While a fundamental teaching of Christ is to love one's neighbor, many US Christians have been seduced into accepting and valorizing the excluding rhetoric of "Make America Great Again," which easily translates to "Make American self-interest our primary priority."

An important aspect of meaning is the need to be recognized. Our need for connectedness is dependent on someone recognizing us as worthy of belonging. We feel appreciated by others when they make us feel connected relationally. The philosopher Charles Taylor recognized this need, writing that

> our identity is partly shaped by recognition or its absence, or by the *mis*recognition of others, and so a person or group of people can suffer real damage, real distortion, if the people or society around them mirror back to them a confining or demeaning or contemptible picture of themselves. Nonrecognition or misrecognition can inflict harm, can be a form of oppression, imprisoning someone in a false, distorted, and reduced mode of being.[12]

Recognition affects our needs satisfaction for control. Minorities, the poor, the marginalized, the oppressed all experience a lack of recognition when their dignity is denied. We see this all too often with refugees and those seeking asylum because of political unrest or dissent. In the United States, as I am writing this, there are detention camps on the southern border that have forcefully separated parents from their children, because the recognition that they are equal in human dignity has been elided because of political ideologies of racial exclusion and political expediency.

Because of my experiences of the vicissitudes of life, I know that this world is not always safe. Relations of domination are ubiquitous. Physical threats are ever present, whether I want to think about it or not. Relationships can be fragile, and if broken, heartbreaking. There are those who do not always have my best interest at heart. Humans can be a selfish lot. Violence is recorded daily in the press. Thieves want to steal our stuff, so we put locks on our doors. We pay enormous amounts of money for security, either in defense spending, or home security services. Even the moment of birth is fraught with danger, and the body being as fragile as it is, we spend billions on healthcare. We do all this in order to satisfy the need for security. While the threats to our physical well-being are obvious, there are myriad threats to our sense of self and its well-being. Our worlds of meaning incorporate this need and its satisfiers. Vern Redekop writes that "security, as an identity need, deals with the security of the person in the identity group, in the present and in the future. Security implies physical, emotional, intellectual, and spiritual safety."[13] Even walking into a room of friends or relatives can demonstrate our need for security. While I like hanging out with Bill, Tim, Sarah, and Ron, I know that given the chance Tim will say something sarcastic and make me feel stupid in front of the others. To be safe from embarrassment I have learned to strategize how not to set Tim off. I want to feel safe wherever I am. I learn to play the field, though I may not be conscious of the details. With Sarah I can be more open and vulnerable, and my disposition toward her reflects this. The same goes with the others. I have shaped my bodily hexis (*the storehouse of deep-rooted dispositions*) to fit the situation in order to meet my need for security.

The same goes in other realms of social life. We are taught that certain groups are a threat to our well-being, and we form dispositions toward members of these groups, or at least the idea about members of these groups, since we may never have actually met any. Redekop points out, "[t]he degree of security one needs is a result of fear, which is itself a function of past experiences."[14] Our past experiences, both our personal experiences, as well as the experiences of our national and ethnic groups, transmitted through narratives of history and myth, can create a deep, and possibly delusional, fear of the "other."

Humans are agents, that is, each has volition and has the need to be able to act freely in order to endeavor to satisfy one's needs. "To meet the demands of this identity need, an action must be a matter of choice. And if it is truly a matter of choice, it implies some control over the immediate social and physical environment."[15] The tragedy for millions of peoples in human history has been the enslavement of free action due to a variety of social, political, and cultural forces. This includes literal slavery, as well as social and cultural ideologies that have acted to subjugate to subaltern status ethnic, racial, gendered, and national "others."

Our "worlds of meaning" incorporate the need to feel connected to others who provide us with a sense of worth, which helps to elevate our self-esteem, giving us confidence that we belong in our social space. Our sense of connectedness is tied to our ability to control the relational environment around us, giving us confidence that our basic needs will be met through the cooperation between ourselves and others. We keep threats at bay when we feel satisfied that our need for control is met. Because there are in fact real threats to our *selves* we need to have a sense of security. We create barriers and protective strategies to keep out forces that we believe will harm us in some way. This need is based on experiences of harm, either directly, or through the narratives of our social and cultural memory. And, as agents, we need to be able to act in order to acquire the objects satisfying our needs. Each of these identity needs must have sufficient satisfiers for us to feel a sense of well-being. A major issue in the acquisition of a sense of self at peace with our world/s is/are the means by which we acquire and satisfy these needs. As I stated in the previous chapter, we are not born with the biological hardware that guides us to the proper objects that will bring us to a feeling of wholeness in those areas of our lives shaped by our ontological needs. Desire has replaced most of our instincts. Because desires are not preformed to know the means to satisfy one's needs, they require models to help guide them to the objects of satisfaction. This is the basis for human relationality, and it is the basis of human conflict. Desire draws us to one another. As dependent creatures, we rely on each other for the resources we need to reach a place of well-being. At the same time, the limitations of human finitude, as well as concupiscence (distorted desires), mean that we many times lead one another astray by our misguided, and sometimes malevolent, ideologies that distort our call to love. The issue that I now want to explore is the mechanics of social and cultural transference. How do we learn what objects will satisfy our ontological psycho-socio-spiritual needs? What influences shape the direction of our desires? René Girard has offered profound insights about our mimetic nature that helps us to answer these questions.

MIRROR NEURONS

Before I begin my examination of René Girard's mimetic theory, I want to say a word about recent neuroscientific discoveries concerning the mimetic nature of the brain. Recent neuroscientific studies reveal that the human brain has evolved neuronal structures that give humans the natural, biologically grounded, capacity to imitate others. Jean-Michel Oughourlian argues, based on the works of such neuroscientists as Antonio Damasio and Vittorio Gallese, that the human brain is wired to act mimetically. This is due to the existence in the brain of "so-called mirror neurons." Oughourlian states that "[t]he mirror system puts humans in a prerational resonance with other humans. It makes the 'individual' capable of identifying the other's gestures, of interpreting the other's actions and intentions and of understanding and imitating them and may even constitute the underlying neurophysiological foundations of empathy as well as explaining the determining factors in human action."[16] Oughourlian takes note of Gallese's grounding of "our emotions and cognition in basic interrelational mechanisms." Nidesh Lawtoo notes the work of Giacomo Rizzolatti and Corrado Sinigaglia, who have found that

> the 'primary' function of the 'mirror neuron system' concerns their 'role linked to understand the meaning of the actions of others.' According to this view, we don't understand others only through the mediation of our minds (though we certainly do that too). At the most basic level, we understand others through an 'embodied simulation' that gives us an immediate access to the psychic life of the other.[17]

These findings give a biological grounding to Girard's theory of mimetic desire, discussed below.

MIMETIC DESIRE

It is not a recent revelation that humans imitate one another. Many ancient Greek thinkers, such as Plato and Aristotle, were very much aware of the mimetic nature of humans. Plato understood imitation, or mimesis, as representational. Objects in the material world represent eternal unchanging forms. Objects in the material world are suspect for Plato *because* of their mimetic nature. The real are the unchanging forms, while the material world lacks the fullness of reality, and is mutable. The material world is a mere copy. The real is immutable. We should focus on the original and not the copy. All copies are imitations, many of them bad ones. Aristotle also recognized the mimetic nature of humans but had a more positive opinion about this than Plato. Matthew Polotsky writes that Aristotle understood imitation as "second nature to human beings from childhood, one of our advantages over other animals being that we are the most imitative creatures in the world. It is by imitation that we first learn."[18]

Prior to the insights of Girard, the idea that mimesis is representational was a long-established perspective among artists, poets, novelists, and dramatists. For example, a chair represents for Plato a material representation, a copy, of the form of a chair. Actors on the stage represent the characters they are portraying. A painter paints a representation of objects. It might be in the realist style or expressionist; in either case it represents an object in the mind of the artist. There is no doubt that at one level mimesis is representational, otherwise we would never be able to learn from others. We learn language through imitation, for example. Daily we experience representational forms of imitation. Andrew Meltzoff writes that "the type of imitation that bears on appearance, this disposition to imitate the action one observes in another, is . . . neither facultative, something one does or does not do by choice, nor is it aleatory, something that depends on uncertain contingencies: it is neurological, automatic, and necessary."[19]

The insight that René Girard offers us is that mimesis is more than just representational. As Robert Hamerton-Kelly states,

> *imitation is not just a replication of external action or style, nor in internal emotion of affect, but fundamentally in imitation of desire.* I imitate the other's desires, that is, *I want what he wants*—however differently I might express and pursue that identical goal . . . Girardian mimesis imitates primarily and specifically, not the whole range of external and internal actions, but the desire of the other (emphasis in original).[20]

Girard came to this discovery when reading and teaching courses on literature. He noticed that certain authors recognized the mimetic nature of desire. Girard saw that these authors realized that desire was imitative, and derivative. Girard dismissed what he called romantic writers because of the prevailing illusion in their narratives that the desire for particular objects was motivated by a direct and autonomous value believed to reside in the object itself. In other words, it is the perceptiveness of the individual that autonomously discovers the intrinsic value of the object. The romantic lie is the belief that the value of an object is independent of human desiring shaped by mimetic modeling, and that the recognition of value is autonomously discovered. If this were true, then one could argue that nationalism has intrinsic value emanating from the ontological value inherent in the nation. Thus, a challenge to nationalism is a challenge against reality. The enlightened novelist is one who recognizes that autonomous recognition of inherent value is an illusion. Objects of human construction have no essential value beyond what is given them by human beings.

Girard's initial discovery of the mimetic nature of desire is expounded in his first book on the subject, *Deceit, Desire, and the Novel*. In this work Girard highlights the role of mediators/models of desire. As stated previously, our desires do not have predetermined contents. Our attention is drawn to objects through the mediation of models. There are two types of models according to Girard: exterior and interior. As an example of exterior modeling, Girard uses the story of *Don Quixote* by Miguel Cervantes. In the novel, Don Quixote is motivated to be a great knight and turns to the exemplar of knights, in his estimation, Amadis of Gaul. By choosing Amadis as his model, Don Quixote gives his will over to the knight in order to embody the qualities of knighthood Amadis represented to him. Not only does Don Quixote imitate Amadis' behavior, he even begins to see the world through the eyes of Amadis. The objects in the world take on a new meaning when mediated by Amadis' perspective. For Girard, Amadis has become the mediator of desire for Don Quixote. For Don Quixote "chivalric existence is the imitation of Amadis in the same sense that the Christian existence is the imitation of Christ."[21] Michael Kirwan states that,

> Don Quixote effectively abandons any independent judgment (*sic*) of his own. He has no independent 'self'. Girard illustrates this state of affairs geometrically, by declaring that desire has a *triangular* structure. Instead of desire being a single linear relation (subject A desires object B—'Quixote desires to be a perfect knight'), we have three elements: A only desires B because C (in this case, Amadis de Gaul) has directed his attention towards it. Since Quixote's desires are channeled or mediated by Amadis, point C of the triangle is called the 'mediator' or 'model'.[22]

What distinguishes exterior mediation and interior mediation is the distance between the model and the imitator. This distance is measured in time, level of prestige, and one's place in the social hierarchy. Another aspect that differentiates exterior and interior mediation is that in exterior mediation there is no possibility for conflict between the model and the imitator. The greater the distance between the model and imitator, the less the possibility for conflict or rivalry.

The closer in proximity between the model and the imitator, either in time, prestige, or hierarchical parity, the greater the possibility for conflict and rivalry. As most have heard, if not experienced, one of the most contentious forms of rivalry is sibling rivalry. This has to do with the closeness in proximity siblings have in all three categories. In both exterior and interior mediation, the imitator, for whatever reason, esteems another as worthy of imitation. The primary models of course are our parents. Because of the natural relational bonds between a child and a parent, the child will naturally learn to focus desires on the objects observed to be valued by the parent. As the child grows, this attention to objects offering needs satisfaction will be imitated from other significant individuals or groups held in esteem. Desire, as understood by Girard, is triangular. Objects that we believe will satisfy ontological psycho-socio-spiritual needs are never unmediated. We learn what to desire through observing and imitating others.

The objects of mimetic desire are multiple. They include physical objects, tastes, style, beliefs, dispositions, status, prestige, power, values, and ideologies. The objects in each of the many categories offer the individual a promise of satisfaction for the fundamental ontological needs giving rise to intrinsic and instrumental desires. When we experienced hunger in infancy, we felt a desire to relieve the pain and displeasure. Our parents provided food typical of the culture they were living in. As we grew, we took it for granted that the types of food offered to fulfill our hunger needs were normative, and we learned to value *our* cultural foods. We habituate an intrinsic desire for familiar foods. The way we dress ourselves, the rituals we learn from our family and social groups, and the myriad social practices we adopt from our cultures become normative for us. We learned to desire these ways of dress, rituals, and social practices, because these objects were mediated through significant models in our socio-cultural milieu. I will ask my students to look around the room and notice what everyone is wearing. While no one is dressed exactly the same, each is wearing clothing that is typical and normative for American students to wear. Interestingly, I have Muslim students who, for the most part, dress like typical American college students. But when I visited the local mosque during Ramadan, I noticed one of my female Indian Muslim students dressed in traditional Indian clothing. In this context, traditional clothing was normative. We make our choices of needs satisfaction within the structures shaped by our chosen models. We reproduce these structures in our actions. This is not always reproduced exactly as modeled. We have agency and can choose to modify our actions. But there are no modifications that are not modeled in some way. I cannot dress like a Martian, because I have never seen a Martian, except fictional ones.

Value formation is also formed and structured by mimetic desire. Anything we learn to value has been mediated through a significant other. When I was a member of an evangelical Protestant church, I learned to value the interpretation of the Gospel as it was taught to me by those I deemed worthy role models. I believed that they knew the truth. Having formed attitudes of respect for their knowledge and expertise, I had no reason to doubt them. When I encountered situations in my life where what I was taught to believe did not appear to fit the actual state of things, I began to waver in my esteem for my mentors. This led me to seek other mentors from whom I might gain a better sense of what was truly "gospel." This has been a long journey, nowhere near completion.

Oughourlian states that "desire is the heart and the energy of the relation to the other, the first movement that carries us toward life."[23] If not for desire we would not be able to experience love, be drawn toward the other, have any type of meaningful relationships. When it comes to relationships of love, the increase of desire is a positive. The greater desire for the other, the stronger the bond. But the downside of mimetic desire is that it can easily take a negative turn when the objects of desire are scarce. Notice a child playing with a toy. She seems to be finding a great deal of pleasure in it. Then introduce another child into the same room and watch how she is drawn to the same toy. Out of all the toys in the room, the one the first girl is playing with is deemed more valuable, more fun, than all the others. But there is, alas, only one of its kind. So, the second girl asks if she can play with it. The first girl refuses, and an argument ensues. Before long the two girls may go beyond pushing and pulling and begin to attempt real damage on the other. This dynamic is called by Girard *mimetic rivalry*. This occurs when the object of desire, modeled by another, cannot be shared by both because of the limitations of resources. Oughourlian states that mimetic rivalry "is always rooted in one of the two following claims: the claim of the self for the ownership of its own desire; and the claim of desire for its anteriority, its seniority over the other's desire, the other desire that has generated it, on which it is modeled."[24] In other words, I desired the toy before I saw the other child playing with it, and my desire to play with it trumps those of the other child, so I am going to take the toy away from him. The illusion in all of this is the belief that desire and the supposed value intrinsic to the object arose from an autonomous perception of value resident in the object. Value was perceived without mediation. Such a perspective denies the socio-relational formation of values. If a value is essential to an object, then there is no need for mediation.

THOUGHT EXPERIMENT

Think about what you value. Of course, there are so many things that it may be difficult at first to choose just one. But think about something in particular, especially something that is really valuable to you. It may be a material object, a relationship, or an idea—such as a moral conviction, a strongly held principle. First, examine what need is filled by valuing whatever you presently have in your mind. Let's say you are thinking of the person with whom you are presently in relationship. In this case there may be more than one need, for example, a need for connectedness (intimacy), a need for sex (to procreate as well as intimacy), a need for meaning which the relationship offers by giving your life purpose, and so on. Now ask yourself, where did you learn to form your desire for this particular person? One way of responding is to list the qualities that this person has that you find attractive. Now ask yourself; why do I find those qualities attractive? There are those who don't find your partner's qualities attractive, but you do. If you think about it long enough, and you could access the archived experiences of your life, I dare say that someone modeled those qualities as attractive to you and you experienced pleasure in those qualities. If you like people who are kind, there was at some time, or times, in your life where you experienced the pleasure of being treated kindly. If you like intelligence in your partner, you experienced at some time intelligence in some other as pleasurable. On and on. People are also attracted to more negative qualities in others. These too have somewhere along the line been modeled. Those who we imitate, as stated above, have some significance for us. There are qualities about them that we find worthy of emulation.

Now imagine that you desire greater cultural capital, that is, you desire the acquisition of certain qualities, such as education, intelligence, sophisticated tastes and style, status, privilege, and so forth. You may want these qualities because they empower you to attain what you deem as higher and better standing in society, and greater access to the resources you deem attractive. With greater social capital you have more control over your environment, you are free from the dictates of others. Being boss is better than being an employee. You get to run the show. Having status gives you a greater sense of self-esteem. You feel like a winner, while the failure in attaining social status and recognition makes you feel like a loser. If you think that you are above such petty ambitions, imagine being in a small group of people with whom you are not that familiar. You want to fit in, be a part of the conversation. As a discussion flows along you are thinking about how to contribute, show that you have some knowledge of the topic. Then an idea comes to mind and you risk sharing it, hoping the others see your cleverness. You speak and suddenly the conversation abruptly stops. They look at you like you just said the stupidest thing they ever heard. You are embarrassed, your face turns red. You want to crawl under a rock, or at least get out of the room as quickly as possible. While this experience is not exactly the same as wanting to climb the social ladder, the same dynamic is still happening. We all want to be esteemed, to be desired. This gives us a sense of belonging, being appreciated, recognized for our worth. Now that you have made an apparent fool of yourself, you find the environment threatening, unsecure. These people's judgments make you feel insecure, and you want to retreat and lick your wounds.

Now imagine yourself back in your room after this terrible event. You keep rehearsing the event in your mind, wondering where it all went wrong. Then, to make yourself feel better about yourself, you begin to think that just maybe "I am not the problem, it is those dimwits who simply couldn't grasp my superior intelligence. It is really their issue; they are to blame for my embarrassment because of their dull wittedness. To heck with them, they can go. . . ." Now you feel a tad better. Girard notices something very important in this dynamic. While it is common to compete over material objects, especially when they are scarce (crude oil has led to multiple conflicts) there is another form of desire based on our ontological needs. These desires lead us to conflicts that go beyond material goods—though material goods may be ancillary to these other desires.

In order to understand this other form of desire, let us imagine two different scenarios. First scenario: When Michele was in high school, she decided she wanted to be a pilot. This came about after she saw a documentary about Chuck Yeager. Yeager and his aeronautic feats so captured her imagination that she became focused on this goal. In the process she read everything she could about Yeager and watched YouTube videos of his flights. Yeager was her hero. She wanted to be just like him. She saw in Yeager a sense of élan that she desperately wanted to embody. Yeager became her Amadis of Gaul. She saw the world through his eyes.

Second scenario: Tom and Jerry are good friends, but it is obvious that Jerry is the wittier one, quicker with the repartee, and charming to boot. Tom is very much attracted to these qualities in Jerry, but one of Tom's problems is that, when they are in a group of friends it seems that everyone tends to gravitate toward Jerry. While they are friendly with Tom, he simply isn't held in as high esteem as Jerry. Tom slowly begins to resent this, because he wants to be admired in the same way. He also wants the acclamation and admiration. The problem is that he is simply not the best at conversations, and that he always has a witty comeback—two hours too late! Over time this resentment increases, and he finds himself becoming more and more agitated the more time he spends with Jerry. Now when the group gathers, he begins to make little biting comments whenever the others show deference to Jerry. He finds his animus toward Jerry growing stronger. Finally, he simply can't take it anymore and one day, in the midst of a gathering with the group, Tom tells Jerry to go. . . . The friendship ends, and now the two former friends have become enemies. Tom sees Jerry as an obstacle to his desire for recognition, thus effectively scapegoats Jerry as the reason for his frustration and lowered self-esteem.

These two scenarios have both a common element and an important difference. Let us look first at the common element. In chapter two I examined ontological needs that give rise to desire. I have argued that our ontological needs are due to our creatureliness, manifesting in us feelings of ontological lack. We require that these needs be satisfied to gain a sense of well-being, a sense of self, a sense of fullness. What is lacking in our "selves," according to Girard, is *being*. Sebastian Moore would interpret this as a loss of unity/oneness that results from self-awareness, which leads to a sense of separateness and a loss of a sense of desirability (see Conclusion). Our needs, giving rise to nondirectional desire, motivate us to seek satisfaction by means of imitation. We look to significant others to direct us to object satisfaction. This is what is happening in both Michele and Tom. They both have engendered particular desires based on fundamental needs. Michele was drawn to aviation because of Chuck Yeager's influence. He became the model for her desires. Pursuing the vocation of a pilot helped shape her need for meaning and purpose in life. Tom needed to feel a sense of recognition and fashioned his understanding of what this entailed by the example he saw in Jerry. In both cases Michele and Tom wanted something they believed was present in their models. Chuck and Jerry had qualities that Michele and Tom felt lacking. In Girardian terms, Chuck and Jerry had more *being*, and Michele and Tom wanted this being to fill the sense of lack in themselves.

The difference in these cases has to do with the distance between the model and the imitator. Chuck Yeager is an exterior mediator of desire for Michele. The two will never clash because of their social distance; Yeager has already accomplished what Michele has yet to attain, and he does not fear that Michele will steal these accomplishments, his prestige and status, his personal élan. Michele will probably never meet her hero. It is different with Tom and Jerry. There is almost no social difference between them. Jerry, in this case, acts as an interior mediator of desire for Tom. Tom desires to fill his need for recognition with Jerry's qualities of charm and wit. Since he can't, he begins to resent Jerry. This resentment morphs a friendship into a rivalry. Girard calls this type of desire *metaphysical*. We each desire a fullness of being due to our ontological lack. We desire the being of others, especially those we believe to have an abundance of being as manifested in qualities we find attractive. The glossary section of *The Girard Reader* offers a definition of metaphysical desire. The term interdividual in this definition is Girard's and Oughourlian's term for the idea that human personhood develops in interrelational dynamics formed through mimetic desire. The definition given is rather lengthy, but I feel it helpful to quote its entirety.

> *Metaphysical Desire.* As mimetic or interdividual beings we associate being or reality with the other, the model or mediator. Our deepest desire is not for things or objects, but to *be*. In struggles with the model-rival, and particularly when the subject seems to come to a dead-end against the model-obstacle, it becomes apparent from a mimetic analysis that the subject wants the being of the model-mediator. This is the source of fascination, hypnosis, idolatry, the "double," and possession. The experience of the double occurs when the model-obstacle as overpowering other is so internalized that the subject does not experience a distinction of self and the model-mediator. The subject is thus "possessed" by the other. The extreme alternatives are suicide or murder of model-obstacle. Other possibilities are schizophrenia, escape into a new identity, and liberation through the release experienced in love and forgiveness. This latter is the work of a good or conversionary mimesis.[25]

As we go about life's journey, directing our desires toward objects we believe will satisfy our ontological needs (though we are rarely cognizant that this is what we are doing), we develop strategies, inner maps, that we hope will guide us to the attainment of our quest for well-being, for fullness, for more being; a conviction of our desirability. We are guided in this venture by the many model/mediators we encounter and to whom we relate. All the while, we develop, structure, and reinforce emotional feelings that allow us to enter new situations with confidence, having the resources of previous experiences. We become acclimated and familiarized with the objects of needs satisfaction, while they create a sense of normativity for us. Conflicts arise in the realm of intrinsic and instrumental desires. The desire for meaning, security, control, connectedness, recognition, and action, as appetitive desires, are positive, in that they draw us out of ourselves into relationships with others. It is what makes us social creatures, reliant upon one another in order to attain each one's welfare and flourishing. It is in the objects of desire (intrinsic) and the means-ends of desire (instrumental) where the trouble lies. The mediators of our desires are fallible human beings, who themselves have imitated other fallible human beings. What are presented to us as the true ends for ontological satisfaction, that is, in metaphysical terms, the true, good, and beautiful, are, in so many cases, cheap copies that promise fulfillment, but deliver simulacra, empty copies. We seek finite objects to fill infinite desires. We become addicted to the simulacra and lose sight of the real thing. And because so many of these objects are scarce, we tend to struggle with each other for possession, whether for material goods, or for the pyscho-socio-spiritual objects we feel lacking in ourselves and see in others. In attempting to possess the objects of desire from our finite mediators/models, or when our mediators/models become ends in themselves, both give rise to practices of idolatry. Idolatry is a relational dead-end. It is spiritual suicide.

It also has social consequences. Mimetic rivalry, while giving rise to interpersonal conflict, can also lead to social division, and social violence. By attaching our desires to temporal ends, such as status and class privilege, we can turn the quest for greater being into acts of social exclusion.

THE SCAPEGOAT MECHANISM

In his examination of mimetic desire, Girard recognized an important effect that takes place when individuals fail to attain the objects of desire. Intrinsic desires inform objects with value. For example, among many White Americans there is implicit value to being White, with various attendant privileges. For many of these White Americans there is the added reality, and value, of their being Christian (see chapter six). This is implicit for many Whites, and White Christians, because the formation of this value, modeled by others in their *field*, is a cultural given. It becomes, unconsciously for the most part, a part of one's habitus. When there is a perceived threat to one's status as privileged, animosity toward those believed to threaten one's privilege—one's cultural capital—arises and can lead to violence. Instead of recognizing or even questioning the validity of White and Christian privilege, those who feel threatened tend to place blame for the perceived loss of privilege on a convenient victim. When a whole group of people, in this case White Christian Americans, have a long tradition that supports and valorizes social hegemony feel their hegemony threatened by a subaltern group there are the makings of social conflict. This animus can be both internal and external. That is, it can be directed against an "other" within one's national boundaries, as well as the "other" from a different nation. It is not important that those perceived to be the cause of loss of status are in fact guilty. What matters is that these "others" act as convenient scapegoats in order to direct the group's animus. These "others" are sacrificed—excluded, imprisoned, marginalized, murdered, or colonized for the sake of national interests—in order to maintain the status quo.

In Girard's mimetic theory, conflict arises due to a loss of difference between antagonists. In the case of White Christian supremacists, the loss of social and cultural capital to non-White, non-Christian groups creates fear. This is related to feelings of loss of privileged status. Girard relates this loss of difference to what he calls doubling. Doubling, in Girard's mimetic schema

> refers to the progressive and mutually reinforcing de-differentiation of subjects that occurs by virtue of an intensification of mimesis. That is, mimesis encourages, through positive feedback, an increasing symmetry between antagonists, which emerges despite increasing attempts at differentiation; it tends toward the erasure of significant differences between individuals—those differences that mark their sociopsychological identity and position within a particular order.[26]

In other words, the privileges that attend to White Christian hegemony symbolize/model to subalterns the value and desirability of such privileges, and through mimesis form desires for the same cultural, symbolic, and economic capital. Thus, doubling occurs. As non-White, non-Christian others form their desires on the model of White and Christian privilege, the model itself becomes a rival, because in most cases the model is unwilling to give up its position and power. For the model, then, in desiring to maintain hegemony, the imitator also becomes a rival. As a means of legitimating and justifying positions of hegemony, narratives bolstering and reinforcing cultural and symbolic capital will be created and disseminated.

Nathan Colborne notes that in isolated individual mimetic rivalries the conflict that arises over the loss of difference may be dealt with "through psychological repression or sublimation or, at worst, a fistfight or two."[27] But when the rivalry consists of large groups of people, such large-scale rivalry can bring about a social crisis. If, for example, wealthy and privileged Whites begin to draw the ire of poor, and culturally powerless Whites, the scapegoat mechanism allows those with hegemonic cultural capital to safeguard their positions of privilege and power. This is accomplished by shifting the focus from their own complicity in the marginalization of fellow Whites onto an arbitrary victim. While Girard notes that the surrogate victim is innocent, the perpetrators of victimage will claim support for their choice of victim with legitimizing rhetoric, indicting the chosen scapegoat as the cause for social instability. Colborne writes that the chosen victim "becomes the focus of the intense social anxiety spawned by mimetic rivalries spiraling out of control and becomes seen as the cause of this social breakdown. . . . The social body . . . now forms itself as a unified body against this scapegoat."[28]

Scott M. Thomas writes that "the antagonism of doubles relates to nationalism, fundamentalism and religious resurgence as a way of responding to the problems of modernity—identity, authenticity, meaning—which are problems that relate to the collapse of difference in society."[29] The irony of doubling is that, as differences begin to lessen the rhetoric of difference increases. For example, while the antagonists mirror each other's desires and actions—thus, doubling—each claims to be substantively different from the other. "Our cause is just because we are just, while they are perpetrators of injustice. Thus, our violence is righteous, theirs is evil." In relation to the ideology of nationalism, Thomas states that "[a] nationalist can take what are considered to be (by the outsider) the neutral, minor, facts about people—language, religion, culture and history—and construct a narrative in which they are transformed into major differences."[30] Thomas further notes that in the field of political science studies researchers have pointed out "the important role of political leaders and political institutions"[31] in the reinforcement of purported differences. In chapter four I discuss the role of both political and religious leaders in fulfilling the role of Antonio Gramsci's "intellectuals" in the dissemination of such rhetoric.

It is important to note that having mediators/models is not a negative thing. In fact, we must have them in order to know how to direct our desires in finding objects of satisfaction. We are creatures who imitate. Many mediators/models are life giving, guiding us closer to what is the true, the good, and the beautiful. Of course, this is an evaluative statement. With any evaluative judgment there is a measure. In this case the measure for a Christian is the will of God, as manifested in the life and teachings of Jesus Christ. However, on closer observation, it becomes obvious that interpretations of the teachings of Jesus Christ are not so easily agreed upon. Go to three different churches and you will get four interpretations.

Despite the profession by Christians that Jesus is the definitive manifestation of the will of God in human expression, the fact remains that we are all historically culturally bound beings. We live in times and cultures that have traditions. These traditions, many of which are in the form of national, ethnic, gendered, and economic narratives, mediate cultural identities, shaping one's sense of needs and object satisfaction. These various social structures inform our habitus, our way of being in and interpreting the world. Culture influences our emotional feeling states, our beliefs about acceptable object satisfaction. Cultural constructs, when acquired through the structuring of social learning, shape our self-identities, as plastic as they may be in the modern world. These identities give us an anchor, a perceived sense of place in our social and cultural landscape. Many facets of our identity are positive, life giving, self-affirming, helping us more confidently enter into mutual and loving relationships. Being called through our models in forming caring and empathic dispositions opens the possibility of crossing over boundaries to identify with and relate positively with social, cultural, ethnic, and religious "others." The teachings of Jesus compel us to form these types of dispositions toward others—love your enemy, forgive seven times seventy, do unto others, feed the hungry, and so on. At the same time cultures can instill in our habitus dispositions of exclusion, and they may use illegitimate interpretations of the gospel to legitimize this. Culture has on offer a number of ideologies, from downright malevolent, to enlightened self-interest. Every Christian, no matter their place of origin, is a mixture of structures, a mixture of ideologies. We all see the world through multifaceted hermeneutical lenses. These in turn elicit and inform our emotional responses to experiences of the world. The challenge for the Christian is self-awareness, self-knowledge. Do our various hermeneutical lenses view the world by the mediation of the gospel? What *is* the gospel? If we are naturally interpreting reality through lenses formed through imitation, how do we know the best hermeneutical strategy to best interpret the will of God? What then is the hermeneutical key to interpreting the gospel? How do we recognize the true, the good, and the beautiful, and not cheap imitations? How do we learn to desire the true, the good, and the beautiful, and overcome our addictions to imitations of false copies?

It is my goal to attempt to offer possible ways of answering these questions. While I cannot, and will not, claim to possess *the* key, the definitive answers to these questions, I do believe some hermeneutical strategies, *keys*, are better than others. Because our hermeneutical lenses are shaped by concepts that inform our meaning worlds, embodying feelings and dispositions toward the world, I want to examine an aspect of our conceptual structures. This has to do with the nature of *ideology*. As I discussed above, the formation of values is intimately connected to relationality. We imitate and form our meaning worlds through the interplay of social relations and ontological identity needs. An important aspect of this interrelational formation is the construction of ideas about the world that either open us to the other, willing to see the other as having dignity and worthy of respect, or close us to the other, especially in relation to groups of people we define as "other," the *"them"* to our *"we."*

NOTES

1. Oscar Nudler, "On Conflicts and Metaphors: Toward an Extended Rationality," in *Conflict: Human Needs Theory*, ed. John Burton (London: Palgrave Macmillan, 1990), 177.
2. Ibid, 178.
3. Ibid.
4. Paul Sites, "Needs Analogues of Emotions," in *Conflict: Human Needs Theory*, 18.
5. Vern Neufeld Redekop, *From Violence to Blessing: How an Understanding of Deep-Rooted Conflict Can Open Paths to Reconciliation* (Ottawa: Novalis, 202), 33.
6. Ibid.

7. Oscar Nudler, "On Conflicts and Metaphors: Toward an Extended Rationality," in *Conflict: Human Needs Theory*, 190.
8. Paul Sites, "Needs Analogues of Emotions," 13.
9. Ibid, 13.
10. Ibid, 14.
11. Ibid, 15.
12. Charles Taylor, "The Politics of Recognition," in *Multiculturalism: Examining the Politics of Recognition*, ed. Amy Gutman (Princeton: Princeton University Press, 1994), 25.
13. Vern Neufeld Redekop, *From Violence to Blessing,* 40.
14. Ibid.
15. Vern Neufeld Redekop, *From Violence to Blessing*, 41.
16. Jean-Michael Oughourlian, *The Mimetic Brain* (East Lansing: Michigan State University, 2016), xviii.
17. Nidesh Lawtoo, *(New) Fascism: Contagion, Community, Myth* (East Lansing: Michigan State University Press, 2019), Google Play Ebook.
18. Matthew Polotsky, *Mimesis* (New York: Routledge, 2006), 16.
19. Quoted in Jean-Michel Oughourlian, *The Genesis of Desire*, 89.
20. Robert Hamerton-Kelly, "A Theory of Religion and Violence," *Paper Presented to the UCLA Dept. of History*, Jan. 2008, http://www.hamerton-kelly.com/talks/Theory_of_Religion_and_Violence.html (accessed 5–8–2010).
21. René Girard, *Deceit, Desire, and the Novel: Self and Other in Literary Structure* (Baltimore: The Johns Hopkins University Press, 1965), 1–2.
22. Michael Kirwan *Discovering Girard*, (Lanham: Rowman & Littlefield, 2005), 16.
23. Jean-Michel Oughourlian, *The Genesis of Desire*, 11.
24. Ibid, 22.
25. René Girard, *The Girard Reader*, ed. James G. Williams (New York: The Crossword Publishing Co., 1996), 290.
26. *The Australian Girard Seminar: Exploring, Commending and Advancing the Mimetic Theory* http://www.australiangirardseminar.org/?page_id=745 (accessed 9–12–19).
27. Nathan Colborne, "Violence and Resistance: Towards a Politics without a Scapegoat," *Toronto Journal of Theology* 29, 1 (2013), 111–112.
28. Ibid.
29. Scott M. Thomas, "Culture, Religion and Violence: René Girard's Mimetic Theory," *Millennium: Journal of International Studies* 43, 1 (2014), 325.
30. Ibid.
31. Ibid.

Chapter Four

Ideology, Beliefs, and Social/Group Influence

In modern parlance the use of the word ideology tends to mean some kind of thought, worldview, or perspective that is false, misleading, and possibly threatening. For the person on the street ideology tends to be associated with politics, especially in this politically divisive and divided time. There have always been bogus ideas forming bigoted, prejudicial, and marginalizing worldviews. Ideology seems to have always been a social and cultural given. The reality is that the etymology of the word is of recent origin. The word was coined as late as the latter part of the eighteenth century in France. It was given birth, in fact, at the beginning of the French Revolution, an ideological event if there ever was one.

In this chapter I will examine two aspects of ideology. First, I will trace its development from its first use in the last decade of eighteenth-century France to its present understanding by various thinkers. Second, utilizing the discipline of social psychology, I will examine social psychological discussions of ideology, and the role of social groups in the transference and maintenance of ideological viewpoints shaping individual and group identity. As we will see below, ideologies are forms of beliefs, and, as we noted in chapter two, beliefs are intimately related to emotions.

IDEOLOGY

The term ideology was coined by the French philosophe Antoine Destutt de Tracy in 1796. For de Tracy the term did not have the pejorative connotation it would later acquire. For de Tracy the term referred to "an ostensible 'neutral' science of ideas that sought to trace how 'sensation' became thought."[1]

The term would receive its pejorative status when de Tracy and his confreres began to fall afoul of Napoleon, who saw these *ideologues* as obstacles to his own imperial designs. He viewed these ideologues as peddling "liberal and republican ideas," which conflicted with his autocratic ambitions. Thus, at the beginning of its life, ideology "assumed two contrasting meanings: ideology as a science of ideas (de Tracy) and ideology as a set of false, even subversive, ideas (Napoleon)."[2]

Although the term was only coined late in the eighteenth century, its referent had precursors, "most notable in the writings of Francis Bacon. His book *Novum Organon* (originally published in 1620) argued for a rigorous scientific approach to the world that dispel the 'idols' and 'phantoms' that he believed had held human thought captive since antiquity."[3] In this work Bacon adapts the biblical concept of idolatry, dividing mistaken concepts and ideas into four classes of idols. David Hawkes summarizes these classifications as, first, the "idols of the tribe," which refers "to the presuppositions and prejudices which enter the mind as a result of living in society."[4] This is the practice of elevating social conventions to the status of "eternal verities, and so products of the mind are mistaken for absolute truths."[5] Second, the "idols of the cave," which "are the mistakes which arise from the purely personal predilections of individuals."[6] Third, the "idols of the Marketplace," which indicates "the mental distortions which result from ignorance of the creative power of linguistic representation: 'For men believe that their reason governs words; but it is also true that words react on the understanding'."[7] Hawkes notes that Bacon labels these "three kinds of 'idol' 'native', or inherent in the human mind, and he therefore sees them as unavoidable."[8] These contrast with the fourth class of idols, the "idols of the theatre," "which includes all closed philosophical systems which try to force empirical reality to accord with their own formal patterns," which "is termed 'adventitious'."[9] This means that "these idols are originally extraneous to the mind and they can therefore be expelled."[10] So then, Bacon sees these two classifications, "between those false ideas which arise spontaneously out of everyday social life, and those which are introduced with a degree of calculation, usually with the purpose of perpetuating a particular form of power or control."[11]

The phenomenon of the rise of ideological inquiry in the period of the Enlightenment is attributed to the decline of traditional religious structures in the West. Traditional religious worldviews and social structures began to be challenged by various intellectuals, giving way in some quarters to the exaltation of Reason and Science. As commonly agreed upon conceptions of the world, informed by Christian theological constructs, as well as long held folk norms and beliefs, no longer holding meaning for Enlightenment rationalists, religion was perceived to be a set of superstitious beliefs maintained by an elite clerical order desirous of maintaining social control. In the nineteenth century ideology would become the focus of social analysis, given special attention by Karl Marx and Friedrich Engels.

MARX AND IDEOLOGY

Marx, in *The German Ideology*, argued against Hegel's "false" understanding of consciousness. Marx believed that Hegel's view was in fact an inversion of how consciousness is actually formed. Hegel began with examining human consciousness, proceeding "from this to an investigation of material reality."[12] For Marx, it was the other way around. One begins with the reality of one's actual life in the world. The social and material realities of one's life, that is, forms of material production, social classes, and economic structures shaping these classes, determine human consciousness. As Marx states:

> The production of ideas, of conceptions, of consciousness, is at first directly interwoven with the material activity and the material intercourse of men, the language of real life. Conceiving, thinking, the mental intercourse of men, appear at this stage as the direct efflux of their material behaviour. The same applies to mental production as expressed in the language of politics, laws, morality, religion, metaphysics, etc., of a people. . . . Men, developing their material production and their material intercourse, alter, along with this their actual world, also their thinking and the products of their thinking.[13]

So then, ideology "is a function of the social relations of production,"[14] and cannot be understood "without reference to the social structure, the social relations and the nature of actors who convey it."[15] To believe that consciousness shapes actual, material, life, and not the other way around, is a form of *camera obscura*, a turning of reality on its head. Such a view is seen as *false consciousness*. The Marxian idea of false consciousness has been a matter of controversy among many scholars. Because of its usefulness for my argument, I will discuss this in more detail below.

By associating ideology and class, Marx, along with Friedrich Engels, declared that the ruling class determined the ruling ideas. As Michael Freeden states, "[i]deological illusions were an instrument in the hands of the rulers, through the state, and were employed to exercise control and domination; indeed, to 'manufacture history' according to their interests."[16] Dominant ideological constructs shaping consciousness among social and cultural groups are determined by the means and modes of production. With the rise of capitalist economies, the market determines class consciousness, with the producer class shaping dominant paradigms of consciousness driven by the need for the consumption of goods, to ensure higher profitability. For Marx, "the genesis of Enlightenment thought, with its emphasis on personal autonomy, flows not from a 'natural' social contract, but from a need to create consumers for a market economy."[17] In Marxist lexicology the distinction between material modes of production and ideological constructs is known as base and superstructure. Marx claimed that base shapes superstructure, that is, the modes of production shape the ideas informing consciousness, forming ideological paradigms. For example, in the middle ages feudal relations between lords and peasants were given legitimacy by theological constructs that saw social hierarchy fitting a divine pattern. A social structure that mirrored the divine hierarchy was believed best suited for social harmony. This was believed despite economic inequality that overlooked issues of poverty and political oppression that led to so much suffering and injustice. Legitimation was given in the form of assurances that docile willingness to endure suffering without active resistance would be rewarded in the afterlife. Thus, as Marx saw it, the masses of suffering poor were medicated with the opium of pie-in-the-sky promises of eternal reward. This helped to maintain social hegemony for the rich and elite.

While there is little doubt that modes of production, that is, economic structures of a given society, influence human consciousness, Marx's insistence that modes of production determine the formation of consciousness is somewhat reductive. Humans have concerns other than economic well-being. Desire for intimate relationships, and concerns over meaning and purpose, play significant roles in shaping consciousness. At the same time, Marx's insights should not be dismissed out of hand. Along with these other concerns, that is, relationships, meaning, and so on, there is the issue of power. Economic status plays an important role in fulfilling various identity needs, such as security and control. Wealth can offer to fulfill these needs, for example, better access to health care, protection from crime by living in better neighborhoods, greater influence in shaping political policies that ensure one's status and concerns, and so forth. Wealth can offer better access to higher education, leading to higher status and higher-class affiliation. Each of these in turn is influenced in some measure by modes of production. The desire for relational intimacy may be delimited to members of one's own economic class, educational level, and so on. Meaning and purpose may be shaped by the categories of class and status, themselves informed by capitalist economic constructs. What it means to be successful can be influenced by the reigning paradigms informing concepts of success, based on a capitalistic economic worldview. When other forms of prejudice are introduced into the mix, attitudes and actions of exclusion can lead to further injustice. Racial bigotry in a capitalist society can lead to acts of exclusion by denying despised minorities access to certain jobs. Fear that particular ethnic groups may gain ascendency in the job market influences immigration policy. This, despite the reality that immigrants in most cases help the economy, and, in some cases, are vital to economic success.

Reigning paradigms have a significant influence on the formation of one's understanding of the meaning of life, and in turn can become Baconian "idols" shaping hegemonic conscious structures shared by social groups. Meanwhile legitimations and justifications, that is, ideological constructs, for adherence to these idols may incorporate, even be legitimated, by religious beliefs. These beliefs in turn may be exclusionary, determining who is included in social acceptability, and who is to be excluded. Underlying these religious ideological legitimations for exclusionary attitudes is a desire for social, cultural, and economic hegemony. For many Christians in the United States, these reigning, hegemonic ideological constructs are reinforced by various leaders among the various denominations, both Protestant and Catholic, as well as the larger dominant social and cultural institutions. Jeannine Hill Fletcher, whose insights I examine in chapter six, implicates universities and theological schools' complicity in US history as purveyors of the ideology of White Christian supremacy.

ANTONIO GRAMSCI AND HEGEMONY

The Italian Marxist Antonio Gramsci is well known by students of ideology for his concept of *hegemony*. An important insight of Gramsci's was a corrective to Marx's reductive exclusive claim that base forms the superstructure, by recognizing that ideologies have formative influences in the shaping of cultural values and beliefs. Existential concerns not exclusively tied to economic concerns have played influential roles in people's formation of meaning and purpose. In medieval Christendom hegemonic beliefs and structures, shaped by theological and folk traditions, informed worldviews, shaping feelings and attitudes about the world and one's relationships with others, both ingroup and outgroup relations. Social structures at this time tended to be conservative, maintained through hierarchies legitimized by claims of divine authority, mediated through both Church and civil authorities. With the decline of Christendom, and the rise of nation-states, with its attendant separation of Church and State, means of social cohesion found other avenues to bring homogeneity of norms among social groups in order to maintain social cohesion and social harmony. In many cases this took the form of ideological constructs.

These constructs, Louis Althusser notes, do not always appear to be explicitly conscious. While ideologies have cognitive content, they do not always appear in the forefront of cognitive perception. Rather, these ideological structures, many times, lie below the surface of conscious awareness, informing emotions, feelings, and attitudes. Althusser writes

> ideology has very little to do with 'consciousness'. . . . It is profoundly unconscious. . . . Ideology is indeed a system of representation, but in the majority of cases these representations have nothing to do with 'consciousness': they are usually images and occasionally concepts, but it is above all as structures that they impose on the vast majority of men, not via their 'consciousness'. They are perceived-accepted-suffered cultural objects and they act functionally on men via a process that escapes them. . . . In ideology men do indeed express,

not the relation between them their conditions of existence, but *the way* they live the relation between them and their conditions of existence: this presupposes both a real relation and an '*imaginary*', '*lived*' relation.[18]

Hanna Samir Kassab highlights the important link between ideological conceptualization and emotions. Kassab notes Freeden's definition of ideology as "clusters of ideas, beliefs, opinions, values and attitudes usually held by identifiable groups, that provides directives, even plans for action for public policy-making in an endeavor to uphold, justify, change or criticize the social and political arrangements of a state or other political community."[19] Kassab argues that "emotions influence ideas and create politics."[20] Kassab states that

> The conflict over ideology is rooted in emotion and determinations of what is morally right and natural. If society considers certain ideas as natural, then we must consider them to be part of the structure of knowledge that guides and encourages certain behaviors over others. Whether or not you accept or reject them is something that comes from within given one's own experiences and so forth. This fact results in a reaction based on one's emotion: to protect or reject an idea within the structure of knowledge. The affect reaction will bring ideas to either replace or defend the initial idea based on emotion conduct. These ideas then feed into the structure of knowledge, adding to it. The role of emotions, therefore, is absolutely essential to the transformation of society and its structure of knowledge of competing ideologies that exist only to restructure society materially. Ideology is certainly not the reason for violence, but it is the power behind the ideology, emotion, which shapes the ideology and whether or not the ideology is violent or not.[21]

I maintain that these emotions underlying the formation of ideological constructs and beliefs are the result of identity needs seeking satisfaction. Social influences play a primary role in how beliefs about how to satisfy these needs are shaped. Threats to need satisfaction induce fear, which in turn leads to attitudes and behaviors of confrontation, conflict, and exclusion. While how these attitudes manifest differ from situation to situation, motivations for attitudes and action begin with emotional responses. These emotions are reinforced by one's social group, which I discuss below.

In a hierarchical and traditional culture dominant worldviews, as stated above, were maintained by a type of social homogeneity, more easily maintained in rural cultures than urban ones. With the expansion of urbanization, as well as a decline in homogenous religious structures, Gramsci noted that ideological conformity took on a new form of mediation. In the world of medieval Christendom, social order was maintained through hierarchical structures accepted as divinely ordained, while, with the collapse of these dominant belief structures, post-Christendom society looked to other forms of authority for maintenance of social order. Gramsci noted that functionally the previous ruling classes were essentially conservative in the sense that they did not tend to construct an organic passage from the other classes into their own, i.e. to enlarge their class sphere "technically" and ideologically: their conception was that of a closed caste. The bourgeois class poses itself as an organism in continuous movement, capable of absorbing the entire society, assimilating it to its own cultural and economic level.[22]

As class affiliation became more porous, the dominant classes, in order to maintain class status and position, as well as legitimation for economic superiority, relied upon "intellectuals" to disseminate legitimations for class boundaries. These intellectuals are not necessarily those among the academic elite, though some come from this arena. Rather, they are those who disseminate the worldviews of the ruling class through the various bureaucratic and social structures prevalent in modern society, be they civil associations, political organizations, or religious institutions. As MacLellan notes, "the worldview of the ruling class was so thoroughly diffused by its intellectuals as to become the 'common sense' of the whole of society, the *'structure of feeling'* in which it lived" (emphasis mine).[23] Daniel Bar-Tal notes that a society's beliefs (ideology is a form of belief) must not only be acquired and assimilated by members of society but must be "disseminated if they are to be acquired and considered by society members as social beliefs."[24] Transmission of beliefs takes place through a variety of channels. "These range from the informal and personal, such as interpersonal interactions in small groups, to institutionalized formal channels of information, including cultural, political, and societal sources."[25] These forms of dissemination transmit the beliefs (ideology) of either the dominant social and cultural paradigms, or the ideologies held by purported leaders within the various social groups. Intellectuals are those who manage the dissemination of beliefs, articulating in various forms and formats hegemonic ideological concepts.

Gramsci's focus was the working class, examining how it acquiesced to the ideologies of the producer class. For my purposes, I see a parallel in the dissemination of ideological constructs mediated through, to use Gramsci's term, "intellectuals" in the Christian Churches. These would include, but not be limited to, pastors, theologians, and various lay ministers. This also includes politicians whose claims to Christian membership give them a position of influence among some Christian groups. It would also incorporate social and cultural presumptions and assumptions about the contents of the message of Jesus that have been coopted and hijacked by commonly held ideologies believed to be compatible with his teachings.

Chapter 4
KARL MANNHEIM

Karl Mannheim's book, *Ideology and Utopia*, has had a significant influence on scholarly discussions on the issue of ideology. His goal was to "extend the insights of Marx," in order "to produce a comprehensive theory of ideology."[26] Mannheim's work has become a matter of controversy among a number of scholars dealing with issues of ideology, especially those concerned with the discipline of the sociology of knowledge. Mannheim placed all conceptions about the nature of reality under the rubric of ideology, claiming that the study of ideology was not to favor any ideological perspective as though it were somehow a perspective transcendent to social construction. He writes that the "general form of the total conception of ideology is being used by the analyst when he has the courage to subject not just the adversary's point of view but all points of view, including his own, to the ideological analysis."[27] Mannheim thus "refused the choice between an objectivity based on timeless principles unmediated by historical change and a relativism that would abandon any search for truth."[28] Despite the fact that Mannheim rejected the "presuppositions of both views,"[29] his argument had the practical result of relativism. If there is no objective, transcendental ground upon which truth is founded, the construction of all human conceptions about the world are exactly that, human constructions, having merely human origins. Thus, truth statements claimed by any group must be examined in light of the social and cultural agendas engendering ideological positions. Ideologies are thus

> attitudes which correspond to the world of the past and utopias to describe ideas which are advanced for their time. In his interpretation, historical change means that some ideas are now outdated; if they live on, it is only as ideologies which belong to the past and serve to legitimate the existing order, to defend the status quo or maintain a nostalgia of the consequential benefit of dominant or conservative social forces, whereas the ideas which are oriented to replacing the established order or which inherently carry this promise belong to the category of utopia.[30]

The problem that arises from this perspective—that is, all truth claims are ideological constructs formed in the matrix of historical, social temporalities—is that determination of the veracity of any truth claim pivots on evaluations of functionality. All truth claims are determined by social, cultural, and/or political feasibility. No ideological position can be evaluated as false, because there is no ahistorical, asocial, acultural perspective that can determine the truth or falseness of an ideological position. Thus, one cannot declare, as Marx did, a state of false consciousness. The result of Mannheim's argument is captured in the following conclusion given by Helmuth Plessner. Plessner turns Marx's understanding of false consciousness from a misguided understanding about the formation of consciousness, (i.e., from the contents of mind to real life, rather than real life to the contents of consciousness) to a determination that false consciousness is the fallacious belief that there are transcendent, ontological truth claims. Plessner writes:

> By 'ideological' we do not mean here a state of false consciousness that can be corrected by historical development and through human intervention, for there is no standard against which to judge the respective 'worlds' in which the social formations exist. The style in which a primitive person thinks, desires, and feels cannot be compared to that of a highly civilized one. We can only get a sense of a particular world and of the way its people see themselves by way of the objectifications of this style of thinking, desiring and feeling in the medium of the culture. From this point of view, consciousness is inherently false or ideological if it fails to recognize that its own way of positing values is existentially bound and if, in consequence, it proclaims the absolute validity of its values and meaning contents. This consciousness is not ideological because of its transcendent hypostases of an otherworldly reality, but because it claims to possess aesthetic, logical and ethical *objectivity*.[31]

Thus, the definition of ideology has come to mean something quite different than it did for Marx. As Plessner concludes, rather grimly,

> As a superstructure, it now refers to the spiritual and sensuous expression of practical or natural, vital 'interests' or drives; it now refers, as it were, to the incorporeal, cultural and value equivalent of the corresponding psychophysical base. The religions and sciences, the nations and arts, the different moralities and legal systems, the entire worlds of objectification within which human lives are wasted, remain pointless. There is no real basis for their claims. They are simply expressions of life itself which requires them in order to *be* life. This puzzling detour through a willed, known, believed and enacted infinity is, in the final analysis, a mere reflection of the peculiar being called 'man'. Life strives for more life and for more than life; for this reason, man is ideologically simply by virtue of the fact that he is a living being. He is the ideological animal.[32]

So then, we find ourselves in a world of relativistic truth claims that are in fact falsifications of consciousness, in that they mistake cultural constructs for transcendent truths. This obfuscates the reality of social agendas, believed to be claims about reality, as nothing more than quests for positions of power and status. There are then no truths, only more persuasive claims. We find ourselves, if this is correct, in a Nietzschean nightmare in which truth is simply, as Nietzsche stated,

> a mobile army of metaphors, metonyms, and anthropomorphisms—in short, a sum of human relations, which have been enhanced, transposed and embellished poetically and rhetorically, and which after long use seem firm, canoni-

cal, and obligatory to a people: truths are illusions about which one has forgotten that is what they are; metaphors which are worn out and without sensuous power; coins which have lost their pictures and now matter only as metal, no longer as coins.[33]

If one takes seriously the implications of both Plessner's and Nietzsche's position, that is, all moral judgments and convictions are matters of human construction, then the consequences for moral evaluation becomes a matter of preference and power. The relativist can offer a variety of moral philosophies that regulate human moral behavior, from social contract theory to enlightened self-interest. The problem with this lies with the issue of ultimate justice. If moral truth claims are solely of human construction, thus matters of power, how is one to make claims of justice beyond issues of preference and power? For example, if a demagogue attains total authority over a state and is backed by the forces of the military, what moral high ground can be argued if both the demagogue and the subjugated ground their more actions on preference, power, and the desire for self-determination? If there is no absolute standard for moral evaluation, and there is no ultimate transcendental justice, then moral judgments are ultimately a matter of power. In other words, whoever has the greatest power determines moral standards of right and wrong. This is the will-to-power formula found in Nietzsche's later writings. Despite the argument that Nietzsche did not actually intend this interpretation, many German fascists came to this conclusion and valorized the power of domination. So then, if there are no universal, transcendental truths, then all moral claims are simply ideologies that have been *embellished poetically and rhetorically, and which after long use seem firm, canonical, and obligatory to a people*. Despite the sincerity of convictions held by those believing in transcendental moral absolutes, if there is in fact no such reality, then we find ourselves in a world in which ideologies are successful or unsuccessful depending on the status of power. If there are in fact moral absolutes, then those claiming this position must determine the nature of these absolutes; what these moral precepts require in terms of social relations and behavior. If one's moral judgment and action is grounded in the teachings of Jesus then the question is, how did he understand the nature of power in his own social context?

IDEOLOGY AND POWER

John B. Thompson has defined ideology in reference to power, especially as it relates to conflict. He writes that

> The study of ideology is a controversial, conflict-laden activity.... The theory of ideology invites us to see that language is not simply a structure which can

be employed for communication or entertainment, but a social-historical phenomenon which is embroiled in human conflict. . . . To study ideology, I propose, is to study the ways in which meaning (or signification) serves to sustain relations of domination.[34]

In his analysis of ideology, Terry Eagleton makes distinctions between ruling belief systems and ideology. He states that "the term ideology lies in its capacity to discriminate between those power struggles which are somehow central to a whole form of social life, and those which are not."[35] Eagleton challenges thinkers like Foucault who "abandon the concept of ideology altogether, replacing it with the more capacious 'discourse.'"[36] If the struggle between two competing points of view is simply a matter of discourse, how is one to distinguish an argument between a husband and wife over a matter of mundane domestic concerns, and that of a discourse over gender roles? Rather, the use of language must be put into the context in which it is used, and by whom it is being used. "Ideology is less a matter of the inherent linguistic properties of a pronouncement than a question of who is saying what to whom for what purposes."[37] Eagleton notes, linguistic idioms can be ideological:

> [T]he language of fascism, for example. Fascism tends to have its own peculiar lexicon (*Lebensraum*, sacrifice, blood and soil), but what is primarily ideological about these terms is the power-interests they serve and the political effects they generate. The general point, then, is that exactly the same piece of language may be ideological in one context and not in another; ideology is a function of the relation of an utterance to its social context.[38]

Ideology's relation to power, I believe, is vital. The motivations, attitudes, and goals that lie behind the use of ideology are of greatest importance. Analysis of ideology is vital to understanding motives of power among various groups and institutions, be they religious or political. This is a matter of security and survival, as well as a matter of human flourishing. In the context of meeting identity needs, the struggle for power, how it is acquired and used, relates to issues of hegemony, which in turn facilitates class and ethnic dominance. This in turn informs and forms attitudes and perceptions concerning issues of meaning, belonging/connectedness, control, security, recognition, and action, each shaping one's sense of self. Power, in this situation, can affect self-esteem and confidence. Having greater social and economic power can give one a sense of well-being, greater self-esteem, and greater confidence about one's security in one's social field. Greater social and economic power, as well as social status, gives a sense of greater control over one's environment. Threats to these identity needs will tend to lead to conflict, with attendant motivations, attitudes, and goals for the shoring up of one's position of strength in one's social location. In all, power, in terms of dealing with fear of loss to identity needs satisfaction, is a means of overcoming, dominating, and eliminating perceived threats. In politics this is observed in the enacting of policies that protect the hegemony of the wealthy classes, despite their demographic minority, or the marginalization of and acts of injustice toward subaltern classes.

If there is no transcendent reality grounding any claims to truth, ideology will be an endless struggle between human groups. These struggles will continue to be battled out with the conviction that the struggle for dominance is a worthy and necessary goal, regardless of the cost to others—all this, despite the logical conclusion that in the end none of it ultimately matters. The suffering, the effort, the anxiety, that is experienced in the struggle for dominance in whatever arena, is ultimately, to quote Shakespeare's Macbeth, like an actor that *struts and frets his hour upon the stage, and then is heard no more: it is a tale told by an idiot, full of sound and fury*. Ideology is thus not a matter of truth, but of power. But what if there is a transcendent reality grounding truth claims? If there is, we can then begin to discuss issues of false consciousness, beyond Plessner's position which holds that false consciousness is simply a matter of attributing a transcendent reference to truth claims.

Eagleton has resisted the modern scholarly attempt to relativize ideology, in which evaluations of truth are dismissed among postmodern thinkers who, "under the influence of Friedrich Nietzsche,"[39] have conflated issues of interests, "generated by the nature of" human "bodies: interests in eating, communicating with one another, understanding and controlling their environment and so on,"[40] with relations of power that have political import. "The political effect of this move is to blur the specificity of certain forms of social conflict, grossly inflating the whole category of 'interests' to the point where it picks out nothing in particular."[41] For Eagleton, then, ideology is not a matter of interests, which are viewed homogeneously as competing ideological discourses. Rather ideology is a matter of epistemology. Eagleton notes that there is

> a fairly unpopular notion of ideology nowadays, for a number of reasons. For one thing, epistemology itself is at the moment somewhat out of fashion, and the assumption that some of our ideas 'match' or 'correspond to' the way things are, while others do not, is felt by some to be a native, discreditable theory of knowledge. For one thing, the idea of false consciousness can be taken as implying the possibility of some unequivocally correct way of viewing the world, which is today under deep suspicion. Moreover, the belief that a minority of theorists monopolize a scientifically grounded knowledge of how society is, while the rest of us blunder around in some fog of false consciousness, does not particularly endear itself to the democratic sensibility.[42]

If there is a transcendent reality that gives ground to truth claims, we then face an important and difficult situation. As the Christian faith tradition will no doubt attest, there is most certainly a transcendent reality, in which truth is very much an eternal and objective reality. While accepting such a transcendental reality, allowing for the possibility of having our ideas "match" or "correspond to" the way things are, the question arises: *how can we know that our ideas match or correspond to the way things truly are?*

There is little doubt that various Christian practices, and legitimations for said practices, have been deeply and profoundly ideological. These ideologies act as legitimations for obtaining power in order to attain and maintain social and economic hegemony. This has given rise to acts of violence and marginalization toward groups perceived as threatening social and economic hegemony. How is one to determine, within a Christian worldview, what is ideological and what is truth? By what standard is one to evaluate truth claims? Christians have strong convictions that truth is a matter of *Revelation*. The will of God has been revealed through scripture, and preeminently by the incarnation of God's *Logos*, God's Word, Jesus Christ. All well and good, but all one must do is drive around any city or town in the United States and see a plethora of churches, established by some group claiming access to the whole unvarnished truth, while claiming that others have somehow corrupted that truth. How is one to evaluate these claims? That is the rub (*Shakespeare again*). I would be foolhardy to claim that I in fact had the fullness of truth. In that case I should simply start my own denomination, which I have no interest in doing. No one denomination or sect of Christians can claim full possession of divine verities. But I will make the bold claim that some interpretations (*hermeneutical lenses*) of the divine will are better and more faithful to the revelation found in the gospel of Jesus Christ. This will be the focus of the next chapter, in which I will look at the revelation of God in Christ from the perspective of power and relationality. How did Jesus understand power in relation to others, as well as to political and economic structures of his social world? If ideology is a concern about power, especially power over the other, then the truth of God's revelation must be able to shed light on how humans are to use power in social, cultural, and economic relations. The acquisition of certain anti-gospel cultural ideologies by Christians, both individuals and institutions, have done great harm to the proclamation of the kingdom of God commanded by Jesus. I concur with David Koyzis' view of ideology from a Christian perspective. Koyzis writes,

> So what is ideology? . . . I view ideologies as modern types of that ancient phenomenon idolatry, complete with their own accounts of sin and redemption. From the beginning of its narrative, Scripture inveighs against the worship of idols, false gods that human beings have created. Like these biblical idolatries, every theology is based on taking something out of creation's total-

ity, raising it above that creation, and making the latter revolve around and serve it. It is further based on the assumption that this idol has the capacity to save us from some real or perceived evil in the world.[43]

I would add that behind idolatry is a desire for control. Idols are formed in the image of their makers, each projecting upon the idol one's unconscious desire to play God, without admitting such motives, or even recognizing such motives. The pursuit to fulfill ontological identity needs conforms to misguided perceptions of control, where temporal ends are deemed of infinite value. These idolatrous constructs, believed to have transcendent existence, are in reality the projection of one's, or one's group's, God complex. The insidious reality is the fact that in many cases individual attachment to these idolatrous ideologies is reinforced and rewarded by social approval, even among professed Christians.

Before turning to an examination of Jesus and power in chapter five, I first want to examine how we acquire ideological convictions—convictions contradicting Christian commitments to the teachings of Jesus. In this discussion, I want to emphasize the embodied nature of ideological convictions. While ideology, as discussed by social psychologists, is a form of knowledge—belief is a form of knowledge, thus an examination of the sociology of knowledge below—it is important to remember that consciousness incorporates and forms one's habitus, the dispositional lens by which we perceive and act in the world.

BELIEFS AND GROUP INFLUENCE

While many social psychological studies do not make reference to the works of Girard, one can see that Girard's explication of mimetic desire fits well with many theories elucidating the role of groups on the formation of individual desires, beliefs, and values. The structuring of an individual's habitus, that incorporates ideological content, can be seen in the clinical and experimental works of various social psychologists.

Daniel Bar-Tal examines in his work the role that shared beliefs play in the formation of group and social identity and behavior. What follows is a summary of his conclusions. First, he notes the integral part that shared beliefs play in group membership. Bar-Tal distinguishes two types of beliefs, "personal and common beliefs."[44] While individuals may have personal beliefs within their conceptual world, they are only socially relevant if they have social consequences, such as being shared with others, thus influencing others. Second, "common beliefs can be shared by a few individuals, a small group, the members of a society, or even the majority of human beings."[45] Among larger social groups, an *ethos* denotes "the configuration of central societal beliefs," which "provide central characterization to the society and gives it a particular orientation."[46]

There is a powerful "psychological mechanism" effecting a group or society in the recognition of shared beliefs. These shared beliefs demonstrate "important cognitive, affective, and behavioral consequences, both for group members as individuals and for the group as a whole, especially when their content concerns themes related to the groups life."[47] Shared beliefs can influence the type of "social reality that group members construct, the sense of solidarity and unity that they experience, the intensity and involvement of group members with these beliefs, the conformity expected from group members, the pressure exerted on leaders, and the direction of action taken by the group."[48] An example of this as I am writing is the controversy surrounding the hearings of Brett Kavanaugh, candidate for, and eventual Supreme Court Justice, which were complicated by accusations of sexual misconduct. Many evangelicals and conservative Christians—Protestant and Catholic—were faced with the dilemma of two moral issues vying for consideration. On the one hand was the issue of sexual impropriety, and the attendant abuse of power—in this case, attempted rape—and the issue of abortion. Many who believe that the issue of abortion is more important found a variety of reasons for disregarding Kavanaugh's behavior, some going so far as to believe that Dr. Christine Ford, Kavanaugh's accuser, was the instrument of a liberal, left-wing conspiracy. The group belief in a pro-life agenda gives a sense of solidarity and group affiliation to a variety of individuals who otherwise have several differences on other social, political, and religious issues. The shared belief among the various social groups that abortion is a sin, helps to form conceptual constructs informing the idea of self-categorization. The theory of self-categorization, based on the research of Henri Talfel, proposes "that individuals form social identity by being psychologically connected to social groups through their self-definition as members of social categories."[49] There are "emotional and psychological implications,"[50] in this categorization process. It is "meaningful for intergroup relations because [Talfel] assumed that people are motivated to maintain positive self-evaluation through differentiation between ingroups and outgroups."[51]

Bar-Tal notes that the recognition of shared beliefs "instigates a general sense of power among group members on the basis of the aroused sense of similarity, which indicates unity and solidarity, and on the basis of the confidence in these beliefs, which arouses a sense of rightness. Group members feel strong and influential, believing that they are right in their opinions and can influence the decision making of their leaders and the course of group action."[52] David Matsumoto and Jessie Wilson, noting the social nature of humans, state that affiliation to a group offers the advantage of power in satisfying various needs in order to adapt to one's environment. Groups form because of the need for social harmony. Thus, both physical needs as well as social needs are met through group association. From the formation of group affiliation arises the basis of culture. Matsumoto and Wilson define culture as

> the complex set of ways that emerges when a group use the basic tools inherent in its members to address the problems presented by their ecological context in order to meet biological needs and social motives. Culture is a set of solutions developed over time to solve the problem of how to survive. For all these reasons, the great complexity of human social life can easily lead to social chaos. Human cultures, therefore, evolved to help deal with this complexity, prevent social chaos, maintain social order, and ensure efficient group functioning, by giving meaning to this social complexity. Human cultures allow humans to make greater differentiations in their social lives, and institutionalize much of it. Thus, we define human culture as a unique meaning and information system, shared by a group and transmitted across generations, that allows the group to meet basic needs of survival, by coordinating social behavior to achieve a viable existence, to transmit successful social behaviors, to pursue happiness and well-being, and to derive meaning from life.[53]

In the formation of culture, groups shape meaning, creating scripts that are transmitted from generation to generation. These scripts, informing the hermeneutics of one's worldviews, shape in turn the emotional responses to social experiences. Matsumoto and Wilson define emotion, in this context, as "transient, bio-psycho-social reactions designed to aid individuals in adapting to and coping with events that have immediate implications for their well-being."[54] Maintaining that emotions are "the universal psychological processes that are an inherent part of basic human nature," Matsumoto and Wilson "believe that emotion primes the individual to engage in behavior, by activating and coordinating cognitive, bodily, and motivational states."[55]

Andrzej Nowak, Robin R. Vallacher, and Mandy E. Miller examine the role that social influence plays in the formation and maintenance of group solidarity and conformity. They note that one of the fundamental conceits that humans share in is the "belief that we are the masters of our own destiny."[56] This belief that "one's actions are autonomous, self-generated, and largely impervious to external forces," while offering the perception of self-autonomy that enables one to "face uncertainty with conviction and challenges with perseverance," is to be "dismissed as philosophically untenable to the extent that it reflects naïve assumptions about personal freedom."[57] Nowak et al. state that people have "a natural tendency to bring their beliefs, preferences, and actions in line with those of the people around them, and this tendency becomes manifest in the absence of overt or subtle manipulation strategies."[58] It is this "penchant for interpersonal synchronization," that "enables a mere collection of individuals to become a functional unit defining a higher level of social reality."[59] Nowak et al. explicate the various ways in which groups maintain conformity to social norms through various methods. Social norms provide, at the group level, "continuity, stability, and coordination of behavior among individuals."[60] Thus, means of maintaining norms become important in order to maintain social cohesion. If some deviate from these social norms, threatening social harmony, groups utilize methods of either enforcing conformity or ostracizing the offenders. Nowak et al. describe various experiments that demonstrate how social groups effect conformity for most individuals. The overall conclusion of these experiments is that many people are susceptible to what is known as groupthink. "Groupthink essentially entails 'a deterioration of mental efficiency, reality testing, and moral judgment that results from group pressure.' Rather than examining all possible courses of action, people in the grips of groupthink expend their mental energy on achieving and maintaining group solidarity and opinion unanimity."[61]

While there is always the possibility for agency, that is, freedom to dissent from the group, humans are drawn to conform because of their need to belong. The desire to connect tempts individuals into forgoing personal beliefs that counter those held by the group. In Girardian terms, the group acts as a model for imitation. The more esteemed the group, the greater the mimetic force impresses the norms and values of the group upon one's meaning world. The social norms within the group offer the means by which individuals map their route for satisfying identity needs. Many of these norms fall under the category of ideology. In turn, by self-categorizing within a particular ideological structure, individuals are naturally drawn to likeminded others, creating in the process outgroups who are experienced as threats. As Harry C. Triandis and David Trafinow state,

> In the process of maximizing self-esteem people identify with various social groups. Social categorization results in intergroup discrimination and ingroup favoritism. Individuals pick the groups with which they can compare their ingroup, and the dimensions for comparison, in such a way as to maximize the favorability of the judgment of their ingroup. In judging whether or not an attribute of their group is favorable they use the values of their culture. . . . Cultural distance results in perceived dissimilarity. Dissimilarity together with frequent contact results in conflict.[62]

Every individual is thrown into a mix of social groups and structures— family, peer groups in school and sports teams, religious associations, political party, work groups—the list can go on. In each of these the individual is faced with a variety of social norms, values, conventions, taboos, attitudes about status and class, and so on, in which one must navigate and adapt. Social pressures attempt to conform individuals to the dominant values, norms, and so forth, in order to maintain social and group coherence and conformity. While there is no doubt that some individuals "comply" with the norms and values of a group in order to maintain a sense of belonging and security, research shows that ingroup influences tend toward acceptance of norms and values rather than mere compliance. Diane M. Mackie and Crystal L. Wright state that "when group concerns are salient people conform more to ingroup norms."[63] Mackie and Wright note studies that found "heightened social identification has been determined to cause the conformity to group norms typically found in deindividuation paradigms," with one meta-analysis showing "that deindividuation (heightened, almost exclusive, group identification) increased normative behavior."[64] This parallels Girard's insight about the mimetic formation of a worldview. As with Don Quixote, who saw the world through the vision of his hero Amadis of Gaul, individuals imitate and construct the worldviews of significant members of their ingroup. Christians, like everyone, are thrown into a mix of social groups and influences. Regardless of religious confession, identity needs are a shared ontological reality, and how one seeks to satisfy them is profoundly shaped by social influences. As an individual learns the rules of the many social fields of play, habits of responses to life situations are formed, shaping a habitus and dispositions that become second nature. Accepted norms, values, and beliefs—including ideologies—become engendered in the emotional structures of consciousness. Thus, accepted ideologies take on feelings of veracity. Emotions, attitudes, and motivations thus become normative, and ideological worldviews become concretized in the emotional structure of the individual.

All of this is problematic from a Christian point of view. How to navigate the dictates of the Gospel and those ideologies that are normative in one's social group can easily lead to cognitive dissonance. One cannot maintain dissonance for very long before the tension between two contradictory worldviews will create inner stresses that may have deleterious effects on the psychic and spiritual life of the believer. Typical responses to dissonance are the creation of reasons/legitimizations/justifications for holding a view that contradicts one's religious convictions. One way is to deny or reject interpretations of the Gospel that challenge one's ideological constructs. This is more easily done when one's ingroup reinforces this by holding and disseminating a particular ideological perspective. While I can identify a number of ideological constructs that, I believe, contradict the revelation of God's will as manifested in the life and teachings of Jesus, there is one that I find to be a matter of contemporary concern. This is the ideology of nationalism, specifically as it has developed in US history. Nationalism has become more prevalent in the last few years. I believe it contradicts the will of God as revealed in the life and teachings of Jesus, yet many Christians have somehow found justifications for adhering to this ideology as though it were compatible with the Gospel. I find that adherence to this ideology indicts Christian complicity in the misuse of power. Nationalism as an ideological vision can be tied to identity needs, and, I am convinced, is idolatrous.

Before examining the ideology of nationalism, the next chapter is a historical and exegetical examination of the life and teachings of Jesus. I am specifically concerned with how Jesus expresses his ideas, *attitudes*, and *emotions* concerning human relations. How do the life and teachings of Jesus manifest the will of God concerning the nature and use of power and the treatment of the powerless, the marginalized, the poor, and the oppressed? How is a Christian's habitus to be formed by the life and teachings of Jesus? I will argue that the teachings of Jesus give lie to ideological visions that justify exclusion, attitudes of superiority, and acts of dominance. Nationalism is a modern ideological worldview that embraces these practices and contravenes the teachings of Jesus. Because I am primarily interested in examining Jesus' teachings and actions in his own socio-cultural-economic-political context, I will limit my discussion to the synoptic gospel accounts.

NOTES

1. James M. Decker, *Ideology* (Palgrave Macmillan, New York, 2004), 10.
2. Ian MacKenzie, "The Idea of Ideology" in *Political Ideologies: An Introduction*, ed. Robert Eccleshall, Alan Finleyson, Vincent Geoghegan, Michael Kenny, Moya Lloyd, Iain MacKenzie, and Rick Walford (New York: Routledge, 2003), 4.
3. Ibid, 3.
4. David Hawkes, *Ideology*, 2nd Edition (New York: Routledge, 1996), 36.
5. Ibid.
6. Ibid.
7. Ibid.
8. Ibid.
9. Ibid.
10. Ibid.
11. Ibid.
12. David MacLellan, *Ideology*, Reprint Edition (Ballmoor: Open University Press, 1996), 10.
13. Quoted in Ibid, 11.
14. Michel Wieviorka, "An Old Theme Revisited" Sociology and Ideology" in *Sociology and Ideology*, ed. Eliezer Ben-Rafael (London: Brill, 2003), 84.
15. Ibid.
16. Michael Freeden, *Ideology: A Very Short Introduction* (New York: Oxford University Press, 2003), 6.
17. James M. Decker, *Ideology*, 53.
18. Louis Althusser, *For Marx* (New York: Verso, 1969), 233.
19. Michael Freeden, "Ideology, Political Theory and Political Philosophy" in *Handbook of Political Theory*, ed. Gerald F. Gaus and Chandran Kukathas (London: Sage, 2004), 6; quoted in Hanna Samir Kassab, *The Power of Emotion in Politics, Philosophy, and Ideology* (New York: Palgrave Macmillan, 2016), 5.
20. Ibid.
21. Ibid, 16.
22. Antonio Gramsci, *The Gramsci Reader: Selected Writings, 1916–1935* (New York: New York University Press, 2000), 258.
23. David MacLellan, *Ideology*, 27.
24. Daniel Bar-Tal, *Beliefs in Society: Social Psychological Analysis* (Thousand Oaks: Sage Publications, 2000), 60.
25. Ibid.

26. McLellan, *Ideology*, 36.
27. Quoted in Ibid, 40.
28. Ibid.
29. Ibid.
30. Michel Wieviorka, "An Old Theme Revisited," 85.
31. Helmuth Plessner, "The Conception of ideology and its vicissitudes," in *Knowledge and Politics: The Sociology of Knowledge Dispute*, ed. Volker Meja and Nico Stehr (New York: Routledge, 2015), 245–246.
32. Ibid.
33. Quoted in David Hawkes, *Ideology*, 7.
34. John E. Thompson, *Studies in the Theories of Ideology* (Berkeley: University of California Press, 1984), 2, 4.
35. Terry Eagleton, *Ideology: An Introduction* (London: Verso, 1991), 8.
36. Ibid.
37. Ibid, 9.
38. Ibid.
39. Terry Eagleton, *Ideology*, 10–11.
40. Ibid.
41. Ibid.
42. Ibid.
43. David T. Koyzis, *Political Visions and Illusions: A Survey and Christian Critique of Contemporary Ideologies* (Downers Grove: InterVarsity Press, 2003), 15.
44. Daniel Bar-Tal, *Beliefs in Society*, xv.
45. Ibid.
46. Ibid.
47. Ibid, 4.
48. Ibid.
49. Ibid.
50. Ibid.
51. Ibid.
52. Ibid, 12.
53. David Matsumoto and Jessie Wilson, "Culture, Emotion, and Motivation" in *Handbook of Motivation and Cognition Across Cultures*, ed. Richard Sorrentino and Susumu Yamaguchi (Cambridge: Academic Press, 2008), 542–543.
54. Ibid, 545.
55. Ibid, 545, 548.
56. Ibid, 384.
57. Andrzej Nowak, Robin R. Vallacher, and Mandy E. Miller, "Social Influence and Group Dynamics" in *Handbook of Psychology: Personality and Social Psychology*, Vol. 5, ed. Theodore Millon and Melvin J. Lerner (Hoboken: John Wiley and Sons, 2003), 383.
58. Ibid.
59. Ibid.
60. Ibid, 393.
61. Ibid, 398.
62. Harry C. Triandis and David Trafinow, "Culture and Its Implications for Intergroup Behavior" in *Blackwell Handbook of Social Psychology: Intergroup Processes*, ed. Rupert Brown and Samuel L. Gaertner (Oxford: Blackwell Publishers, 2003), 374, 377.
63. Diane M. Mackie and Crystal L. Wright, "Social Influence in an Intergroup Context," in *Blackwell Handbook of Social Psychology: Intergroup Processes*, 291–292.
64. Ibid.

Chapter Five

Jesus' Summons to Hospitality and Table Fellowship

In a class I was once enrolled in on the life and writings of Francis of Assisi, a question was raised by one of my classmates along the lines of "what would Francis do," in lieu of our contemporary situation. What I was not expecting was the professor's response, a Franciscan brother well studied in the early Franciscan tradition. He stated, quite emphatically, "Francis wouldn't do anything, HE'S DEAD!" The point was, and is, that while it is important for Franciscans, and those inspired by Francis, to read and reflect on Francis' life and writings, as well as writings about Francis, one should not do so as though imitating Francis were a matter of simply applying Francis' literal practices to a very different social and cultural reality. For example, Francis forbade friars to ride horses, because only the wealthy could afford to do so. Yet, we now have horsepower, in the form of cars, trains, and planes, and even many poor persons can afford to own at least a cheaper vehicle or buy a ticket for a train or plane fare. What is called for is to discern the underlying principles that guided Francis in his actions and determine how these principles can be applied in our contemporary world. So, while a friar may be able to make use of a car (the registration would not be in his name), he should not be utilizing the services of a Cadillac or Rolls Royce, as they are symbols of wealth and privilege.

In my examination of the life of Jesus in his own historical situation, I want to attempt to do what this Franciscan brother advised above with his admonition concerning imitation of what Francis did. Because our contemporary social, cultural, political, and economic realities are so different from first-century Palestine, what I hope to do is to examine the principles and intentions guiding Jesus in his attitudes, teachings, and behavior regarding others in his social environment. In contextualizing Jesus' attitudes, and so on, I will then excise the underlying principles and intentions found in these areas of his life and ministry so that we can utilize them for better judging the will of God as manifested in the life and teachings of the Word made flesh. Because Christians are called to imitate Christ, to be conformed to the image of Christ, it is imperative to know what we are to imitate, what we are to be conformed to.

REVELATION

Christians believe that the written witness, the Bible, was, and remains, inspired by the Holy Spirit in order to reveal what pertains to salvation. The Second Vatican Council's document *Dei Verbum* states that

> In His goodness and wisdom God chose to reveal Himself and to make known to us the hidden purpose of His will by which through Christ, the Word made flesh, man might in the Holy Spirit have access to the Father and come to share in the divine nature. Through this revelation, therefore, the invisible God out of the abundance of His love speaks to men as friends and lives among them, so that He may invite and take them into fellowship with Himself. This plan of revelation is realized by deeds and words having an inner unity: the deeds wrought by God in the history of salvation manifest and confirm the teaching and realities signified by the words, while the words proclaim the deeds and clarify the mystery contained in them. By this revelation then, the deepest truth about God and salvation of man shines out for our sake in Christ, *who is both the mediator and the fulness of all revelation.* (*DV* 1: 2 emphasis mine)

It must be noted that, although Christians believe that Jesus is the definitive manifestation of the revelation of God in human form, there is an important distinction between revelation, that is, God's self-disclosure in Christ, and the written witness to God's self-disclosure. While there is a close relationship between the revelation of God in Christ and the written witness, they are not one and the same. Regardless of God's gracious revelation of God's self, humans are socially and culturally bound creatures, who must utilize the social and cultural conceptual constructs that are always and everywhere limited by historical realities. There is as well the limitation of human knowledge. Every relational encounter is filtered through a hermeneutical lens that has been shaped by the social and cultural milieu of the individual. Tyron Inbody notes that, while Christians profess a sense of immediacy in their experience of God,

> the way Christians know the reality, character, and presence of God involves more than the immediate knowledge of God. The God the Christian knows is mediated to us through the history of Israel and the story of Jesus embodied in the Scripture and interpreted by the church. . . . Scripture understands revela-

tion primarily to be God's *indirect self-disclosure* through the "acts of God" which are discerned within the events of Israel's history and the story of Jesus' life, death, and resurrection. (emphasis in original)[1]

A more than cursory examination of the four gospels demonstrates that Jesus' life and teachings were not written verbatim by the four authors/ communities composing the four canonical texts we find in the New Testament. Each gospel composer made selective decisions concerning what was to be incorporated into the corpus. This had much to do with relevant concerns about the historical realities of each one's social and cultural milieu. Each author obviously considered the theological, spiritual, and communal needs facing their respective communities. Each in turn had his (I am taking it for granted the authors were male) own theological lens shaped in his particular historical context. Rather than being problematic, what on the surface appears to some as a case of theological co-optation of the teachings of Jesus by the four authors—some claim significantly changing the original context and intent of Jesus' teachings—is instead, I believe, a further confirmation that the revelation of God in Christ must be interpreted for changing social and cultural circumstances, while being faithful to the underlying principles found in Jesus' teachings. Jesus' teachings, his attitudes, his worldview, and his emotional responses were deeply informed by his own social and cultural reality and time. He was a first-century Jew, a Galilean, within particular political and religious structures, and this is reflected in his words and behavior. If the teachings of Jesus remain locked within their first-century milieu, they will lose their social and practical import for those living in very different social, cultural, economic, and religious structures. God became human in Jesus of Nazareth. Being human means that we are necessarily social, as discussed in previous chapters. As social creatures we are formed by existing social and cultural structures. Thus, for God's salvific revelation to have real affect in our lives, it must meet us where we live, in the social and cultural reality of our lived historical experiences. Jesus taught, acted, and emoted within his own social reality and thus was able to touch the lives of those he encountered and with whom he related.

It is not my intent to write a chapter on the historical Jesus. The last several decades have seen an explosion of research resulting in a myriad of books, thousands of articles, and a plethora of TV specials on the historical Jesus. I invite interested readers to discover these for themselves. Rather, it is my intention to examine, with the aid of several of these scholarly examinations, the relevant principles underlying the teachings, attitudes, feelings, and acts of Jesus that I believe offer us a better hermeneutical *key* to understanding the will of God in relation to how we are to shape our attitudes and behavior toward others and society in our present historical context. This, in turn, requires us to examine the formation of our own attitudes, desires, and emotions as they have been formed by a plethora of cultural influences, many of which are antithetical to the teachings of Jesus. Mine will not be an exhaustive examination of every aspect of Jesus' teaching and behavior. Instead I will select from a variety of gospel passages and accounts that deal specifically with Jesus' concerns about relationality, acts of inclusion, attitudes on the use and abuse of power, attitudes about acquisitiveness, and how his emotions reflected and demonstrated his understanding of and commitment to the will of God.

THE SOCIAL AND CULTURAL WORLD OF JESUS

The social and cultural world that Jesus inhabited had many differences from our own. A significant difference is the perception of the individual. Modern sociology and psychology characterize Western contemporary personhood under the moniker *individualism*. Clifford Geertz defines individualism, especially in its American expression, as "a bounded, unique, more or less integrated motivational and cognitive universe, a dynamic center of awareness, emotion, judgment and action organized into a distinctive whole and set contrastively both against other such wholes and against its social and natural background."[2] We moderns, inhabiting an individualistic consciousness informing our habitus, have taken the introspective, inner psychological self as an obvious reality, finding it difficult to imagine any other way of perceiving consciousness and personhood. The individualist formation of identity is uniquely volitional, with a natural tendency to highlight and celebrate distinctions. But as I attempted to demonstrate in chapter three, we are by nature mimetic, forming desires, values, and preferences through the processes of imitating others, and we delude ourselves with the illusion of autonomous formation. We are still compelled by the need to belong, to fit in, to be accepted, and complete nonconformity is therefore usually only the purview of the mentally unbalanced. Regardless, because of the aggrandizement of distinction and uniqueness, the illusion of autonomous individualism is maintained, leading to the celebration of perceived difference.

Bruce Malina notes that among first-century Mediterranean societies, there was a very different concept of the person. He states that there was simply no awareness

> of the personal, individualistic, self-concerned focus typical of contemporary American experience. Given Mediterranean social experience, such self-concerned individualism would appear deviant and detrimental to other group members. For group survival it would be dysfunctional, and hence dangerous. Behavior that indicates self-concerned individualism is noticed, but it is disdained and variously sanctioned.[3]

Recognizing the differences of perception about the individual, between the individualist and collectivist, is vital in grasping the meaning and intent of the various teachings and acts of Jesus. Most modern Western readers of the Bible naturally interpret its texts from an individualist perspective, within the social and cultural structures of a post-Enlightenment, post-Freudian psychological worldview. The search for spiritual comfort and salvific assurances has become a matter of private striving, in many cases neglecting the social import of Jesus' commands.

Another important example of social and cultural differences between the world of Jesus and our own has to do with the relationship between the institutions of State and Religion. Americans have enshrined as a civil dogma the separation of Church and State. This means that, ideally, no one religious institution, denomination, or sect is to have hegemony over social policy and jurisprudence, or individual conscience. Religion has become a matter of individual choice, a private affair. There are no legal repercussions for abstaining from or adherence to any particular religious ideology or doctrine, other than, maybe, upsetting one's family. This has become a matter of an individual's rights, along with other rights respecting personal autonomy. For first-century Jews, the idea that the functioning of the State could somehow be divorced from religion would have been unimaginable. The law, as codified in Torah and interpreted by experts from the various sects of Jews, shaped the heart of communal identity, behavior, and jurisprudence. Fidelity to the law was believed by many to have real world consequences. In determining the reasons for national tragedies, such as the Babylonian exile, as well as Greek and Roman domination, many interpreted these tragedies as the result of the people's unfaithfulness to the commandments (*mitzvoth*) of God. And because individuals were collectivist in their consciousness, rather than individualists, each would, as Malina states,

> define themselves rather exclusively in terms of the groups in which they are embedded; their total self-awareness emphatically depends upon such group embeddedness. To paraphrase M. Bowen (1978), one might say that such persons are immersed in and share "an undifferentiated mass as well." And they believe that other persons are part of such an undifferentiated mass as well.[4]

Behavior on the part of the individual reflects and affects the group. Maintaining social control among one's identified group was paramount for the well-being of the group. Thus, deviant behavior, attitudes, and ideas tended to be viewed at minimum suspiciously, and maximally as subversive and dangerous. For example, family structures in Jesus' world were strictly prescribed, embedded in an honor-shame society in which it was expected that children sought to enhance the honor of the family. In renouncing these prescriptions, by reimagining family as those who followed his interpretation of the law (Matthew 12: 46–50), Jesus, in effect, renounced his own kin. He thus brought shame to his family. As family was, and remains, the fundamental institution of any given society, changes in its structure affect the larger society and culture. By forming familial commitments to something other than blood/kin ties, as Jesus did, offending cultural traditions believed to be normative, was obviously scandalous and threatening to his contemporaries.

The majority of the conflicts that Jesus' Jewish interlocutors had with him was over the correct interpretation of the law. Correct interpretation was not merely an intellectual one-upmanship. It was a matter of faithfully recognizing the will of God, how it was to be applied for the whole of the Jewish community. Disagreements led to division and the formation of various Jewish sects, some of whom condemned other Jews as no better than *goyim*, gentiles, thus outside the perimeter of the covenant. Who belonged to the covenant community was a hotly contested, and variously prescribed issue. As we will see below, understanding Jesus' teachings, behavior, attitudes, and emotions within the social and cultural world of his time, one gains a deeper insight into his understanding of the will of God. From the principles underlying his teachings, behavior, and so on, we can then apply them to our contemporary reality.

THE KINGDOM OF GOD

The dominant emphasis in the teaching of Jesus is the kingdom, or rule, of God. Jesus' use of the phrase "kingdom of God," or "kingdom of heaven" is found prominently in the Synoptic Gospels. Donald A. Hagner states that

> the kingdom is to be thought of not as a place but rather as the experience of an era in which a new relationship with God, based on the new saving activity of God in Jesus, is made possible. At its heart is the idea of the restoration of the perfect rule or reign (hence "kingdom") of God—that is, the recovery of what was lost through the sin of the garden of Eden. It is a dynamic rather than a static concept. It is the experience of the saving sovereignty of God, not only at the personal level but also the cosmic, and with decidedly eschatological connotations.[5]

Thus, in his clashes with the Sadducees and Pharisees, Jesus was not particularly concerned with Torah's "disputed interpretations" as much as he was driven by his understanding of God's coming reign. This helps to clarify Jesus' interpretation and application of Torah to the various situations narrated in the Gospels. While Jesus had no intention of abolishing Torah (Matthew 5: 17–20), his focus was "not oriented to the Torah, but to the kingdom of God."[6] Udo Schnelle maintains that "[t]his decentering is not to be equated with rejection or abolition (of Torah), but for Jesus it was not the gift of the Torah but love of God in his kingdom that was the open door through which every person could come to God"[7]

Jesus' focus on the kingdom of God is given greater clarity when he responds to a scribe's query concerning Jesus' view as to the greatest of commandments (*mitzvoth*).

> One of the scribes, when he came forward and heard them disputing and saw how well he had answered them, asked him, "Which is the first of all the commandments?" Jesus replied, "The first is this: 'Hear, O Israel! The Lord our God is Lord alone! You shall love the Lord your God with all your heart, with all your soul, with all your mind, and with all your strength.' The second is this: 'You shall love your neighbor as yourself.' There is no other commandment greater than these." (Mark 12:28–31 *NABRE*)

By linking love of neighbor to the love of God, Jesus is, in effect, stating that unless one in fact loves one's neighbor, then one's profession of love for God is questionable. From the perspective of a culture in which the dominant consciousness is collectivist, especially when dealing with such issues as purity (to be examined more closely below), determining who qualifies as one's neighbor, thus deserving of one's love, becomes problematic. While Jesus' response to the question of who qualifies as one's neighbor is well known, his response must be interpreted within the cultural structures of his time to get the full import of his inclusion of the "other" as one's neighbor.

THE GOOD SAMARITAN

> But because he wished to justify himself, he said to Jesus, "And who is my neighbor?" Jesus replied, "A man fell victim to robbers as he went down from Jerusalem to Jericho. They stripped and beat him and went off leaving him half-dead. A priest happened to be going down that road, but when he saw him, he passed by on the opposite side. Likewise a Levite came to the place, and when he saw him, he passed by on the opposite side. But a Samaritan traveler who came upon him was moved with compassion at the sight. He approached the victim, poured oil and wine over his wounds and bandaged them. Then he lifted him up on his own animal, took him to an inn and cared for him. The next day he took out two silver coins and gave them to the innkeeper with the instruction, 'Take care of him. If you spend more than what I have given you, I shall repay you on my way back.' Which of these three, in your opinion, was neighbor to the robbers' victim?" He answered, "The one who treated him with mercy." Jesus said to him, "Go and do likewise." (Luke 10:25–37 *NABRE*)

As we examined in previous chapters, the formation of identity is profoundly influenced by one's social relations. Social knowledge and cultural constructs and structures are transferred through modeling and mimesis.

Through the mimetic acquisition of the values and desires of the model, be it an individual or group, the individual acquires a social identity, as well as a sense of personal identity. In a collectivist culture, it is very difficult to distinguish the two. Henri Tajfel's theory of social identity helps to uncover the dynamics of social behavior. While social identity does not fully explicate the individual's sense of self, it nevertheless aids in explicating a good deal about one's sense of self. And, as Philip F. Esler states, "[t]he extent to which group membership contributes to a sense of self varies depending upon the level of group orientation present in the ambient culture."[8] So, the degree to which one's identity is tied to a particular group helps to determine the level of one's sense of self in conformity to the group. In a collectivist culture one's sense of self identity is deeply conformed to what modern social psychologists call groupthink. While groupthink may be viewed in contemporary Western cultures as a form of pathology, groupthink was a natural and normal experience in Jesus' social world. How one perceives oneself in one's social milieu effects behavior. In an individualist culture, there may be an idealization of nonconformity (though in actuality rarely practiced), while in a collectivist culture nonconformity is held in contempt and seen as a threat to the group's social stability and well-being.

Examination of ingroup/outgroup dynamics is helpful for understanding the practice of stereotyping. This "refers to the process of treating all members of an outgroup as if they were the same, usually with the projection of negative attitudes toward them."[9] We see this in our contemporary reality. For several decades the primary enemy of the United States was the Soviet Union. US Christians were taught to believe and perceive all Soviets as godless and dangerous, desiring the destruction of the American way of life. Many Catholics and Protestants, Christians and Jews and Muslims, Blacks and Whites, and so forth, use language, symbols, and characterizations that form stereotypes of the other, defining whole groups into rigidly drawn categories. Esler states that "[t]he dynamics of intergroup categorization and differentiation are more pronounced in a social setting which is collective rather than individualist in orientation, as was the ancient Mediterranean."[10] While it is more pronounced in a collectivist culture, it is present nonetheless even in an individualist culture, as is evidenced in daily parlance, be it private conversations or in social and televised media formats. A glance at Facebook and Twitter, as well as a brief listen to MSNBC and FOX news confirms this reality.

In answering the question about "who is one's neighbor," Jesus chose a Samaritan for his response and example. Why? What's the big deal with Samaritans? Well, there is a history behind the animosity between Samaritans and Jews. In brief: In the eighth century BCE, the Northern Kingdom of Israel (the Kingdom of David and Solomon divided into two kingdoms after the death of Solomon—Israel in the north and Judah in the south) was conquered by the Assyrian Empire (c. 722 BCE). The inhabitants of Israel either migrated to the south, were exiled to other parts of the Assyrian Empire, or else intermarried with other ethnic groups brought in by the Assyrians. Over the next several centuries, those Israelites who maintained their religious traditions developed prior to the Assyrian conquest, formed a community collectively named Samaritans, named after the city of Samaria, founded by Omri, King of the Northern Kingdom in the ninth century BCE. Samaritans maintained certain traditions that distinguished them from their Judahite neighbors in the south. These included their allegiance to their temple at Mount Gerizim, and their adherence to their own version of Torah, the first five books of the Hebrew Bible, while rejecting all other writings that made their way into the Hebrew Bible that some Judahites (e.g., Pharisees) accepted. As for the temple at Gerizim, prior to the fall of the North to Assyria, the Israelites had been accustomed to temple worship and sacrifice at two complexes, one at Dan in the north of Israel, and at Bethel in the south near the border between Israel and Judah. Thus, there would not have been a sense of allegiance to the Jerusalem temple, deemed by the Deuteronomic historian as the prescribed cult center for Yahweh worship.

In the seventh and sixth century BCE, the Southern Kingdom of Judah was conquered by the Babylonian Empire, with the aristocratic class taken into exile to Babylon. While in Babylon, the Judahites (soon to be known as Jews, derived from the name Judah) were able to maintain their loyalty to their God, moving closer to embracing a more definitive monotheism, away from the henotheism that had defined their religious consciousness prior to the exile. In exile a group of literate priests and scribes began to coalesce, edit, and put into a coherent narrative a set of texts that would eventuate into what we know as the Hebrew Bible. These texts would profoundly shape Jewish identity up to this day. When the Persians conquered Babylon around 539 BCE, the Persian king, Cyrus, gave permission for those who had been taken into exile by the Babylonians to return to their lands of origin, and to worship their gods and reinstitute their religious practices as they traditionally had done prior to exile. Not all Jews (I will use that moniker from now on) taken into exile returned to Judah, having found a reasonably comfortable life in their new home. Those who did return went with the expectation that the temple would be rebuilt and the sacrifices to their God reinstituted. The Samaritans, having their own temple at Gerizim, were not particularly interested in this venture, and many were opposed to it. As things developed, Jews and Samaritans would come to identify themselves as distinct from the other, developing animus between themselves. This animus would at times translate into acts of violence against the other. Negative stereotypes about the other would develop that made interaction between the two groups conflictual. This negative view of the other was still very much present in the period which Jesus was living and teaching. As far as Jews were concerned,

Samaritans were on par with the *goyim*, the gentiles, and while they shared some religious ideas and practices, they deemed Samaritans as outside the covenant.

It was a common belief for Jews of Jesus' time that one's neighbor was a member of one's ethnic/religious group, or among some Jewish sects, a member of one's religious sect. Thus, to love one's neighbor meant to love those in one's own group. One was responsible for the members of one's group, but not necessarily for those outside the group. As for how much one owed one's neighbor as a manifestation of love, this was debatable and was indeed debated among experts of the law. In the process of listening to the story Jesus tells about the man beaten, robbed, and left for dead, the lawyer may have been attempting to parse in his mind the various laws regarding the situation that a priest and a Levite find themselves. Esler imagines the lawyer at this point thinking, in the light of contemporary Jewish law, that Jesus is

> discussing the question 'Were these two Israelite men, associated with the cult and therefore subject to higher legal standards than ordinary Israelites because of their connection with the cult and no doubt well versed in the law by virtue of their positions, justified in not treating the man as a neighbor?' He would have been expecting that the next person along the road would have been an ordinary Israelite.[11]

If the priest and Levite were to exercise their cultic responsibilities in the immediate future, and were unsure whether the individual was in fact a Jew or not, or dead or not, they might legitimize their not aiding the man with the argument that they needed to maintain ritual purity in order to fulfill their ritual obligations without having to go through the required purification rites. There was a qualitative difference between the priest and the Levite. Priests were the only ones legally able to offer sacrifices at the temple, while Levites, being understood as inferior in status to the priests, could not offer sacrifices, but could help in the other services of the temple that did not involve sacrifice. Thus, the Levite could theoretically have stopped to help without too much inconvenience. But in this case the Levite chose, as Jesus tells it, to pass by. Maurice Casey states the following concerning the Levite's situation and action:

> Levites were *not* however subject to the restrictions placed on the behaviour of priests at Lev. 21: 1–4. There was therefore no doubt as to what the Levite in this parable should do: he should save life if the man were alive, and he should bury an untended corpse if he were dead. Like the priest, however, the Levite passed by on the other side because he wanted to avoid corpse uncleanness, and he declined to see whether he could save a wounded person in case he might be dead. That is why this is a more dramatic example than the previous one.[12]

At this point in the story, the lawyer may have been thinking that the next character would naturally be another Jew, a non-priest or Levite in this case. While the priest may have had legal arguments on his side for not stopping, and while one might give the Levite a pass, considering possible scenarios that might acquit him for his choice to pass by, a regular Jew had no cultic obligations, and could thus afford becoming unclean for a time. He could more easily justify his offer of aid, if he found evidence that the man in need was in fact a Jew.

It is at this point that Jesus' story takes a turn that is not expected by his interlocutor. One can only imagine the jolt the lawyer, and any others listening to Jesus, must have experienced when Jesus introduces a Samaritan! Let us try to put ourselves in the story by contemporizing it. While there are obviously significant differences in culture and religious attitudes between first-century Jewish religious views and modern twenty-first-century religious sensibilities, this is only meant to approximate the emotional response felt by those listening to Jesus' narrative.

> *One day an Asian woman was on her way to Mass. Being a conservative Catholic, she practiced the old tradition of wearing a head scarf to church. As she was driving along a country road a deer ran out in front of her car. She swerved to avoid the deer, careening into a ditch. Hitting her head on the steering wheel knocked her unconscious and bleeding from her temple. A few minutes later a White man was driving by on his way to church, slowed down when seeing the damaged car. When he saw that the woman was Asian, he drove on, as he held White supremacist attitudes towards non-Whites. A few minutes later a woman on her way to church was driving by, saw the headscarf and concluded that the woman was a Muslim, so she drove on. Next came an Imam from the local mosque on his way to breakfast with some friends. Seeing the car in the ditch he pulled over to see if anyone was in the car. As he walked to the car, he saw a bumper sticker that read "Jesus is the only way." While he found this a bit off putting, he continued to the driver side window. When he saw the injured woman unconscious and bleeding, he called 911, and gave whatever aid he could to the woman. The next day he went to the hospital to check up on her, and when he found that she did not have insurance, decided to pay her bills. The day she was to be released from the hospital, he met her at the entrance and drove her to her home.*

For anti-Muslim Americans, this story may be somewhat discomforting. Now imagine how the crowd listening to Jesus must have responded, especially with the long history of animosity between Jews and Samaritans. Jesus was indeed being provocative.

While biblical scholars have offered a variety of exegetical interpretations on this story, let us attempt to excise the underlying principle that informs Jesus' narrative and apply it to our contemporary social and cultural locale. In a collectivist consciousness we can confidently offer the supposition that both the priest and Levite had been formed to believe that they had responsibilities to those within their own group. These responsibilities enjoined both prescriptions and proscriptions. They had also been educated in the cultic responsibilities of their status and occupation. In terms of conflicts between both issues, how was one to determine the correct action in terms of aid to the man on the side of the road? At the same time, the Samaritan had as well been enculturated and socialized to see the Jews as *other*, outside the confines of his ethical responsibility to give aid. Noting that the man on the side of the road had been stripped of his clothes, which may have given some indication of group affiliation, we may give a legal pass to the priest and Levite, since there was no obvious indication of the man being a member of their group, thus eliminating any ethical responsibility for giving aid. The same is true for the Samaritan, who could have decided not to take a chance on helping a possible sworn enemy. In each case, Jesus notes that all three men "saw" the man on the side of the road. As Arland J. Hultgren notes, "[v]isually the three were equals. But the first two persons simply 'saw with the eyes' and noticed a problem to be avoided, whereas the third 'perceived' and wanted to look into the situation, and consequently he was moved by pity to do something."[13]

It is important to see that what differentiated the three men in this story, as Jesus told it, was the emotional response to seeing the man lying, possibly dead, on the side of the road. We are not told what particular emotions the priest and Levite had in this encounter, but we are told that the Samaritan was *moved* by pity. He felt sorry for the man. His emotional response moved him to overcome whatever his cultural and social formation might have taught him to think in this situation. In this case we are justified to conclude that the Samaritan's compassion for a fellow human being in dire need of aid informed his actions, actions that might have been condemned by his own group. Let us recall that when Jesus, in Luke 9:51–56, had set his face to go to Jerusalem, sending messengers to Samaria in order to make preparations for him while he stayed there, the Samaritans rejected him because of his intent to go on to Jerusalem. This so angered his disciples that they asked if it was permissible to call down fire on the whole lot of Samaritans. Of course, Jesus was less then pleased with this request.

The question thus arises about how we, as disciples of Jesus, are to respond to the question of who we are to understand to be our neighbor, and by what determinates we are to offer or reject aid. Who have we, and do we, determine to be within the confines of our mercy? Let us now examine other teachings of Jesus, in order to draw from them underlying principles that help to shape our contemporary interpretation and application.

SERMON ON THE MOUNT

Any examination of the teachings of Jesus must include the *Sermon on the Mount* in Matthew's gospel. Again, my examination will not be exhaustive, but will highlight those aspects of the Sermon that inform what I believe is a better hermeneutical key in interpreting the will of God in the formation of our social and cultural beliefs and practices.

In the Beatitudes Jesus offers what many would consider idealistic platitudes that simply cannot realistically be taken literally. While the prescriptions and promises do appear improbable in a world where the poor and suffering seem rarely to find relief or release, Jesus in fact believed that what he was teaching was not only possible but was incumbent upon his disciples to pursue and strive for, as the very heart of their discipleship. Jesus' vision of the kingdom of God was not a form of radical idealism. It was a conviction that with God all things are possible, even the very transformation of humanity. This involves the transformation of the whole of the individual, inside (intentions), and out (actions). And, as I have insisted above, looking at Jesus' teachings in light of his social and cultural reality, his words make more sense.

Looking at the political situation of first-century Palestine, one is justified on one level in judging Jesus' Beatitudes as a bit delusional, offering false hope. Since 63 BCE both Judea and Galilee had come under the suzerainty of Rome. Whether this meant rule through puppet kings like Herod the Great or his son Herod Antipas, or through the rule of Roman governors, such as Pontius Pilate, the result of this rule was debilitating for many throughout Palestine. While many students have been taught that the Romans developed what has been called the *"Pax Romana,"* Geraldo Zampaglione notes that "almost all the Roman writers agreed that spreading peace . . . meant subjecting other peoples to Roman domination."[14] Jesus rejects this form of "peace" in Matthew 20: 25–26. He counters this form of brutal domination and oppression with a call to form a very different kind of kingdom. As Warren Carter states,

> In the biblical tradition peace is closely tied to the doing of justice, God's will, that ensures access to adequate resources and protection from the greedy and oppressive (Ps 72). The rest of Jesus' blessings in Matt. 5: 3–12 evoke these traditions and envision a different future. They are subversive words that question the status quo, evoke visions of a different future, and mandate an existence of alternative practices in the present.[15]

A major result of Roman domination was the economic effect on the lower classes. Herod Antipas ruled in Galilee during the period of Jesus' ministry. Antipas evidenced a bit of his fathers' penchant for building, initiating the rebuilding of the city of Sepphoris, just across the valley from

Nazareth, hoping it to become "the ornament of Galilee." This project, along with others, had a negative impact on the economic lives of peasant landowners in the adjacent villages. Resources needed to maintain the luxurious lifestyle of the rich and powerful among Antipas' court and the subsidizing of retainers drew heavily from the local region. Along with the requirement to offer up these resources in the form of taxation, there was the added burden of tribute payment to Rome required of Antipas and other Roman suzerains. Philip Esler describes the lot of peasants in this period as follows:

> By the time peasants had paid taxes to the local political ruler and often to the local temple as well, there might be little left to support themselves and their families. Hunger was common, and the peasantry could even be drafted into military service or made to work on construction projects. Poor harvests generally meant that the peasants had to borrow at high interest rates, with the loans often secured against their next crop or their land itself. A very visible sign of this was the way in which the elite acquired peasants' land, by taking over fields that had been used to secure loans. It was very common for peasants to be forced off their land in these circumstances and to become tenant farmers, landless labourers or even beggars. These pressures sometimes led to the flight of peasants from the land altogether and to the consequent break up of families.[16]

This had the effect, as Seán Freyne points out, for the margins of the "smaller landowners and their families" to be "reduced, driving many of them to penury and brigandage."[17] Being forced off the land due to their inability to make payments, the resulting deserted lands would be confiscated by the wealthy, creating large and economically successful estates. In some cases, these large estates would operate through middlemen at the behest of absentee landlords, who were living lives of privilege and comfort away from their property, shielding them from the harsh life of those required to produce wealth for their absentee masters. It is this reality that gives us a clearer understanding for the content of Jesus' parables that incorporated "absentee landlords, farm stewards, slaves, hired servants and day laborers, often recruited or possibly pressganged from the surrounding villages, such as those on the Nazareth ridge."[18]

Though the circumstances have changed, an analogous situation has arisen in the modern world in which thousands of refugees have been forced, by poverty and ecological disasters, off their land, seeking survival through immigration. In many cases this dire situation has resulted from the forces of economic imperialism and environmentally devasting acquisitive consumption due to neoliberal capitalistic policies. In many cases the United States' attachment to a neoliberal capitalistic ideology, as well as economic imperialistic policies have helped to create this international crisis. In response to this situation many Christians have condoned policies that punish asylum seekers and economic refugees in search of economic survival. In some cases complicity in demonizing the victims of years of American economic imperialism is grounded in attitudes of White Christian supremacy.

It is to the desperate economic and political oppression of many peasants, farmers, and artisans, as well as the decadent lifestyle of the rich and powerful, that Jesus' message of the kingdom was directed. Seeing the suffering that greedy acquisitiveness and dominating and oppressive power had on the lives of people drew from him both a deep compassion for the poor and oppressed, as well as righteous anger toward their oppressors. This included those religious authorities who colluded with the reigning power structures. As Freyne states, "[i]t was to hard-pressed people such as these villagers that Jesus' declarations of beatitude were addressed and intended as good news."[19] For many Christians, limiting the teachings of Jesus to such historically contingent circumstances appears to relativize the eternal significance of his message. The problem with this view is that it diminishes the significance of the incarnation. As Marcus Borg states, "to take seriously the Christian understanding of 'incarnation' means precisely that God in Christ did become enmeshed in the circumstances of human life in a particular time and place, which need not (and perhaps cannot?) exclude the turbulent political questions of that time and place."[20]

While the teachings of Jesus have eternal salvific import, I would argue that this is not limited to the issue of life after death. The community of Jesus, the Church, is not simply about saving souls for heaven. As Karl Rahner writes, "[a] Christian community should not be a service station, where people come just to satisfy their individual need for piety and salvation. Such a community also has political and social obligations that should be clearly mentioned from the pulpit."[21] Jesus is calling for a transformation of consciousness that includes the whole person, body, mind, and emotions, for the sake of life in the here-and-now, as well as the life to come. His teachings in the Sermon on the Mount concerning internal motivations evidence this. It is not enough *not* to commit adultery, one must change the inner compulsions that lead to adultery. One must not only *not* murder, but must change the very intentional root, grounded in anger, vengeance, or hatred that leads to murder. This inner transformation is to have real effect on the world, for the flourishing of society, the well-being of each person. The Beatitudes are not idealistic rhetoric from a starry-eyed dreamer, but a summons from the Word of God become human to a vocation that God has predestined for humanity, both on earth as it is in heaven. Anna Wierzbicka argues that Jesus' teachings are a matter of both/and in regards to how life is to be lived in our social life on earth, and as well the hope for the life to come. She states that

> [t]he idea that God's recompense for human suffering may come after a person's death is sometimes rejected by commentators who want to interpret

Jesus' teaching as a sociopolitical manifesto and who focus on social justice as an urgent task for the here and now. But in fact one perspective need not exclude the other, and in the light of the Gospels as a whole there is no reason to think that Jesus' "good news" was meant to apply exclusively to future sufferers rather than to all sufferers, without restrictions.[22]

In stating that the poor, those who mourn, the meek, those who hunger and thirst for righteousness, those who are merciful, the clean of heart, and the peacemakers are blessed, Jesus is in a sense laying out the constitutive nature of the kingdom of God as he understood the nature and the will of God. In Deuteronomic terms, blessings from God come from fulfilling the law of the Lord. If this is the case, then it seems that Jesus has turned the tables on the concept of blessing, even the common understanding of the nature of God. From the logic of Deuteronomy, the poor, the mourning, and the suffering would appear to have fallen under the curse of the law. But from the vantage point of economic and political practices of the time, a clearer vision is offered for why people experience poverty, suffering, and grief. In many cases these are not the result of personal sin, but rather the imposition of economic and political structures that advantage the rich and powerful, while oppressing the poor and powerless. Sin is on the part of the oppressors, not the oppressed. Righteousness, then, becomes less a matter of ritual purity (what goes into the body is not what defiles, but what comes out—the violation of which would seemingly incur the curse of God), but rather the use of power over others that leads to poverty, suffering, and grief. Those who then thirst for righteousness, an emotional response to the desire for right relationship with God, must then discard the normative social and cultural constructs that elevate power as domination, and take on the yoke of servitude. This service includes the active pursuit of transforming systemic structures that cause poverty, suffering, and grief. This requires both personal and systemic transformation. This in turn requires of the disciple of Jesus to reflect on the social, political, economic, and cultural constructs that have been assimilated into his or her worldview that feel normative and true, but in fact are the antithesis of Jesus' teachings. One way of beginning this reflection is to consider who has been included in one's construction of "us" and "them." In the next chapter I will examine how the ideology of nationalism as an aspect of modern life influences the construction of "us" and "them," but here I want to examine two further aspects of the teachings of Jesus. These have to do with the practice of *hospitality* and *table fellowship* that formed attitudes of inclusion/exclusion in Jesus' socio-cultural-religious world. In examining the religious precepts and prescriptions of first-century Palestinian Jews that inform the structures and conceptual constructs shaping hospitality and table fellowship, we can discover the principles underlying

Jesus' practice, attitudes, and teachings concerning these two issues and apply them to our contemporary situation.

HOSPITALITY

It is important to note that while the practices of hospitality and table fellowship in the ancient world had many overlapping qualities, they were not necessarily the same in terms of prescriptions and proscriptions formed by social and religious interests. This had to do with the fact that certain Jewish sects, while subscribing to the general Mediterranean practice of hospitality, prescribed rules concerning who was allowed into one's table fellowship. Inclusion and exclusion had to do with issues of purity, which I will discuss below.

According to John Navone, the practice of hospitality in Mediterranean cultures was "a social process by means of which the status of someone who is an outsider is changed from a stranger to guest."[23] This process had three stages. First, the host had to discern, by evaluating and testing, whether the stranger's admittance as guest would not be a threat to the group's line of purity. Second, in lieu of the rules of patronage, admittance of the stranger followed the "culture-specific code of hospitality" that required the imposition of certain obligations on "both host and guest."[24] Third, the transformation of stranger to friend transpired, as long as the codes of honor were satisfied. Otherwise, the stranger might become an enemy if the codes of honor were breached or violated. Navone notes that the Hebrew Scriptures portray God playing host in many encounters between God and the Hebrew peoples. God's act of hosting is analogous to human practices of hospitality. These in turn become examples for God's people to imitate.

Jesus is also portrayed in the gospels as acting as host. We see this, for example, at the wedding feast in Cana, in which he helps keep the festivities going by turning water into wine (John 2:1–10). He feeds thousands who have come to listen to his message of the kingdom (Matthew 14: 15–21; 15: 32–38). He offers himself as spiritual food in John 6: 30–51. In a scene following the resurrection, Jesus begins as a guest and ends up becoming host, as he feeds the two disciples on the way to Emmaus (Luke 24: 30). Navone states that in the gospel of Luke, Jesus' life and ministry portray him "as a divine visitation to the world, seeking hospitality. The One who comes as a visitor and guest becomes host and offers God's hospitality through which the entire world can become truly human, be at home with God and one another, and know salvation in the depths of their hearts."[25]

In Jesus' proclamation of the reign of God, he often uses the image of the kingdom as a place "associated with the production of food and drink or homelike refuge for God's creatures." This is seen in several of Jesus' parables. In Matthew 22: 1–14, for example, Jesus compares the kingdom of God to a king who puts on a wedding feast. Over the course of the story the king invites members of all levels of society. At the Last Supper Jesus tells his disciples that, while he will not be eating the Passover dinner with them again in this life, they will gather again at the "eschatological and messianic banquet" in the life to come (Matthew 26: 20–29; Mark 14: 17–25; Luke 22: 14–20).[26] Waldemar Janzen notes that who Jesus "invites and those from whom he accepts hospitality"[27] is a central aspect of his message. This is both good news, for those who accept Jesus' invitation—usually those denied hospitality in other social situations—and an offense to those who are scandalized by those to whom Jesus extends hospitality. Acting in the name of God, Jesus opens his invitation to all, and "if any are given preferential treatment, it is to those with greater need."[28] Janzen states that this openness, while "characteristic of hospitality in the ancient world and evident in the Old Testament," had been "overlaid by careful distinctions between the worthy and the unworthy."[29] The regulations of hospitality offered by various Jewish sects and others had taken into account such concerns as "social status, religious purity, national origin, wealth, and power."[30] By refusing to take these concerns into consideration, or be restrained by them, Jesus "evokes release and joy in some, and deep enmity in others."[31]

PURITY, IMPURITY, AND TABLE FELLOWSHIP

Jacob Neusner states that ancient Israel shaped two vital and important concepts about purity and impurity that would be incorporated into later Judaism. These concepts played an important role in the ritual practices of Jews in the time of Jesus. First, "purity and impurity are cultic matters."[32] That is, they had to do with one's relation to the sacrificial system centered in the Jerusalem temple. Being in either state dictated one's ability to participate in the sacrifices and rituals surrounding sacrifice. For most of Jewish history until the period of the Hasmoneans concerns over ritual regulations were the purview of the priests. They did not apply, in most cases, to the average Jew in his or her day-to-day existence. Second, "they may serve as metaphors for moral and religious behavior, primarily in regard to matters of sex, idolatry, and unethical action. Purity furthermore closely relates to holiness."[33] And since the land was believed to be holy, it must therefore "be kept holy."[34]

While the concepts of purity and impurity may have acted as moral metaphors for religious behavior, ritual impurity was not necessarily moral in its actual implications. Due to the nature of life, it was taken for granted that most Jews would be in a state of impurity much of the time. As Robert Goldenberg points out, "the Torah offered no criticism of this state of affairs."[35] The only concern was to be aware of being in a state of impurity when coming into contact with sacred things. One was "to avoid any contact with the sacred"[36] if one was in a state of impurity. This meant the forbiddance of entering the Temple precincts or touching sanctified meat or the utensils used to prepare and serve sacred foods. To do so was believed to be a profoundly grave matter in which acts of purification would be required. The day of atonement took into account the possibility of sacred objects being made unclean by accident, by having everything associated with the performance of sacrifice being subjected to purificatory rites.

Again, the regulations concerning purity and impurity were primarily the concern of priests who were responsible for maintaining the sanctity of the sacrificial system. Most non-priestly Jews did not have to concern themselves, except for occasions that required purity. But there developed sometime in the Hasmonean period, in the second century BCE, a group of mostly lay Jewish men who would incorporate into their daily lives practices of ritual purity that typically only applied to priests. Goldenberg states

> The Pharisees' innovation was that they extended the rules of purity and impurity into their everyday lives. They ate ordinary meals as if these were sacrificial feasts. No one could be pure all the time, but this became the focus and the goal of their religious lives. This commitment required people to master a great many complicated rules, and it demanded a high degree of attention to countless minute details. It also unavoidably caused a degree of separation from people who were unwilling or unable to maintain this rigorous discipline, and this possibly explains the strong feelings of other people toward the group.[37]

It is this development among the Pharisees, a popular movement among many in both Judea and Galilee, that would inform the contentious narratives in the gospels portraying the antagonistic relationship between Jesus and this sect. An important aspect of this tension was over the issue of table fellowship.

One instance of this tension over the issue of table fellowship is found in the Synoptic Gospels. This had to do with Jesus' eating with tax collectors and "sinners" at a dinner hosted by Levi/Matthew (Matthew 9:9–13; Mark 2: 14–17; Luke 5: 27–32). As to the identity of who deserved the appellation "sinner," Mark Allen Powell states that "who would be included among the generic designation 'sinners' is not absolutely clear, but the context suggests that the reference is to people who, like tax collectors, could be denigrated on the basis of their vocation."[38] Regarding tax collectors, their "sin" was a matter of ethnic and religious treason. Tax collectors in this situation were Jews who chose, either out of necessity or greed, to serve either local rulers, like Antipas, or the Romans, to collect tolls and other forms of taxation that brought a good deal of economic hardship on many Jewish farmers and artisans. Powell maintains that Jesus' willingness to share table fellowship with such company was "deemed scandalous because it appears to imply acceptance and/or approval of the sinners (though, of course, not necessarily of their behavior)."[39] In his defense of such behavior, Jesus claimed to be acting, in an analogous sense, as a physician. These individuals, due to their social/religious disease, had been quarantined/excluded from society. This act of exclusion, in a collectivist consciousness, was tantamount to being excluded from the covenant, and it effected a loss of identity. By offering hospitality and table fellowship, Jesus was effectually inviting them back into the community of the covenant and offering back their identity as members of God's beloved. In an analogous way, White Christian supremacy acts a regulation to attitudes of table fellowship, demarcating who is worthy to be invited to the table of national hospitality and who is to be rejected (see chapter six).

It is important to note here that by inviting the types of people Jesus did, he was in danger of becoming impure/unclean by sharing sanctified food made unclean by unclean hands, as well as touching utensils made impure by impure hands. There is no indication in the texts of the gospels that Jesus finds this alarming, nor does he chastise anyone for being in states of uncleanness. On one occasion the Pharisees are surprised that Jesus did not wash/purify his hands before he ate (Luke 11: 38). Powell maintains that, along with Jesus' gracious offer of free healing, his willingness to offer table fellowship "provided a vision of 'shared egalitarianism' that challenged Jewish notions of privilege and favoritism by ignoring the boundaries between slave and free, male and female, pure and impure, patron and client, rich and poor."[40] Jesus embodied God's loving and inclusive nature through his acts of hospitality and table fellowship. I am convinced that his motivation was engendered by his deep emotional compassion for those excluded by the religious ideologies informing his social and cultural world. This world also included that of Roman social and cultural practices and norms. Powell states that "Jesus struck at the very heart of the Roman social system, which was based on patronage and brokerage and inevitably privileged a few and left many more on the margins."[41] In both his acts of hospitality and table fellowship, Jesus models for his disciples, of every era, the need of welcoming those excluded, marginalized, and denigrated due to the many social, cultural, and economic ideologies and policies that legitimate exclusion and marginalization. This includes refugees and immigrants fleeing oppressive situations. Corneliu Constantineanu notes this welcoming aspect of the gospel imperative, writing:

> The proclamation and embodiment of this divine welcome is the ultimate goal of theology and mission. But 'welcome' represents also one of the greatest needs of our present world: a world of inequalities, of suffering, of estrangement, of exclusion and violence. . . . We see the need of people to be listened to, understood, accepted and welcomed. And this represents a great opportu-

nity and a call for Christians, because offering welcome is both an integral part of Christian identity and an imperative for mission. In a world like ours, where exclusion and hurt and suffering is the order of the day, the church has a great opportunity to offer a different way of understanding, relating to and welcoming the other. Christians can and must make a difference; but for this to happen, hospitality must become a priority.[42]

In chapter two I argued, using the *Humean Theory of Motivation*, that the foundation of action is desire, which in turn is intimately connected to belief. Desires are shaped by modeling and mimesis (chapter three). Our models come from our social and cultural landscape. From this arena comes the formation of ideologies that inform our worldviews and actions (chapter four). As we develop over a lifetime, we shape our habitus, which in turn shapes our dispositions in our social relations (chapter one). An aspect of our dispositions is the formation of views concerning the "other." Our models give us direction regarding the proper response to the "other." We embody these dispositions in the form of emotions, many of which become second nature, causing a "natural," many times automatic, response to the "other." Our emotional responses *feel* true, thus reinforcing our reasoning concerning our views of and reactions to the "other." One's hermeneutical lens, formed over many years, shapes conclusions manifested in feelings of veracity concerning our understanding of the world, giving shape to the formation and habituated attachment to various intrinsic and instrumental desires. One's ontological appetitive identity needs for meaning, security, control, belonging, recognition, and action, are believed to be satisfied by the various intrinsic and instrumental desires we incorporate into our embodied emotional formation. Over time our embodied emotional responses become more concretized, forming a kind of second nature, thus making transformation more difficult when presented with alternative perceptions of the world. Many of our intrinsic and instrumental desires are, from a Christian hermeneutical perspective, idolatrous. That is, how we satisfy our appetitive identity needs/desires through intrinsic and instrumental desires become substitutes for the divine, from which our true fulfillment can be satisfied.

For many Christians in the modern world, and specifically in the United States, the embodied incorporation of ideologies that are, I am convinced, antithetical to the teachings of Jesus, has done real damage to Christian credibility. These various ideologies not only demonstrate a contradiction in Christian practice but are both heretical and idolatrous. While a much longer book could investigate a plethora of non-Christian, idolatrous ideologies, I have chosen to focus on one because of its immediate and devastating impact on our Christian practice and witness. In the next chapter I will focus on the issue of American Christian nationalism, which has become more and more visible the last several years and has brought with it a great deal of divisiveness, exclusion, and marginalization. Many Christians subscribe to aspects of American cultural values that are believed to define the American character. Many of these values, some of which used as evidence of American exceptionalism, are either directly in contradiction to the teachings of Jesus or can tempt one away from the teachings of Jesus. By subscribing and giving loyalty to these various values, many Christians wittingly or unwittingly seek to fulfill identity needs, believing temporal ends to be the resolution to experiences of ontological lack. The desire and pursuit for greater being in the temporalities of life are idolatrous. This in turn invariably leads to conflict and exclusion.

NOTES

1. Tyron Inbody, *The Faith of the Christian Church: An Introduction to Theology* (Grand Rapids: Wm. B. Eerdmans, 2005), 57.
2. Clifford Geertz, "'From the Native's Point of View': On the Native of Anthropological Understanding" in *Meaning and Anthropology*, eds. Keith H. Basso and Henry A. Selby (Albuquerque: New Mexico University Press, 1976), 225; quoted in Bruce Malina, *The Social World of Jesus and the Gospels* (New York: Routledge, 1996), 37.
3. Ibid, 38.
4. Ibid, 64.
5. Donald A. Hagner, *The New Testament: A Historical and Theological Introduction* (Grand Rapids: Baker Academic, 2012), 68.
6. Ibid.
7. Udo Schnelle, *Theology of the New Testament* (Grand Rapids: Baker Academic, 2009), 143.
8. Philip F. Esler, "Jesus and the Reduction of Intergroup Conflict: The Parable of the Good Samaritan in the Light of Social Identity Theory," *Biblical Interpretation*, 8, no. 4 (2000), 327.
9. Ibid, 328.
10. Ibid.
11. Ibid, 341.
12. Maurice Casey, *Jesus of Nazareth: An Independent Historian's Account of His Life and Teaching* (New York: T & T Clark, 2010), 303.
13. Arland J. Hultgren, "Enlarging the Neighborhood: The Parable of the Good Samaritan (Luke 10: 25–37)," *Word and Worship*, 37, no. 1 (2017), 74.
14. Geraldo Zampaglione, *The Idea of Peace in Antiquity* (Notre Dame: University of Notre Dame, 1973), 135; quoted in Warren Carter, *Matthew and Empire: Initial Explorations* (Harrisburg: Trinity Press International, 2001), 33.
15. Ibid.
16. Philip F. Esler, "The Mediterranean Context of Early Christianity" in *The Early Christian World*, Second Edition, ed. Philip F. Esler (New York: Routledge, 2017), 12.
17. Seán Freyne, *Jesus, a Jewish Galilean: A New Reading of the Jesus Story* (New York: T&T Clark, 2004), 45.
18. Ibid, 46.
19. Ibid, 47.
20. Marcus Borg, *Conflict, Holiness, and Politics in the Teachings of Jesus* (New York: Continuum, 1984, 1998), 24.
21. Karl Rahner, *Theological Investigation: Volume XXII* (New York: Crossroads, 1991), 132.

22. Anna Wierzbicka, *What Did Jesus Mean: Explaining the Sermon on the Mount and the Parables in Simple and Universal Human Concepts* (Oxford: Oxford University Press, 2001), 49.
23. John Navone, SJ, "Divine and Human Hospitality," *New Blackfriars*, Vol. 85, 997 (2004), 330.
24. Ibid.
25. Ibid, 333.
26. Waldemar Janzen, "Biblical theology of hospitality," *Vision: A Journal for Church and Theology*, 3, 1 (2002), 11.
27. Ibid, 12–13.
28. Ibid.
29. Ibid.
30. Ibid.
31. Ibid.
32. Jacob Neusner, "The Idea of Purity in Ancient Judaism," *Journal of the American Academy of Religion*, 43, 1 (1975), 16.
33. Ibid.
34. Ibid.
35. Robert Goldenberg, *The Origins of Judaism: From Canaan to the Rise of Islam* (Cambridge: Cambridge University Press, 2007), 103–104.
36. Ibid.
37. Ibid, 104.
38. Mark Allen Powell, "Table Fellowship," in *Dictionary of Jesus and the Gospels: Compendium of Contemporary Biblical Scholarship*, ed. Joel B. Green (Downers Grove: IVP Academic, 2013), 927.
39. Ibid.
40. Ibid, 929.
41. Ibid.
42. Corneliu Constantineanu, "Hospitality and Welcome as Christian Imperatives," *Transformation*, Vol 335, 2 (2018), 111.

Chapter Six

Nationalism as Idolatry

As discussed in previous chapters, the formation of our habitus and identity have multiple influences. Who we think we are is important to how we respond to issues that confront us in our daily lives. Issues of identity inform our loyalties. Our membership in a particular nation-state informs an important aspect of our identity. Nationality has become an influential part of how we define ourselves: I am an American, you are a Canadian, or a Mexican, and so on. We travel with documents that remind us of our national identity. Even our language and accents reinforce national identity. David Miller states, saying that one's national identity is integral to who one is,

> is not saying something that is irrelevant or bizarre in the same way as, say, someone who claims without good evidence that she is the illegitimate grandchild of Tsar Nicholas II. . . . It says simply that identifying with a nation, feeling yourself inextricably part of it, is a legitimate way of understanding your place in the world.[1]

In daily parlance, we have formed stereotypes based on national identity: the "ugly American," the "nice Canadian," the "poor Mexican"; Italians are lovers, while Germans are serious and follow rules. While many, for purposes of humor or easy reference, compress national identity to these short stereotypes, there is an awareness of more complex national characteristics that play a role in the formation of personal identity. These characteristics are preserved in national narratives—in many cases mythic in nature—that valorize particular qualities, or ethos, enhancing a sense of self-esteem, even a sense of superiority. These narratives offer a sense of belonging to something bigger than oneself and form a sense of loyalty to the nation. Many believe loyalty to the nation, its social, cultural, and political structures, to be a virtue. For a Christian, this issue of national loyalty is problematic. While there is nothing intrinsically wrong with loving one's cultural heritage, overweening loyalty to the nation can have deleterious effects on those not included in the definition of national membership. Thus, from a Christian theological perspective, nationalism, which requires some level of loyalty to the nation, is idolatrous, if one's loyalty to the nation contravenes the will of God.

In my discussion of nationalism below, I note that nations have their own unique qualities due to their distinctive histories. While there may be some shared similarities among the many nationalisms, American (USA) nationalism has *at least* three distinct elements that have informed its character. These elements are: 1) a tradition of exceptionalism, interpreted in both religious and secular categories. 2) White supremacy, and 3) Christian supremacy. While attitudes of White supremacy can be found in other White majority countries, attitudes and conceptions of the superiority of Whiteness in America have taken shape in the context of both ethnic diversity and Christian majority status. The wedding of White supremacy and Christian supremacy, having a long history of social and cultural hegemony in the United States, has accumulated for White Christians profound levels of cultural, economic, and symbolic capital. It has played a significant role in the formation of attitudes concerning American exceptionalism, as well as attitudes, dispositions, and acts of marginalization and exclusion of non-White, non-Christian others. In other words, these characteristics have, and continue to inform explicit and implicit judgments of many White Christian supremacists, as well as other US Christians, regarding who deserves hospitality and a seat at the table of American fellowship. Immigration and refugee policies have demonstrated the influence of these characteristics in much of US history. Attitudes toward people of color, including African Americans, Asians, and Latinos have demonstrated too often that hospitality is extended to those among one's own White Christian community, not unlike those religious sects discussed in chapter five. The segregation of Christian Churches demonstrates the extant of welcome to one's table of Christian fellowship. Religious bigotry grounded in a sense of Christian supremacy is demonstrated in recent policies of limiting immigration and visas to dominantly Muslim countries. In all of these areas, many US Christians have helped form these attitudes and policies, giving authority to the nation-state to enforce these interests. In turn, many US Christians follow the lead of the nation-state which incarnates the beliefs and ideologies that give the promise of fulfilling identity needs formed by the mythic narratives of exceptionalism and White Christian supremacy.

DEFINING NATIONALISM

The study of nationalism is vast, with a plethora of views regarding its birth, development, and structure. It is not my intent to review this expansive material. It would take a book-length study to cover a fraction of the subject. I will instead focus on how nationalism informs identity, and how it informs actions and reactions to others, especially with regard to inclusive and exclusive attitudes and behavior. Having reviewed a number of studies on nationalism, I have culled from several of these works aspects I find relevant to my thesis, which is, as stated in the Introduction:

> *many American Christians have assimilated into their identity ideologies that are antithetical to the teachings of Jesus the Christ. I maintain that appropriating identities that contravene, what I believe is a (as best as I can discern from my examination of the gospels) true Christian identity ultimately leads to idolatry.*

I have chosen among the many works on nationalism theorists who I believe offer insights that are, in my opinion, most salient to modern American (USA) experiences. While there are scholars who see some aspects of nationalism as benign, it is my contention that, from a Christian theological perspective, nationalism is at its heart idolatrous. William T. Cavanaugh writes that for many members of modern nation-states, "[n]ational identity becomes one's primary loyalty, and that highlights what separates one's nation from all others."[2] Nationalist ideology, when incorporated into one's self-identity, seeks satisfaction for ontological identity needs in desired ends that commit one's loyalty to, and faith in, the nation and its interests over the teachings of Christ. The will of God is our proper and true end, and where commitments to the nation contravene and contradict the will of God, conversion is called for.

Because of the morphological nature of nationalism scholars of nationalism note the difficulty of finding one simple definition for the term. There is no one type. This seems obvious to me since how a group of people perceive their identity as a group is determined by a diversity of social and cultural traditions. These include a shared memory among a national group for its origins, development, rituals, myths, and other cultural artifacts. Noting that the term nationalism is sometimes used synonymously with similar terminology, such as state, scholars of nationalism make important distinctions between these terms. The terms state and nation are sometimes used interchangeably. According to Philip Spencer and Howard Wollman, the "conflation of the terms nation and state, which may seem simple common sense to many people, is in part a tribute to the power and efficacy of nationalism as a political movement, committed to a certain view of the world."[3] John Coakley offers the following definitions for these two terms:

> A state is a self-governing territorial entity with central decision-making agency which possesses a monopoly of the legitimate use of force in ensuring compliance with its decisions on the part of all persons within its decisions on the part of all persons within its borders. . . . A nation is an ethnic group whose members are mobilized in the pursuit of political self-determination for that group. . . . Nationalism is either (a) a form of political mobilization that is directed at rectifying a perceived absence of fit between the boundaries of the nation and the boundaries of the state; or (b) the ideology that justifies this.[4]

Miller offers insight regarding what elements form a sense of nationality. He states that there are five elements that "serve to distinguish nationality from other collective sources of personal identity." These are: "a community (1) constituted by shared belief and mutual commitment, (2) extended in history, (3) active in character, (4) connected to a particular territory, and (5) marked off from other communities by its distinct public culture."[5] Coakley's use of the term "ethnic" is defined as a large group of people "whose members are linked by certain cultural characteristics—including the sense of sharing a common past—which they and others see as defining a social boundary between members and non-members of the group."[6] For my purposes, I see American Christians as a distinct group belonging to Coakley's definition of ethnicity, in terms of defining cultural boundaries between members and non-members, but not in terms of biologically shared traits. Miller's five elements can be found in American Christian nationalist's imagined community. They share basic religious beliefs and commitments and claim a particular history. Miller describes the third element as "communities that do things together, take decisions, achieve results, and so forth. Of course this cannot be literally so: we rely on proxies who are seen as embodying the national will—statesmen, soldiers, sportsmen, etc."[7] American Christian nationalists are deeply convinced that God has bequeathed them the land they call the United States, and have a profound sense of American exceptionalism.

Coakley's definition of nationalism notes that in its attempt to form political mobilization, ideological constructs justify such mobilization. In light of the ideological nature of nationalism, I concur with Spencer and Wollman's evaluation that "nationalism is an ideology which imagines the community in a particular way (as national), asserts the primacy of this collective identity over others, and seeks political power in its name, ideally (if not exclusively or everywhere) in the form of a state for the nation."[8]

Katherine Verdery notes that the concept of nation "has become a potent symbol and basis of classification within an international system of nation-states."[9] Most Westerners tend to think of "peoples" in national, or nation-state categories. When people travel abroad, a typical question they encounter is what country they come from. Most respond with an identity informed answer, such as *"I am* an American." The concept of nation "names the relation between states and their subjects and between states and other states; it is an *ideological construct* essential to assigning subject positions in the modern state, as well as in the international order" (emphasis mine).[10] The concept of nation acts as a symbol, which in turn informs personal and group identity. Verdery states that

> [a]s a symbol, nation has come to legitimate numerous social actions and movements, often having very diverse aims. It works as a symbol for two reasons. First, like all symbols, its meaning is ambiguous. Therefore, people who use it differently can mobilize disparate audiences (both internal and international) who think that they understand the same thing by it. Second, its use evokes *sentiments and dispositions* that have been formed in relation to it throughout decades of so-called nation-building (emphasis mine).[11]

Verdery argues that nationalism uses these symbols as a means for shaping discourse and political action. National symbols are invoked to draw from people feelings and sentiments so that they can shape responses to the use of these symbols, however that may manifest. "Nationalism is a quintessentially homogenizing, differentiating, or classifying discourse: one that aims its appeals at people assumed to have certain things in common as against people thought not to have any mutual connections."[12]

As stated above, scholars have argued that defining nationalism is difficult. One of the reasons for the difficulty is nationalism's morphological nature. One size does not fit all. So then, this begs the question of whether the concept is actually helpful, and whether one can glean any sort of common traits among the varieties of nationalisms. Are there core qualities and components of nationalism that can be observed in its multiple manifestations?

Michael Freeden offers helpful insights to these questions. In asking whether nationalism is a distinct ideology, Freeden notes that an important differentiation between nationalism and other political ideological constructs is the distinction between a full and a thin-centered ideology. A full ideology is one that "provides a reasonably broad, if not comprehensive, range of answers to the political questions that societies generate."[13] As a thin-centered ideology, nationalism acts as a supplement, or an attachment to a full ideological political construct, for example, liberalism, socialism, or conservatism. Each of these political ideologies claim the nation as the locale for one's commitment, while interpreting the proper character of the nation from different political hermeneutical lenses.

Freeden argues that nationalism, at its core, as a distinct ideological construct, contains the five following components. First, priority is given to the particular nation with which a group identifies "as a key constituting and identifying framework for human beings and their practices."[14] When this is realized, a sense of nationhood results. Second, "a *positive valorization* is assigned to one's own nation," which leads it to claim the right to determine "the conduct of its members."[15] Third, "the desire to give *politico-institutional expression* to the first two core concepts" (emphasis in original).[16] Fourth, there is the consideration of the concepts of space and time as "crucial determinants of social identity."[17] Fifth, there is "a sense of belonging and membership in which *sentiment and emotion* play important roles" (emphasis mine).[18]

The first core conceptual component relies upon the formation of perceptions of both the distinctive nature of the nation, that is, its qualities, values, traditions, and the many cultural artifacts believed to be normative for a particular nation, as well as who legitimately constitutes right of membership to the nation. Benedict Anderson notes the imagined quality of these constructs, defining the nation as "an imagined political community—and imagined as both inherently limited and sovereign. It is imagined because the members of even the smallest nation will never know most of their fellow-members, meet them, or even hear of them, yet in the minds of each lives the image of their communion."[19] Gerard Delanty and Patrick O'Mahony note the importance of the "role of intellectuals" in the formation of modern culture, who aid in the construction of modern cultural ideologies. Delanty and O'Mahony give a nod to the influence of religion in the formation and influence on modern ideological constructs, while emphasizing the secular nature of modern society. While there is no doubt that much of Western society can be categorized as secular, it is important to recognize, and I will discuss this more below, that American culture is still very much influenced by religious, and specifically Christian, symbols and cultural constructs. Recognition of this can be observed, to borrow from Michael Billig, in the banal and ubiquitous symbolic manifestations of Christianity in American society.

Billig observes that modern nation-states contain within their social structure's banal symbols that, in their ubiquity, tend to fade into the background of conscious awareness, only coming to awareness on special occasions. A prime example that Billig uses is the national flag. Billig states that the "uncounted millions of flags which mark the homeland of the United States do not demand immediate, obedient attention."[20] As for the purpose of these countless national symbols, Billig argues that "all these unwaved flags" provide "banal reminders of nationhood: they are 'flagging' it unflaggingly. The reminding, involved in the routine business of flagging, is not a conscious activity; it differs from the collective rememberings of a commemoration. The remembering is mindless, occurring as other activities are being consciously engaged in."[21] In an analogous way, throughout American society there are myriads of Christian symbols that "flag" America as seemingly a Christian nation, despite the constitutional declaration that no religious institution has legal hegemony over the citizenry. Yet there is a seemingly natural tendency by politicians and many Christian leaders in merging national symbols with Christian symbols, which acts as a type of flagging that feels natural for many American Christians because it typically lacks critical examination. Phillip M. Bratta gives an example of this merging of national and Christian symbols from a speech by George W. Bush shortly after 9/11. Bratta writes, in mentioning

> the "unfurling of flags," [Bush] uses this statement in combination with "the lighting of candles, the giving of blood, the saying of prayers." These other three behaviors are all associated with religion and echo Christian religious behavior: The light of Christ, the sacrifice of Jesus and blood of Christ, and prayer, which is how one speaks to God. Bush's mention of flag behavior by Americans paralleled with these religious rituals gives sacredness to the flag. Bush evokes the Messianic role and mission of the United States and Americans in the world. Bush's reference subliminally reminds Americans of the belief that they are divinely chosen with a mission to spread Christian principles.[22]

Freeden's second component argues that members of a nation assign a *positive valorization*, which in turn demands of its members prescribed/proscribed conduct. For example, two valorized traditions in American history are beliefs in liberty and equality as fundamental values. While the interpretation of these values is contested, they nonetheless form attitudes in which "true" Americans are committed to protecting them, going so far as to call on its members to take up arms, if needed, to defend them.

It is in Freeden's third component, the attempt to form a political structure in which the *sense of nationhood . . . can be represented*, that one finds the basis of political and national tension and division. Verdery notes that because of nationalism's agenda to form homogeneous societies, disparate political ideologies in the United States have produced a great deal of contention, including violent rhetoric and action among competing political groups. Each group seeks recognition by means of the institutionalization of their agendas. Freeden notes that *all* such political ideologies "seek institutional recognition."[23] In attempting to institutionalize a political agenda, groups actively attempt to block the institutionalization of other political ideological agendas. Abortion is an example of this, with pro-choice and pro-life advocates seeking the institutionalization of their agendas, while actively attempting to impede the other side's attempts to institutionalize their agenda.

In Freeden's fourth core concept, concerning attitudes on matters of space and time, there are attempts among disparate nationalist groups to privatize, and in many cases, gain "exclusive control over, stated space and time perimeters."[24] Freeden states that control over space and time

> constitutes a type of particularism that can be justified in terms of competing notions of national space—geographical, linguistic, cultural, biological. These are generally reinforced by an association of space with time: the continual occupation of land, the inherited ties of family in possessions and blood, the evolving cultural domain of language. Time is usually constructed as an in-

vented continuity designed to cover fragmentary historical evidence. It is occasionally attached to a founding myth and an ultimate destiny.[25]

American Christian nationalist perceptions of God's providential gifting of the American nation has played, and continues to play, a profound influence in American Christian nationalist's conceptions of the nation, in both its belief in American exceptionalism and its sacred mission. For many evangelical American Christians, time also has a sacred quality to it. Many hold a premillennialist conviction, developed in the nineteenth century, that the end of history and the advent of the eschaton is near, and that the role of America in its arrival has been and remains a matter of deep religious conviction.

American Christian nationalists adhere to a belief in a divine election—that God has elected America to be a New Israel, and American Christians are the new chosen people. Andrew J. Bacevich writes,

> [b]elief in the uniqueness of the American experiment is deeply embedded in the nation's psyche. The United States is not only different. It possesses special responsibilities. "We Americans are the peculiar chosen people—the Israel of our time," wrote Herman Melville in 1850. "We bear the ark of the liberties of the world." A century and a half later, this insistence that the United States, a great power unlike any other, retains a special mission to the world survived undiminished.[26]

Joanna Overing writes, "[m]yths of election" such as that held by many American Christians, "state that the nation . . . has been entrusted, by God or History, to perform some special mission, some particular function, because it is endowed with unique virtues."[27] Unfortunately, since many American Christians have included in their belief system other significant national ideologies, such as neoliberal capitalism, the special mission of evangelizing other peoples has also incorporated these ideologies as part of their missionizing endeavors. The addition of neoliberal capitalism to this missionizing endeavor has resulted in a form of economic imperialism. Bacevich has narrated the history of American policies that have legitimatized acts of economic imperialism in his book *American Empire*. Many American Christians have condoned such policies. This may have to do with the fact that capitalism has become *the* sacrosanct economic philosophy in America. American Christians have adopted, for the most part, a belief that neoliberal capitalism and Christian belief and practice are not only compatible, but coextensive. Along with bringing the gospel to foreign lands, there is an associated mission of Americanizing other nations in order to establish a neoliberal capitalist ideology that, conveniently, ultimately benefits American economic interests. When American economic interests are threatened, many American Christians accept foreign policies that take measures to protect these interests, regardless of the cost to human life, or to the destruction of other societies and cultures. Along with a number of interventions in other nations, in order to protect American economic interests, there is also the reality that American acquisitiveness has contributed to the environmental catastrophe that is devastating the planet.

Cavanaugh examines and critiques the tradition of American exceptionalism, which has been articulated and represented in two broad types. He writes that

> [t]he first explicitly appeals to Christian theological concepts such as election of Israel and God's providence. The second appeals to Enlightenment concepts concerning the universal applicability of the American value of freedom. The two types of American exceptionalism would appear to be at odds: the one appeals to a nation under the Christian God, the other to the freedom to have one God, none, or many.[28]

Cavanaugh makes the argument that despite their different approaches, both forms of American exceptionalism "end up in the same place."[29] Cavanaugh contends that "when a direct, unmediated relationship is posited between America and a transcendent reality—either God or freedom—there is a danger that the state will be divinized."[30] By allowing the state to take the place of God in the Christian's loyalty and commitments, the Christian accedes to idolatry.

Cavanaugh narrates the historic transformation of early Puritan views of divine election, visioning this in the confines of ecclesial structures, to a national Christian vision that "embraced the new nation as a whole."[31] Thus, America, the new Israel, becomes "itself a kind of metachurch."[32] This shift in vision now sees the transformation of "a nation under God to a nation as God's incarnation on earth, the nation as Messiah."[33] As noted above, other significant social, cultural, economic, and political ideologies have been incorporated into this messianic complex. Included in the American messianic, missionizing endeavor is the desire to spread the good news of American style democracy, American conceptions of individual rights and autonomous individualism, as well as an American neocapitalist economic ideology that elevates as a priority in foreign relations American self-interests. In other words, the desire to make the world into the image of the United States of America, an idolatrous inversion of being formed into the image of Christ. As will be discussed below, other profound cultural and social ideologies that have been part of American national identity for the length of its history, namely White and Christian supremacy, inform attitudes about American exceptionalism, as well as attitudes and perceptions of what constitutes true American national identity.

Cavanaugh warns that the idolatrization of the state, as has developed in both its Christian theological and Enlightenment forms, contains the "deepest theological danger" which is "that of the messiah nation that does not simply seek to follow God's will, but acts as a kind of substitute God on the stage of history."[34] An example of this in American Catholic history is exemplified in the life and career of Francis Cardinal Spellman, who infamously quoted the phrase first stated by Stephen Dacatur, "My country, may it always be right, but right or wrong, my country."[35] He spoke this "while visiting Vietnam, choosing to side with the president over the pope."[36] John Cooney notes in his biography of Spellman that "[w]henever he spoke out, Spellman reinforced his image as a defender of both Catholicism and Americanism,"[37] which, in some cases seemed to be the same thing. Numerous contemporary conservative Protestant leaders, including such well-known names as Franklin Graham, son of Billy Graham, and Jerry Falwell Jr., as well as others, are often highlighted in news stories defending partisan, especially Republican, policies and agendas. In a *Religious News Service* article, Yonat Shimron reported that Franklin Graham, an outspoken backer of President Donald Trump, "issued a dire warning about the fate of the United States, should the presidential impeachment inquiry started by the U.S. House lead to President Donald Trump's ouster."[38] Graham's backing of the president has been inspired by his belief that Trump is God's choice for presidential leadership. Graham has implicitly, and at times explicitly, wedded the will of God with the policies of the Republican party. Many of these policies are, I maintain, antithetical to the teachings of Jesus as discussed in the previous chapter. Along with Graham, a popular evangelical pastor, Robert Jeffress, a devout Trump supporter, made the claim that "a potential civil war" would occur "if the House votes on impeachment."[39] Jeffress has "accused Democrats of worshipping the pagan god Moloch."[40] While many Democrats are not blameless for holding idolatrous nationalistic ideologies, it is ironic that an ordained minister who has shaped his convictions and loyalties to an idolatrous nationalistic mind-set, has accused a whole political party of idolatry. As with Spellman, Graham, Falwell, and Jeffress, many religious and political leaders and lay Christians claim divine affirmation and biblical legitimation for policies that clearly, I submit, contradict the teachings of Christ. By divinizing the state, making it, as Cavanaugh states, the location of "God's activity in America is that America itself becomes the criterion for locating God's activity in the world."[41]

THE UNCONSCIOUS/BANAL FORMATION OF NATIONALISM

As examined in chapter one, many memories go unexamined that are sedimented in the unconscious structures of a person's psyche, manifesting as appresented emotions. The ubiquity of national symbols, traditions, and norms that individuals encounter in their banal manifestations become embodied, shaping emotional concepts. Attachment to national norms, traditions, and loyalties, embodied in the emotional and attitudinal habitus of the individual, shapes an individual's social practice. In this process, there is a form of non-remembering remembering that influences the formation of one's identity, developing a second nature element in the emotional structures of one's identity. Billig writes, "if banal life is to be routinely practiced, then this form of remembering must occur without conscious awareness: it occurs when one is doing other things, including forgetting."[42] Billig notes that Bourdieu's theory of habitus "expresses well this dialectic of remembering and forgetting."[43] Billig quotes Bourdieu: "The *habitus*—embodied history, internalized as a second nature and so forgotten as history—is the active presence of the whole past of which it is the product."[44] Billig concludes that social life, patterns shaping one's habitus, "become habitual or routine, and in so doing embody the past. One might describe this process of routine-formation as *enhabitation*: thoughts, reactions and symbols become turned into routine habits and, thus, they become *enhabited*. The result is that the past is enhabited in the present in a dialectic of forgotten remembrance" (emphasis in original).[45] The problem this raises for Christian practice is that the inhabited forgotten remembrance may be a narrative that is antithetical to the teachings of Christ, and simply not historically factual. And because they are inhabited as a second nature, they engender feelings of veracity. These feelings of veracity make it difficult to convince a person of alternative, more truthful, narratives. Accepting and embodying nationalist narratives can lead to feelings of anger or fear when these cherished narratives are challenged. Guilt, and a sense of betrayal may occur if consideration is accorded a different hermeneutic. Because of the deeply polarized condition of contemporary American society, the willingness to dialogue, critically examining the merits of one's conceptual worldview in light of another hermeneutical lens, has become quite difficult. A retreat into tribalism has grown up around a digital, social media society, with a tendency to listen to similar voices that strengthens the entrenchment of one's ideological convictions. These ideologies are tethered to sentiments and emotions that shape and inform motivations and reactions to perceived threats.

Freeden's fifth core concept is vital in understanding the motivational impact that nationalist ideology has for individuals and groups. It has to do with "sentiment and emotion as the basis for socio-political ties. . . . All ideologies . . . carry emotional attachments to particular conceptual configurations, both because fundamental human values excite emotional as well as rational support, and because ideologies constitute mobilizing ideational systems to change or defend political practices."[46] In order to attempt to motivate people to act on particular desired political agendas, political leaders will attempt to evoke emotions through the use of emotionally charged rhetoric. Freeden states that "the role of emotion becomes an overriding *con-*

sciously desired value—which is why it contains such useful sets of ideas when recruitment to the flag and sacrifice are predominant political ends." [47] The ability to call forth such emotions depends on the already sedimented presence of emotional concepts and attachments that lie beneath the surface of awareness until they are recalled by some trigger. As discussed in chapter two, latent emotional beliefs are embedded/embodied in memory, remaining dormant until presented with objects that trigger sedimented emotional beliefs. Because of the mimetic nature of humans, leaders are able to trigger these emotional beliefs, and manipulate them for their own purposes. Mimesis results in a form of contagion in regard to groups and crowds. Lawtoo, working with the foundational studies of Gustave Le Bon, Gabriel Tarde, and George Bataille, along with Girard's mimetic theories, describes this reality in his discussion of crowd mentality. Lawtoo illustrates the contagious nature of emotional mimesis in his description of Donald Trump's ability to create a mass pathology among his most ardent supporters. Lawtoo writes,

> [n]ow, if we establish a genealogical link that bridges the origins of mimetic theory with its most recent developments, there are plenty of reasons to take Trump's histrionics seriously. Why? Because the embodied, affective, and performative dimension of his mimetic speeches, mimicry, and gestures triggers mirroring effects that have an influence on what subjects feel and think. These subjects are already susceptible to being affected by mimesis, not only because of the mirroring structure of their brains, or solely because an identification with Trump was already in place, but also because being part of a crowd subjected to a prestigious leader already begins to dissolve the boundaries dividing self and others via a mode of contagious communication that amplifies the mirroring tendencies of *Homo mimeticus*.[48]

Nationalism, as a thin-centered ideology, tends to attach itself to another, fuller, ideological construct. Philip Gorski defines Christian nationalism as the "blending of Christian and patriotic narratives and iconography that blurs or erases the line between religious and political community and identity."[49] Andrew L. Whitehead, Samuel L. Perry, and Joseph O. Baker note the important distinction between American civil religion and American Christian nationalism. They write that

> [c]ivil religion, on the one hand, often refers to America's covenantal relationship with a divine Creator who promises blessings for the nation for fulfilling its responsibility to defend liberty and justice. While vaguely connected to Christianity, appeals to civil religion rarely refer to Jesus Christ or other explicitly Christian symbols (Bellah 1967; Gorski 2017). Christian nationalism, however, draws its roots from "Old Testament" parallels between America and Israel, who was commanded to maintain cultural and blood purity, often through war, conquest, and separatism. Unlike civil religion, historical and contemporary appeals to Christian nationalism are often quite explicitly evan-

gelical, and consequently, imply the exclusion of other religious faiths or cultures (Delehanty, Edgell, and Stewart 2017).[50]

Christian nationalism is the wedding of national attachments and loyalties to an attendant set of biblically informed beliefs. I believe that aspects of these biblical beliefs are misguided, as they misinterpret gospel teachings. In chapter five I argued that there are more faithful hermeneutical lenses by which to discern the will of God through the teachings and actions of Jesus within the context of his socio-political-cultural-economic context. Many American Christians have wittingly or unwittingly incorporated various American social and cultural values into their Christian worldview which, I am convinced, contradict the gospel. I argued in chapter four that Christian faith affirms the existence of objective truth. While certainty regarding the totality of the contents of God's truth and reality are unattainable because of the limitations of human knowledge, there are, as I have argued, better hermeneutical lenses for discerning a more accurate understanding of the will of God. Thus, many ideologically constructed interpretations of the will of God fall within the category of false consciousness, leading in many cases to feelings and attitudes that result in actions and reactions of exclusion. Attachment and loyalty to these ideological constructs, embodied as emotional and attitudinal dispositions, leads invariably to idolatry, because the formation of one's perception of God can be informed by ideological constructs that project one's distorted desires on to one's misguided conception of the divine. This in turn shapes an individual's and group's legitimation for a sense of superiority over others, because "our" God has blessed "us." "Our God is on our side, the righteous ones, and calls us to overcome, and if necessary, vanquish the wicked." Categorization of who is deemed wicked, rejected, sinful, or any variety of other descriptions, leads, when Christian and nationalist loyalties are wedded, to acts of exclusion, whether the rejected are perceived as deviants in the homeland, or others who live in "shithole" countries. It can form attitudes of fear toward certain immigrant groups, or refugees from non-Christian countries, especially Muslim countries.

I want to emphasize that Christian nationalist beliefs are not only the purview of radical and fringe groups, such as the KKK, or radical right-wing Christians. They can also be characteristic of stereotypical, average American Christians who fail to recognize a tacit, unconscious embodiment of Christian nationalist attitudes and sentiments that accepts America as somehow superior to other nations. There follows an acceptance of national policies that sees other nations through a lens of "American interests," regardless of the social, cultural, economic, and environmental damage these policies inflict on other peoples and nations.

An example of a tacit marriage of Christian and national identity is the ubiquitous displaying of the American flag in many Christian churches. Trying to convince a congregation to remove the flag can damage a pastor's career. For an example of this see Craig M. Watts' *Bowing Towards Babylon*. Another example of banal nationalism within American Christian experience is the incorporation of hymns that valorize the nation. As I write these lines, Americans are celebrating Memorial Day. For the Sunday liturgy this week, the music chosen for the final hymn was *America the Beautiful*, a celebration of American exceptionalism in song if there ever was one.

NARRATIVE AND MEMORY

Narrative plays a profound role in identity formation. The stories we learn, tell, and by which we describe ourselves inform our sense of self. We are presented these narratives in our social and cultural environments, our fields. Learning and embodying these narratives gives us a sense of belonging. By sharing common narratives, we feel a sense of belonging within a particular group or community. Membership in particular groups offers the promise of identity needs satisfaction. By acceptance in the group, we feel recognized. In a threatening world, the group can offer a sense of security. Accepting and incorporating the myths and traditions of the group can offer us a sense of place in the ongoing narrative of the group, thus informing our world of meaning. This may in turn inform aspects of our perceived purpose.

Stephen Crites notes that narrative gives us the ability to have a sense of "coherence through time."[51] While our narratives incorporate various strands, or subplots, each tends to meld into a holistic, relatively coherent story that gives shape to the idea of "me." Some of our stories, because of their transcendent qualities, those greater than our individual experiences, are attended by rituals that recall myths of origin. National stories are celebrated at different times, allowing individuals to transcend *chronos* time, the experience of moment-to-moment progressive movement, and enter into *kairos* time, where the past is re-presented and experienced afresh in the present. These rituals, and the stories told to remind people of their national history, reinforce national identity. Identifying with the nation calls forth certain loyalties to the nation. Crites sees that the embodiment of these stories leads to the formation of particular *styles* among groups. I understand his use of "style" as analogous to Bourdieu's concept of "disposition." Different national cultures produce different dispositions, informing a common embodied *hexis*, "the site of incorporated history."[52] Crites calls these types of "fundamental" narratives

> sacred stories, not so much because gods are commonly celebrated in them, but because men's (*sic*) sense of self and world is created through them. . . . For these are stories that orient the life of people through time, their life-time, their individual and corporate experience and their sense of style, to the great

powers that establish the reality of their world. So I call them sacred stories, which in their secondary, written expressions, may carry authority of scripture for the people who understand their own stories in relation to them.[53]

Telling and retelling, in speech and ritual, fundamental narratives creates an imagined connection made with those who are believed to also embrace and embody, the same national memories, origins, and loyalties.

AMERICAN IDENTITY

Each nation draws upon narratives of origins, developing traditions passed from generation to generation through stories. In many cases the traditional narratives are changed, re-created or reinterpreted to fit a new situation or a particular agenda. Such has been the case in the Christian nationalist arena.

In *The Sin of White Supremacy: Christianity, Racism, and Religious Diversity in America*, Jeannine Hill Fletcher highlights a long held narrative in US history of White Christian supremacy. Hill Fletcher argues that at the heart of US social history is a long tradition of White supremacy wedded to Christian theological constructs legitimating both White and Christian supremacy. Hill Fletcher states that

> God's designs for White people and White supremacy were manufactured in the academic spaces of theology and philosophy and given a platform in the pulpit of university ministers and others. Systems of philosophical and theological knowledge allowed White supremacy to appear reasonable in the public square. But it is crucial also to see this *symbolic capital* ultimately informing arguments in the legislative sphere (emphasis mine).[54]

Hill Fletcher's use of the phrase *symbolic capital* is not explicitly defined. Because I believe she is correct in her assessment as to the elevated prestige that White Christians have acquired utilizing theological and philosophical legitimations for White Christian hegemony, a quick explication of this concept is in order.

Symbolic capital is a sociological phrase developed in the work of Pierre Bourdieu and is closely associated to his concepts of cultural and economic capital—the first of which I discussed in chapter one. There is some overlap in symbolic and cultural capital in Bourdieu's work, thus I see both as, in some contexts, synonymous. David Swartz ascribes Bourdieu's use of this phrase to those social structures formed through schemas of differentiation and oppositions. Swartz states that these schemas create networks of oppositions, for example, high and low culture, as well as a plethora of cultural evaluations concerning levels of respect, honor, value, and so on. This affects all aspects of cultural rank and practice. In the totality of these cultural schemas lies "the matrix of all the commonplaces which find such ready acceptance because behind them lies the whole social order."[55] Bourdieu states that "the cognitive structures which social agents implement in their practical knowledge of the social world are internalized, 'embodied' social structures."[56] These social structures are internalized by both individuals and groups "who then unwittingly reproduce the social order by classifying the social world with the same categories with which it classifies them."[57]

White Christian theologians, philosophers, and political leaders, Hill Fletcher argues, successfully created, and reproduced, ideologies of White Christian supremacy, thus obtaining for White Christians a reservoir of symbolic capital—I would include cultural capital—accumulated through three centuries of US history. Hill Fletcher states that

> at the deepest recesses of North American theo-logic is a pattern of thought that repeats itself, a theology of White supremacy that was manufactured within Christian university systems and that counted as knowledge. This pattern of thought is characterized by the theological ideas of God's singular plan, a Christian destiny for all, the value-laden opposition of Christian versus non-Christian, and resultant hierarchy of humanity reflected in skin and status.[58]

The elevation of "White Christian" as a symbol of normativity which has created the belief that true American (USA) identity is measured by the standards of whiteness and Christian affiliation. As Swartz notes, the "social function of classification logic of symbolic representations generates, therefore, a *political effect* to the extent that social groupings identified are hierarchically differentiated and therefore legitimated."[59] Hill Fletcher demonstrates this political effect in her examination of governmental policies enacted over generations of US history that were meant to protect White interests and hegemony, while marginalizing non-White, and in many cases, non-Christian others. Hill Fletcher maintains that the accumulation of years of White Christian supremacy has strengthened White Christian symbolic capital, as demonstrated by such contemporary attitudes and policies that legitimate Islamophobia, as well as the denigration of non-White others among such ethnic communities as African Americans, Asians, and Latinos. Hill Fletcher argues that "[i]n a White Christian nation the environment continues to recognize White and Christian and to not recognize or to misrepresent others."[60] Hill Fletcher demonstrates in her study that presently, Christian supremacy maintains hegemony in US society, and that White supremacy emerges from Christian supremacy, resulting in "death dealing for non-White, non-Christian others."[61]

Hill Fletcher argues that a Christian theological pattern has taken shape in US Christianity, in which God has designed a "Christian destiny for all humankind." This has led, she maintains, to a "sliding scale of humanity" which sees "God's favor on Christians and God's curse on non-Christians, reflected in skin and status."[62] I suspect many Christian theologians and laity would take exception with Hill Fletcher's leveling of Christian revelation as one among many channels by which the divine is revealed and experienced. Her point, as I understand it, is that Christian supremacy, as fostered throughout US history with the complicity of universities and Christian leaders, has led to attitudes and actions that have not only marginalized and oppressed non-White, non-Christian US citizens. It has also formed legitimations for American Christian imperialism, under the guise of bringing the gospel of salvation to non-Christian, and significantly, non-White nations. While Christianity has always been a missionizing religion, Hill Fletcher's argument has, I believe, an important insight, though I might disagree on some theological particulars. As she has demonstrated, the wedding of Christian theology with the ideology of White supremacy has had, and continues to have, deleterious effects on non-White, non-Christian communities in the United States. At the same time, Christian supremacy has played an important role in advancing political policies and endeavors, bolstered by the ideology of American exceptionalism, legitimating acts of American imperialism.

Hill Fletcher's thesis, that White Christian supremacy is a foundational cultural and social reality in US history, from its founding to the present, is bolstered by contemporary social psychological studies that give strong evidence to White Christian hegemony in the United States. I offer an example of such research below. It is important to note here that a significant reason for the continued prevalence of the ideology of White Christian supremacy is its deeply rooted embodiment among so many Whites and Christians. This gives the ideological beliefs of White and Christian supremacy a feeling of normativity. In chapter two I discussed the processes by which feelings, emotions, and desires are embodied. Social and cultural forces play a profound role in the embodying of ideologies that inform feelings, emotions, desires, and attitudes. When individuals and groups experience benefits because of affiliation with a privileged class, ethnic group, and/or religious group, the rewards of such benefits (including cultural, economic, and symbolic capital) become embodied, creating intrinsic and instrumental desires that are not easily dislodged. The benefits that accrue to White Christians form worlds of meaning, which in turn shape strategies to safeguard a meaning world that has become normative. This in turn shapes one's sense of belonging. Threats to one's sense of belonging to a privileged group raise concerns for one's sense of control. Thus, one's sense of loss of power over one's environment can lead to actions of opposition toward those deemed as a threat to one's status and position in the social hierarchy. In many cases, the experience of loss of prestige and power is projected on some "other," or "others," who conveniently act as scapegoats. For many White Christian supremacists, the scapegoat role tends to fall on the shoulders of minorities, especially non-White minorities. For Christian supremacists of any ethnic background, members of non-Christian communities are likely to fill the role of scapegoat.

Unfortunately, feelings and attitudes that reinforce the ideology of White Christian supremacy are, for the most part, unconscious for many who embody them. As demonstrated by social psychological studies, while the ideology of White Christian supremacy might be explicitly rejected by White Christians, there is evidence that implicit complicity to this ideology is, nevertheless, prevalent.

THE SOCIAL PSYCHOLOGY OF WHITE CHRISTIAN SUPREMACY

Carly M. Jacobs and Elizabeth Theiss-Morse have analyzed studies that attempt to capture characteristics believed to describe the stereotypical American. They note studies examined by Devos and Banaji, as well as Cheryan and Monin, illuminating the overriding belief that American=White. In addition to the association of a true American as being "white, specifically of primarily northern European heritage,"[63] Jacob and Theiss-Morse examine the extent to which Americans associate being *Christian* with being American, and whether or not Christianity plays a role in determining national group membership. Jacob and Theiss-Morse note, "religion in general and Christianity in particular are symbolically and explicitly infused in the national narrative and in what it means to be an American."[64] Examples can be found in such things as the printing of "In God We Trust" on currency, as well as having presidential swearing into office by placing one's hand on the Bible. It is common to hear politicians publicly claim, with little or no negative feedback, that America is a Christian nation. While running as the Republican candidate for president, Senator John McCain stated that "the Constitution established the United States of America as a Christian nation."[65] Mike Huckabee, father of Donald Trump's former press secretary Sarah Huckabee-Sanders, and former governor of Arkansas stated, while running for president, "that 'most' of the fifty-six men who signed the Declaration of Independence were clergymen."[66] The reality is "only one member of the clergy signed the Declaration—College of New Jersey president John Witherspoon." Jacobs and Theiss-Morse state that "[t]he lack of controversy surrounding these assertions is indicative of a widespread belief among Americans that the United States is indeed a Christian nation."[67]

Jacobs and Theiss-Morse examine two areas of interest. First, they want to determine the degree to which Americans "associate being American with being Christian."[68] Second, they examine the "attitudinal and behavioral implications of the association between religion and national identity."[69] In this, they want to measure "the extent to which people who do not share a central stereotypical characteristic feel the need to prove they are good, prototypical, national group members."[70] Jacobs and Theiss-Morse, using the social psychological *self-categorization theory*, which holds that once a person determines another person has stereotypical characteristics of a particular group, even if only partially, the individual sharing any aspects of these characteristics is categorized a member of the group. When "people think of the group, a set of descriptive stereotypes automatically, and often unconsciously, comes to mind."[71] John Sanders, summarizing the experimental research of Eleanor Rosch and Carolyn B. Mervis on the relationship between prototypes and categorization, notes four important results from these studies:

> (1) People have much faster speed of processing (reaction time) when responding to exemplars (prototypes) of a category than to a non-prototypical member of a category member. (2) When asked for an example of a category member, subjects typically gave the same exemplars. (3) Category membership is established first for the best exemplars and last for the least representative examples. (4) Of importance to education is that people learn a category more easily and accurately if they are initially exposed to only the most representative exemplars of the category.[72]

Jacob and Theiss-Morse describe prototypical members of a group as those "who hold the key characteristics that allow for assimilation and contrast."[73] Because these characteristics are grounded in what are believed to be widely accepted norms and stereotypes of the group, it is difficult to alter them, having a history that informs the collective memory. Political leaders will reinforce these characteristics "that are prototypical, making it difficult, though not impossible, to alter them." In psychological studies, it has been demonstrated that those members who demonstrate prototypical traits are both "treated differently from, and better than, atypical group members." Studies also show that "atypical members and subgroups are much more likely to have their group identity denied, and therefore are denied benefits that might accrue to group members."[74]

Those who identify with a group very strongly tend to establish "exclusive boundaries" in order to establish "who counts as a group member and who does not." These "strong identifiers" will "prefer to err on the side of *excluding* an in-group member than erroneously *including* an out-group member."[75] Surveys demonstrate that patriotism is a widely shared value among most Americans. Incorporated in this deep love, devotion, and loyalty to the nation are strong feelings about the need to establish tight boundaries around national membership, determining who counts as a member of the national group and who does not.[76]

In their conclusion, Jacobs and Theiss-Morse's research offers strong evidence that many Christians tend to believe explicitly that "America=Christian," while non-Christians tend to accept this belief implicitly. So then, "Christians are much more likely than non-Christians to state explicitly that people have to be Christian to be true Americans."[77] In correlating the two sociological conclusions, America=white and America=Christian, one can see how exclusionary attitudes and behavior are seemingly inevitable. In a *Perceptions of the American People* survey, researchers asked the following question: "Only true Americans should be guaranteed their basic rights, such as freedom of speech and freedom of assembly."[78] Two-thirds of those responding, who associated being "a true American with being Christian agreed with this statement, thereby implying that only Christians (the 'true' Americans) should be guaranteed their basic rights."[79]

The intent of this chapter has been, 1) to describe nationalism, 2) to point out that many US Christians have surrendered their loyalty to the will of the nation, which has developed a mythic narrative of national exceptionalism and White Christian supremacy, and 3) to show that from a Christian theological perspective, nationalism—the act of divinizing the state, making it a surrogate for the will of God, thus claiming the loyalty of many Christians—is by its nature idolatrous. Loyalty to the nation, along with attitudes of White Christian supremacy, have informed attitudes and acts of destructive exclusion. This has brought about the implicit formation of ideologies of White and Christian supremacy, embodied and manifested in dispositions of exclusion toward "others" not fitting the hegemonic categories of Whiteness and Christian. It has in turn given rise to evaluative judgments about who is to be considered a true American. These hegemonic categories have also shaped US policies concerning other states not fitting the categories of Whiteness and Christian, legitimizing what is best understood as imperialism, under the guise, in many cases, of Christian missionizing. I maintain that defense of these categories, these ideologies, is a betrayal of the gospel imperatives of hospitality and table fellowship, as discussed in chapter five.

I have argued throughout this text that, for the Christian, God is the only true end for one's ontological identity needs/desires. Yet, for many, the nation has become the surrogate by which these needs are fulfilled. The question that I believe deserves examination is, what does the ideology of nationalism offer the Christian in terms of identity needs fulfillment. What does the Christian who has put his or her faith in the nation, or the myth of the nation as narrated in light of White Christian supremacy, gain by surrendering his or her loyalty and commitment to the will of this nation? Finally, by what means does the Christian free himself or herself from the bondage of this idolatry? In the Conclusion I will attempt a response to these questions.

NOTES

1. David Miller, *On Nationality* (New York: Oxford University Press, 1977, reprinted 1995), 11.

2. William T. Cavanaugh, *Migrations of the Holy: God, State, and the Political Meaning of the State* (Grand Rapids: Eerdmans, 2011), 38.
3. Philip Spencer and Howard Wollman, *Nationalism: A Critical Introduction* (Thousand Oaks: SAGE, 2002), 2.
4. John Coakley, *Nationalism, Ethnicity and the State: Making and Breaking Nations* (Los Angeles: SAGE, 2012), 11–12.
5. David Miller, *On Nationality*, 27.
6. John Coakley, *Nationalism, Ethnicity and the State*, 12.
7. David Miller, *On Nationality*, 24.
8. Philip Spencer and Howard Wollman, *Nationalism: A Critical Introduction*, 2.
9. Katherine Verdery, "Whither 'Nation' and 'Nationalism'?" *Daedalus*, 122, 3 (1993), 38.
10. Ibid.
11. Ibid.
12. Ibid.
13. Michael Freeden, "Is Nationalism a Distinct Ideology?" *Political Studies* 46, 4 (1998), 750.
14. Ibid 751–752.
15. Ibid.
16. Ibid.
17. Ibid.
18. Ibid.
19. Benedict Anderson, *Imagined Communities: Reflections on the Origin and Spread of Nationalism* (London: Verso, 2006 Revised Edition), 5–6.
20. Michael Billig, "Banal Nationalism" in *Nations and Nationalism: A Reader*, ed. Philip Spencer and Howard Wollman (New Brunswick: Rutgers University Press, 2005), 188.
21. Ibid.
22. Phillip M. Bratta, "Flag Display Post-9/11: A Discourse on American Nationalism," *The Journal of American Culture* 32, 3 (2009), 239.
23. Michael Freeden, "Is Nationalism a Distinct Ideology?," 754.
24. Ibid.
25. Ibid.
26. Andrew J. Bacevish, *American Empire: The Realities and Consequences of U.S. Diplomacy* (Cambridge: Harvard University Press, 2002), 43.
27. Joanna Overing, "The Role of Myth: An Anthropological Perspective, or: 'The Reality of the Really Made-Up'," in *Myths and Nationhood*, ed. Geoffrey Hosking and George Schöplfin (New York: Routledge, 1997), 31.
28. William T. Cavanaugh, "Messianic Nation: A Christian Theological Critique of American Exceptionalism" *University of St. Thomas Law Journal* 3, 2 (2005), 261.
29. Ibid, 262.
30. Ibid.
31. Ibid.
32. Ibid.
33. Ibid.
34. Ibid.
35. Michael Sean Winters, *National Catholic Reporter*, https://www.ncronline.org/blogs/distinctly-catholic/happy-sort-fourth-july (accessed 9/10/19).
36. Ibid.
37. John Cooney, *The American Pope: The Life and Times of Francis Cardinal Spellman* (New York: Times Books, 1984), 154.
38. Shimron, Yonat. "Franklin Graham on impeachment: "Our country could begin to unravel." *Religion News Service*, October 2, 2019. Accessed October 3, 2019. https://religionnews.com/2019/10/02/franklin-graham-on-impeachment-our-country-could-begin-to-unravel/
39. Ibid.
40. Ibid.
41. William T. Cavanaugh, "Messianic Nation," 270.
42. Michael Billig, "Banal Nationalism," 189.

43. Ibid.
44. Ibid.
45. Ibid.
46. Michael Freeden, "Is Nationalism a Distinct Ideology?," 754.
47. Ibid.
48. Nidesh Lawtoo, *(New) Fascism*, Google Play Ebbok.
49. Philip Gorski, "Conservative Protestantism in the United States: Toward a Comparative Historical Perspective," in *Evangelicals and Democracy in America*, vol. 1, ed. Steven Brint and Jean Schroedel, (New York: Russell Sage, 2009), 91.
50. Andrew L. Whitehead, Samuel L. Perry, Joseph O. Baker, "Make America Christian Again: Christian Nationalism and Voting for Donald Trump in the 2016 Presidential Election," *Sociology of Religion: A Quarterly Review* 79, 2 (2018), 150.
51. Stephen Crites, "The Narrative Quality of Experience," *Journal of the American Academy of Religion* 39, 3 (1971), 295.
52. John Thompson, *Language and Symbolic Power*, trans. Gino Raymond and Matthew Anderson (Cambridge: Harvard University Press, 1991), 13.
53. Stephen Crites, "The Narrative Quality of Experience," 295.
54. Jeannine Fletcher Hill, *The Sin of White Supremacy: Christianity, Racism, & Religious Diversity in America* (Maryknoll: Orbis Books, 2017), Google Play Ebook.
55. David Swartz, *Culture and Power: The Sociology of Pierre Bourdieu* (Chicago: The University of Chicago Press, 1997), 84–85.
56. Quoted in Ibid, 85.
57. Ibid, 85–86.
58. Hill Fletcher, *The Sin of White Supremacy*, Ebook.
59. Swartz, *Culture and Power*, 87.
60. Hill Fletcher, *The Sin of White Supremacy*, Ebook.
61. Ibid.
62. Hill Fletcher, *The Sin of White Supremacy*, Ebook.
63. Carly M. Jacobs and Elizabeth Theiss-Morse, "Belonging in a 'Christian Nation': The Explicit and Implicit Associations between Religion and National Group Membership," *Politics and Religion* 6, 2 (2013), 373.
64. Ibid.
65. John Fea, "*Was America Founded as a Christian Nation?*" (Louisville: Westminster John Knox Press, 2011), Kindle.
66. Ibid.
67. Carly M. Jacobs and Elizabeth Theiss-Morse, "Belonging in a 'Christian Nation'," 374.
68. Ibid, 375.
69. Ibid.
70. Ibid.
71. Ibid.
72. John Sanders, *Theology of the Flesh: How Embodiment and Culture Shape the Way We Think about Truth, Morality, and God* (Minneapolis: Fortress Press, 2016), 31–32.
73. Carly M. Jacobs and Elizabeth Theiss-Morse, "Belonging in a 'Christian Nation'," 375.
74. Ibid, 376.
75. Ibid, 377.
76. Ibid.
77. Ibid, 394.
78. Ibid, 395.
79. Ibid.

Conclusion

Healing Our Embodied Idolatry

Christians in every era have believed, or at least have been taught to believe, that they should worship and adore God alone. God is the Christian's ultimate end. Anyone or anything else taking the place of God's will as the primary guide for one's Christian practice is the essence of idolatry. On a practical level, most Christians, whether they realize it or not, have a variety of idols. The temptations leading to this predicament are understandable. It is the nature of human life. Individuals are thrown into a mixture of social and cultural forces and influences beyond their control, needing the resources of others to help in their struggle to survive and grow. We can only build on what we are given.

As a species with little instinctual biological pregivens to direct our ontological identity needs, we are driven by the malleable forces of desire, shaped by the various models we are presented in our social landscape. If there is a biological instinct that has survived our coming to self-awareness, it is the neuronal wiring of our brains that causes us to mirror naturally (re-present) the gestures of others in our immediate vision. This neuronal mechanism also naturally/biologically influences us to mirror the motivations, dispositions, values, mores, and conventions we observe in these same models. As Lawtoo notes,

> the neurosciences have now confirmed the importance of mirroring reflexes in nonverbal forms of communication at the end of the twentieth century . . . the discovery of "mirror neurons" in the 1990s lends empirical support to [George] Bataille's . . . realization that subjects can respond unconsciously, that is, automatically, to (facial) gestures and expressions because the sight of such gestures triggers mirror neurons to fire, causing an unconscious reflex not

only to reproduce the gestures, but also to feel, by way of what used to be called *sym-pathy*, the *pathos* of the other within the ego. . . . [Thus, mimesis is] an affective formation of subjects.[1]

Within the various fields of our social lives we are presented strategies, rules, and motivations to help us attain greater levels of cultural, economic, and symbolic capital in order to flourish, as these are defined within our particular groups and communities. Underlying the explicit quest to succeed in these various fields is the pursuit, primarily unconscious, to fulfill our identity needs, that is, meaning, security, control, belonging/connectedness, recognition, and action. We learn to imitate models who offer the emotional and rational constructs that inform our needs satisfaction. This in turn shapes and develops *simulations* within our embodied emotional structures, so that we *structure*—using Bourdieu's concept—consistent hermeneutics informing our sense of meaning, security, control, belonging/connectedness, recognition, and action. At the heart of this formation is the relational dynamic that is the heart of being human. We come into being, are drawn into personhood, through relational interactions with others. Aspects of the other become, in profound ways, characteristics of myself. This reality about human nature is a mystery, a gift, and the clue to our most significant problems. It is a grace, in that we are drawn into life through these many relationships, and it plays a role in our "fall," our original sin. Because we are finite and embodied, we inherit a sense of separateness and alienation in our coming to full self-reflective consciousness without an abiding experience of fullness of being, a being immersed in the fountain fullness of divine love and acceptance. The moniker "fall" in this context is apropos because our primal experience, as Sebastian Moore notes, prior to self-awareness, is one of fullness. It is an experience of oneness, unity, and desirability. From this fullness we "fall" into an experience of lack as we come to an awareness that we are separate selves, no longer intimately connected to the oneness and unity of all creation, and no longer experiencing a fullness of desirability. Rather, we sense a lack of desirability, which leads us on a quest that in turn leads to a plethora of cul-de-sacs, ending in disappointment.

ORIGINAL SIN: SEBASTIAN MOORE

Original sin "is a distinctly Christian . . . one could argue . . . a distinctly Western Christian belief, based . . . largely on the writings and authority of Augustine."[2] A great deal of ink has been spilled over this doctrine, especially as to how it was originally formulated by Augustine, and later interpreted by theologians like Luther and Calvin, as well as hyper Augustinians in the mold of the seventeenth- and eighteenth-century French Jansenists. While I believe a number of formulations of this doctrine should be abandoned, I do not believe the doctrine as a whole should be tossed out. While Augustine may have misstepped in his understanding of certain aspects of original sin, I do believe his insight, that something is fundamentally distorted in human nature, holds merit.

There are two particular articulations of this doctrine I have found to be compelling, those of Sebastian Moore and Thomas Keating, both of whom were formed in the Benedictine spiritual tradition of *lectio divina, meditatio, and contemplatio* (sacred reading, meditation, and contemplation). Both men were also well read in theology and psychology. While both offer similar insights about original sin and the human condition, each has offered his own unique ways of approaching both the nature and consequences of original sin, as well as prescriptions for bringing about divine healing from its effects.

Humans have evolved as social creatures and are relational by nature. The relational quality of human nature means, for Moore, that we are drawn into personhood by the desire of an "other," an "other" who, in recognizing our desirability, draws us toward the other, toward intimacy, with the hope of union. "Desirable, I desire another and hope to be desired by the other."[3] When experiencing the desire of the other, we experience a sense of arousal. This corresponds with the hedonic principle discussed in chapter two. The pleasure of desirability motivates our move toward relationship/intimacy, giving shape to both intrinsic and instrumental desires.

Underlying Moore's analysis is his use of Freudian categories for the development of the individual, especially in the Oedipal stage. Unlike Freud, Moore does not limit the desire of the child for the mother to feelings of a sexual nature, which Moore felt was too constraining. Girard, in *Violence and the Sacred*, also saw this as problematic in Freud's theory. In the early months of a child's life, before there is an experience of a separate self, there is an unselfconscious experience of unity/oneness with creation. One of the great shocks in early life is the experience of separateness. Moore writes,

> [a]s that most alarming thing, 'conscious separate existence', really gets under way, the need for support becomes enormous. And not for a support of the crutches type that would *mitigate* the venturesomeness of individual reality, but for a total *encouragement* of it. The first powerful sense of self looks ecstatically to the mother for support in an incredible adventure.[4]

Moore notes that the child's complete reliance upon its mother as the means for a total sense of self is "a burden that no one can fully shoulder."[5] Because humans are finite, carrying their own individual sense of incompleteness, thus reliant upon an other/s for a fuller sense of self/being, the mother will not be able to act in a capacity that will offer a sense of fullness of being for her child. The attraction toward the mother is not exclusively, or even necessarily, sexual, though *eros* plays a role. The arousal in being desirable is erotic, a passionate desire not limited to crude sexual stimulation. Because the mother is the primary locus for the child's hopes for desire satisfaction, that is, the mother's recognition of the child's desirability—thus initiating the pull toward psychological personhood—the introduction of the father, who also claims desirability from the mother, is perceived and experienced as a threat to the child.

As an opaque awareness of a loss of unity and oneness with all creation has occurred through an experience of a developing separate self, desiring the paradisiacal experience of the womb compels the child to seek a sense of unity/oneness by means of another's desires. Experiencing disappointment in this quest, first with the intrusion of the father, Moore states that "[w]e might see in this moment, of ecstatic expectation directed to the mother and disappointed into the normal anxious existence of the human animal, *the* human moment, in which we can read all the tragedies and glories of humankind."[6]

Moore takes issue with the traditional articulations of the doctrine of original sin where once humanity sinned according to the Adam and Eve myth, God rejected them, dispelling them from paradise. This expulsion is interpreted as God no longer desiring the humans God has made; thus, they are *constitutionally* undesirable because of their sins. This congenital undesirability is transferred to each subsequent individual who inherits both the inclination to sin, as well as the punishment for the inheritance of this original sin. This punishment consists in the experience of undesirability and alienation from God. Analogically, we see in the experience of the child's coming to a sense of a separate self a sense of expulsion from a paradise of unity/oneness, and now subject to work by the sweat of the brow to find this sense of wholeness of self. It is this early life experience—a sense of rejection by the mother whose attention is drawn to an "other"—that Moore sees as our experience of original sin. He writes,

> [t]his first focus, in which self is all enmeshed with other, is influential over us without a rival. Why would anyone *think* of being him/herself other than the way they *first* came to consciousness? The world on which we first opened our eyes psychologically come to be *the* world. . . . The original habit (and yes, we can think of 'original sin' in this connection) of self-assessment-by-others undergoes a crucial complexification at the second-of-all-crisis, the Oedipal phase.[7]

This experience of rejection and sense of undesirability, or limitation of desirability, infects later beliefs about divine attitudes toward us. The craving for desirability, both by other humans and God, informs one's strategies and struggles to gain a deeper experience of desirability. Moore writes, "[t]he whole of history could be seen as the complex struggle between the original habit binding people into its limited ways, whence come conflicts of every kind, and the gentle pressure of the spirit in people seeking to break out and free them."[8] The original habit/sin consists in a misdirected search for fullness by means of finite objects. The mimetic nature of human consciousness compels us to imitate models we hope can bring us the fullness we crave.

Girard's understanding of original sin correlates with Moore's, in that Girard sees it as the negative use of mimesis. He states that, "[t]he original sin is the bad use of mimesis, and the mimetic mechanism is the actual consequence of this use at the collective level. . . . The mimetic mechanism produces a complex form of transcendence."[9] In archaic cultures this use of mimesis led to the development of rituals of sacrifice, placing blame for social instability, grounded in mimetic rivalry, on some innocent victim, the scapegoat. In order to obfuscate what is in reality a murder, the ancients divinized the victim in order to present the sacrifice as a sacred act, thus acquitting the murderers from charges of actual homicide. But with the revelation of Christ the myths legitimizing murder of innocent victims are revealed as lies, in turn revealing both the innocence of the victim, and the criminality of the culprits. Girard sees these archaic practices of sacrifice, using Durkheim's terminology, as "social transcendence." Girard defines this as

> the idolatrous transcendence from the point of view of the Judeo-Christian perspective. It is an illusory and idolatrous form of the sacred that, nonetheless, can protect the archaic community from greater and more disruptive forms of violence. It is what Paul says also regarding powers and principalities, meaning the secular powers of this world.[10]

Because Christ's revelation exposes the scapegoat mechanism for what it is, humanity can no longer legitimately claim innocence for acts of murder, expulsion, marginalization, and dehumanization. Yet, Christians in every era have fallen back into acts of sacred violence, justifying these acts as biblical, and thus divine. This, in Girard's words, is satanic. Satan, the great accuser is not actually a person, but an aspect of human practice that accuses those who are innocent for the ills and instability of social life. The valorization of nationalism, which is grounded in oppositions, distinction, and claims of difference that subject some to subaltern status, is essentially satanic. Ironically, all of this goes back to the simple reality that we have come to conscious self-awareness with a lost sense of our original desirability and that we therefore create victims.

It is our quest for fullness, an experience of total desirability, and the actual experienced lack of this desirability that distorts our recognition that only in the truly divine—as opposed to the *violent sacred*—is found this fullness. Thus, in our habitual search for fullness, we turn our wrath on those we believe impede our quest. From this arise thoughts and acts of vengeance. As I discuss below, in my examination of Thomas Keating's work, what and who inform our sense of transcendence is learned early and uncritically and can lead to a great deal of conflict and struggle.

Building on Moore's psychological approach to the doctrine of original sin, Neil Ormerod breaks down the tradition of this doctrine in the following formulation:

1. Adam sinned (however we may understand this). From the beginning of human history sin has been part of our condition.
2. Because of Adam's sin, we all suffer (however this suffering may be conceived). Sin has its consequences, not just for the one who sins but for all those around.

Because of this, Ormerod concludes:[11]

3. We are all the victims of Adam's sin.

This is a shift in focus regarding culpability. Ormerod writes, in this schema

> [t]he doctrine of original sin says that, prior to sinning, we are first and foremost sinned against. To be sinned against is to be a victim of another's sin. To be sinned against, especially in early childhood, is to enter into a condition of human brokenness, an interior shattering or distortion of consciousness that muddies our search for direction in the movement of life. To be sinned against in this way, to be thus broken, is the prior state that inclines us all to personal sins of our own.[12]

Being drawn into life and personhood through the desiring of an "other," who in recognizing our desirability makes us feel desirable, we subsequently feel a sense of victimhood when we perceive that our need to feel desirable is denied. The most tragic experience for individuals, especially those exposed to misguided articulations of the doctrine of original sin, either explicitly or implicitly, is that one not only feels undesirable to other humans, but more profoundly, on an existential level, is taught to believe that God rejects one's self due to sin, making one metaphysically undesirable. This is a terrible and tragic lie in Christian theological history. Having lost the original experience of unity and oneness, due to coming to a sense of a separate self, we strive somehow to recapture this initial unity and oneness, this initial experience of pleasure/feeling good. Moore summarizes this quest:

> All our desiring is an attempt of an original feeling-good, an original hedonic sense of myself, to extend itself, to realize itself over the wider field of interaction with others. All desiring is the attempt to realize the dream of myself, of a self-in-bliss which was my original condition in the physical, then the psychic, womb. All desiring is the attempt to be happy, the attempt of an original happiness to extend into the particulars of life.[13]

PROGRAMS FOR HAPPINESS: THOMAS KEATING

If we do not recognize that the need to feel desirable is at the heart of our human reality, we will never be able to get to the root of our motivations. We will not be able to grasp fully the fundamental force shaping our behavior. While others may attempt to enlighten us with their observations and evaluations of our behavior, we will, in many cases, simply miss their point because, as Moore notes, we must have some understanding of what they are talking about. And in order to do this we must have some knowledge about ourselves. Thus, "no emotional healing of me is possible unless I already have a good sense of myself for it to build on."[14] In understanding that one of our deepest motivations is being desirable, we can then, with Moore, acknowledge that it is "because I feel desirable that I like someone else in the first place."[15]

Because we experience rejection in the early stages of our lives—thus, our experience of undesirability—we begin to strategize how best to acquire the desire of another for ourselves. Underlying this quest is a false belief that we are lacking something substantial that would make us desirable. This false belief, increasing in strength over time, motivates our quest for an identity that helps us to feel good about ourselves, increasing our self-esteem. This is accomplished within the *fields* of our social relationships. Thomas Keating, in *Invitation to Love: The Way of Christian Contemplation*, states that

> [o]ur unconscious, prerational emotional programming from childhood and our overidentification with a specific group or groups are the sources from which our false self—our injured, compensatory sense of who we are—gradually emerges and stabilizes. The influence of the false self extends into every aspect and activity our lives, either consciously or unconsciously.[16]

Keating maintains that the quest to prop up our false self-images leads to the creation of programs we believe will bring us the happiness we truly desire. The heart of the spiritual journey for Keating is "toward a confrontation with our motivations and unconscious emotional programs and responses."[17]

Keating states that each person has three basic instinctual needs that require satisfaction. Each of these needs corresponds to the identity needs I have discussed above. Keating sees these needs as safety/security, affection/esteem (corresponding with the identity needs of belonging and recognition), and power/control.[18] The programs we construct to fulfill these needs are the result of the many relational influences we encounter in our daily lives. These programs begin to form early in life, thus becoming sedimented in the unconscious, informing our emotional responses to later conscious experiences. It is in observing our emotional responses, asking ourselves why we experience a particular emotion in a particular setting, that we can begin a deepening of self-knowledge. Keating writes, "[t]he emotions faithfully respond to what our value system is—not what we would like it to be, or what we think it is. Our emotions are perfect recorders of what is happening inside; hence they are the key to finding out what our emotional programs for happiness really are."[19] We can then recognize that "[w]henever an emotional program is frustrated, we immediately experience a spontaneous feeling reaction."[20]

Keating notes that in our personal development we grow through stages of consciousness, forming belief systems, especially in the early stages, which structure our worlds of meaning and value systems. This in turn informs our consciousness in later stages of development at an unconscious level. Two particular stages of development are relevant to this study. The first is the *mythic membership* level of consciousness. Developing between the ages of four and eight, this level of consciousness is "where possessions, competition, success, belonging to a group, and interiorizing the values of a structured society are the order of the day. The child at this age absorbs unquestioningly the values of parents, teachers, peers, and the predominant society in which he is being raised."[21] It is at this stage that the child will begin to incorporate, embody, the mythic narratives of her social and cultural milieu. For many children raised within a predominantly White Christian home and community, it is at this stage that narratives of White Christian supremacy, as well as experienced privileges of being White and/or Christian, will begin to be embodied, shaping value systems that will inform emotional programs. At the same time, many non-White, non-Christian children, experiencing narratives and actions denigrating, marginalizing, and excluding them due to the contingencies of birth, will also form programs for happiness in the light of these experiences. For a myriad of American (USA) children, the narratives of American exceptionalism and superiority will be embodied, again informing emotional programs.

At the mythic membership level, the child does not yet have the means for evaluative, critical rational discernment to determine the veracity of the various value systems presented as true and normative. The mimetic forces drawing the child to imitate those perceived as authoritative is unimpeded by critical rational thought. Add to this mixture the need to feel a sense of belonging, and one can understand how these value systems are easily absorbed into the unconscious emotional structures of the child. In order to belong, to gain recognition, greater esteem, a sense of security, and so forth, the child learns the rules of the field, shaping their dispositions and bodily hexis, which in turn, if mastered well enough, acquires greater cultural capital in the child's social landscape. While the game is learned and embodied in childhood, it informs the dispositions and strategies for success and happiness into adulthood. Although the stakes and the prizes may change, the learned dispositions—desire for belonging, recognition, need for security, control, and power—remain the same, unless something intervenes to change the misguided strategies and programs for happiness. A change in the programs will result in a change in one's meaning world. This is not an easy task. It requires a profound metanoia/conversion, a transformation of one's perceptions about the means and end for true happiness, bringing about a change in consciousness. This will in turn transform the individual's value system.

For many American Christian children, a set of hermeneutics fusing American values with gospel values influence their value systems. This mixture creates a type of dissonance, as the two value systems can be contradictory. From this dissonance arise legitimations and justifications that allow the Christian to elevate certain American values to a divine status. For example, in a Tweet published on September 12, 2019, regarding gun regulation issues arising from a plethora of mass killings in the United States, Sarah Huckabee-Sanders wrote the following: "Democrats say we have guns in America because of 'corruption'. No, we have guns in America because it's our God-given right enshrined in the Constitution."[22] Huckabee-Sanders, a daughter of an ordained Baptist minister, reflects the views of many US citizens, both Christian and non-Christian, elevating the US Constitution to the level of divine revelation, despite the fact that guns are nowhere to be found in the Bible. There is an inability to recognize a deeper call to nonviolence in the teachings of Jesus that overrides any "sacred" right to own a means of mass destruction. Examples of this kind could be reproduced *ad nauseum*. It is such mixing of ideological worldviews with the gospel message that leads to distortions of the message of Jesus, creating divisions, conflicts, acts of exclusion, marginalization, and violence, all under the guise of biblical authority. I maintain that these distortions violate the teachings of Jesus regarding hospitality and table fellowship, where such divisiveness is condemned.

Keating echoes Moore's recognition that with the development of a sense of a separate self comes a sense of separation from an original experience of unity, which instilled a desire to feel good. Keating notes that this sense of separation is more than just a separation of unity with ourselves and others, but also with the divine. He writes that "along with the emergence of full reflective self-consciousness and the sense of personal identity, there arose a growing sense of separation from God."[23] Keating maintains that if "humankind had enjoyed the awareness of divine union as the levels of consciousness unfolded, the emergence of full reflective self-consciousness would not have been experienced as threatening. But instead, the developing levels of consciousness brought a growing sense of alienation from God, oneself, others, and the cosmos."[24] In this we can repeat Ormerod's conclusion that this reality of separateness indicates the consequences of original sin that result in victimization. Keating also sees this dilemma as a consequence of original sin. Keating writes,

> [o]ur pathology is simply this: we have come to full reflective self-consciousness without the enjoyment of divine union—indeed, without any awareness of it at all. Because that crucial conviction, born of experience, is missing, our fragile egos seek every possible means to ward off the painful and at times agonizing sense of alienation from God and from everyone else . . . the poignant character of this sense of alienation from God is described by Augustine as the consequences of original sin.[25]

Keating refers to the next level of consciousness as *mental egoic* consciousness. It is at this level of consciousness that the individual moves beyond "the self-centered instinctual drives and gratifications"[26] developed in early pre-rational stages of development. At the mental egoic stage, the ideal is that the individual will "take responsibility for" him/herself, along with responding "to the needs of our families, our nations, and the human race, including generations yet to come."[27] But tragically, Keating observes, this *"level of consciousness is still not accessed by the vast majority of humankind"* (emphasis mine).[28] This is because "the human condition is still under sway of the false self with its emotional programs for happiness based on the primitive stages of consciousness."[29] While mental egoic consciousness arises at the age of reason, the individual has so embodied the value systems instilled at earlier stages of consciousness that even at the mental egoic stage the child finds it difficult to discern the veracity of these of values. Keating states that we find ourselves at this stage "unfree to reevaluate our enormous emotional and social investment in prerational attitudes. Thus we use our newfound intellectual powers to rationalize, justify, and even glorify our emotional programs and the false values of the culture."[30]

SOMETHING BIGGER THAN MYSELF

Many people have felt the desire to join clubs, associations, religious communities, charity organizations, political action groups, and so on, for the experience of being part of something bigger than themselves. This experience is a feeling of expansiveness, an expansiveness of being. Moore argues that in this exercise to expand one's being is the hope to increase one's sense of desirability, "my sense of myself as desirable."[31] One desires "to be fully actual."[32] It is this experience of full actuality that one "unknowingly"[33] seeks in being a part of a group. Belonging to something bigger than oneself therefore increases one's sense of desirability and the actualization of one's being. This, in terms of identity needs, increases one's sense of meaning, security, control, belonging, recognition, and action.

Whatever group we choose to affiliate with, we naturally, mimetically, inform our value systems, our likes and dislikes, what we believe to be good, true, and beautiful. Moore tells us that in our desiring anything, it is a desire for a "good" which we perceive as desirable, in "which is the dynamic of all being—of all human being certainly, and by a very acceptable metaphoric extension, of all being."[34] The problem is that we have no innate knowledge of what ultimate good, truth, and beauty consists. We must rely upon our models to offer us possible alternatives. Just as a child naturally imitates and learns the language of his/her parents and community, so also does the child imitate the ideologies dominant in his/her cultural milieu. If Whiteness and/ or Christian supremacy is the dominant cultural experience, there is little wonder that the child mimetically absorbs these cultural values into their emotional, embodied consciousness.

Nationalism, as discussed in chapter six, is a social and cultural reality in the modern world. Children are inculcated with national narratives that aggrandize the "good" qualities that structure the essence of the nation. These narratives are offered as "truths" about the nation, regardless of their partially mythic nature. The nation, in all its exceptional glory—its qualities of equality and liberty, its heroes willing to spill their blood for the glory of the nation and its continued existence—is "beautiful." The nation gives one a sense of being part of something bigger than oneself. Citizenship means that one is desired by the nation, resulting in a fuller sense of desirability. For many American Christians, God has chosen the United States as the promised land where He will build a city on a hill, a model for the world; an example of democracy, equality, liberty, and prosperity. Unfortunately, this dream is mixed with perfidious ideologies of exclusion, marginalization, bigotry, and violence. While this imaginative community offers an expansive sense of self which our hearts desire, it is, finally, an illusion, an empty promise, an idol. As such, it can only lead to division, conflict, and death. Fearful that an "other" will rob us of our birthright, *infinite desirability*, we are compelled to create borders, walls, detention camps, lists of undesirables. In the United States, this list includes non-White, non-Christian others, for many Christian nationalists.

HEALING THE IDOLATRY OF CHRISTIAN NATIONALISM

For many Christian spiritual masters, from the patristic age to contemporary teachers like Moore and Keating, the soteriological praxis of Jesus' ministry is that of healer. In Luke 9:1–2, Jesus sends his disciples out to heal the sick and free those bound by demonic forces. As contemporary disciples of Jesus, we too are called to such a healing ministry. One such disease needing healing in the modern world is the idolatry of nationalism. While the prescription for the disease of idolatry is straightforward, the actual medicinal regimen can be difficult and painful. It is analogous to chemotherapy. While the regimen is simple, the misery that accompanies it can feel like death. In a sense, it is a death—the death of the old man/woman. The end result, however, is a new creation, filled with joy, peace, and happiness.

The monastic tradition of *lectio, meditatio,* and *contemplatio* has a lot to offer as a medicinal regimen in our quest to free us from the sickness of idolatry. Deep, meditative reading of the Scriptures, especially the Gospels, can begin to open our hearts and minds to the love, compassion, mercy, forgiveness, and reconciliation of God—the one who desires us into being. Contemplation, in which we place ourselves before the infinite being and source of love, lets the loving, "therapeutic," presence of God heal our attachments that cause us to form practices of exclusion, bigotry, and oppression. Contemplative prayer calls us to a profound experience of divine love, an experience spiritual masters call mystical. Karl Rahner predicted that the Church could only survive as life-giving force in the world if Christians sought this profound mystical experience of transformation. He wrote, "the devout Christian of the future will either be a 'mystic,' one who has 'experienced' something, or he will cease to be anything at all."[35] This something is the presence of love, the love that desired us, and all of creation into being.

Keating offers an example of this method of prayer and reflection. In his insightful reflection on the beatitudes in Matthew 5, he sees each of the beatitudes as addressing the various instinctual drives/identity needs that compel our attitudes and behaviors. While I highly recommend Keating's whole text, here I offer three examples from his work.

In the second beatitude, Jesus says, *happy are those who mourn, for they will be comforted.* Keating sees this as speaking "to the exaggerated demand for affection/esteem and pleasure."[36] Because we become attached/addicted to things that give us a sense of affection/esteem/pleasure, we feel a great deal of tension when these are threatened to be taken away by another. If we have the fortitude to let them go, we initially feel a sense of loss, thus we mourn. By choosing to release an object we previously loved, "we experience freedom from what we formally depended upon excessively and we enter into a new relationship with it,"[37] one that does not expect that object to be our ultimate source of happiness.

The third beatitude, Jesus' claim for happiness for the meek, is interpreted by Keating as "addressing the drive for power."[38] In this beatitude, Jesus calls us to a freedom from overidentification with the need to control every situation, sometimes by means of strategic manipulations. This hyper need for control can lead to abuses of power, that result in acts of domination, even destruction.

Jesus' fourth beatitude promises happiness *for those who hunger and thirst for justice.* In this blessing, Keating sees Jesus addressing our "overidentification with our social group and frees us from the urgency to be accepted and approved by the group."[39] This does not mean that we simply totally reject our group. Rather, it is the recognition that there exist within the various groups with which we are affiliated ideologies that contravene the gospel imperative to love God and neighbor, leading to attitudes and practices that relegate some "other/s" to outsider status, unworthy of hospitality and table fellowship—attitudes and practices we must reject.

These are three excellent brief examples of a method of spiritual healing for our attachments and loyalties to what are in fact idols. Nationalism is such an idol. And because it has been highly valorized, ubiquitously present to our senses—flagged, as Billig says—and sold under the guise of patriotism, it is not only hard to dislodge, it is hard even to recognize as idolatrous. It has been embodied through a variety of narratives of American exceptionalism and White Christian supremacy ingested from childhood. It is experienced as a form of expansiveness of being, offering implicit, and sometimes explicit, promises of gaining greater desirability. And like the demon in Matthew 17:21, this demon/idol, as with many others, may take a good deal of prayer and fasting to dislodge. We are called to the freedom of the children of God, however, so that we may be manifestations of God's profound love, reconciliation, forgiveness, goodness, truth, and beauty in a world torn apart by a satanic need for dominance, control, marginalization, exclusion, and death. We are called to conform ourselves to the image of Christ, who is the perfect manifestation of the *imago Dei* in human form. Our habitus must be re-formed in this image, through the imitation of Christ's hospitality and table fellowship. In Christ are our identity needs truly fulfilled, shaping life giving desires, both intrinsic and instrumental. This in turn will reshape, re-form, our Christian practice.

NOTES

1. Nidesh Lawtoo, *(New) Fascism*, Google Play Ebook.
2. Neil Ormerod, *Creation, Grace, and Redemption* (Maryknoll: Orbis Books, 2007), 68.
3. Sebastion Moore, *Let This Mind Be in You: The Quest for Identity Through Oedipus to Christ* (Minneapolis: Winston Press, 1985), 46.
4. Ibid, 71.
5. Ibid.
6. Ibid.
7. Ibid, 72.
8. Ibid, 75.
9. René Girard, Pierpaolo Antonello, and João Cezar de Castro Rocha, *Evolution and Conversion: Dialogues on the Origins of Culture* (New York: Bloomsbury, 2007), Google Play Ebook.
10. Ibid. Ebook.
11. Neil Ormerod, *Creation, Grace, and Redemption*, 79.
12. Ibid.
13. Sebastion Moore, *Let This Mind Be in You*, 15.

14. Ibid, 14.
15. Ibid.
16. Thomas Keating, *Invitation to Love: The Way of Christian Contemplation*, 20th Anniversary Edition (New York: Bloomsbury, 2012), 3.
17. Ibid, 6.
18. Ibid, 36.
19. Ibid, 26–27.
20. Ibid, 27.
21. Ibid, 35.
22. https://twitter.com/SarahHuckabee/status/1172319208824168455 (accessed 9–22–19).
23. Thomas Keating, *Invitation to Love*, 35.
24. Ibid.
25. Ibid.
26. Ibid.
27. Ibid.
28. Ibid.
29. Ibid.
30. Ibid, 48.
31. Sebastion Moore, *Let This Mind Be in You*, 8.
32. Ibid.
33. Ibid.
34. Ibid, 26.
35. Karl Rahner, *Theological Investigations: Volume VII* (New York: Seabury, 1971), 15.
36. Thomas Keating, *Invitation to Love*, 123.
37. Ibid.
38. Ibid.
39. Ibid, 124–125.

Bibliography

Althusser, Louis. 1969. *For Marx.* New York: Verso.
Anderson, Benedict. 200. *Imagined Communities: Reflections on the Origin and Spread of Nationalism.* Revised Edition. London: Verso.
Augustine. 1910. *The Soliloquies of St. Augustine.* Translated by Rose Elizabeth Cleveland. Boston: Little, Brown, and Company.
Bacevish, Andrew J. 2002. *American Empire: The Realities and Consequences of U.S. Diplomacy.* Cambridge: Harvard University Press.
Barrett, Lisa Feldman. 2017. *How Emotions Are Made: The Secret Life of the Brain.* New York: Houghton Mifflin Harcourt.
Bar-Tal, Daniel. 2000. *Beliefs in Society: Social Psychological Analysis.* Thousand Oaks: Sage.
Berger, Peter and Thomas Luckmann. 1966. *The Social Construction of Reality: A Treatise in the Sociology of Knowledge.* New York: Penguin Books.
Billig, Michael. 2005. "Banal Nationalism." In *Nations and Nationalism: A Reader*, edited by Philip Spencer and Howard Wollman. New Brunswick: Rutgers University Press.
Borg, Marcus. 1984, 1998. *Conflict, Holiness, and Politics in the Teachings of Jesus.* New York: Continuum.
Bourdieu, Pierre and Loic Wacquant. 1992. *An Invitation to Reflexive Sociology.* Chicago: University of Chicago Press.
Bourdieu, Pierre. 1990. *In Other Words.* Stanford: Stanford University Press.
———. 1977. *Outline of a Theory of Practice.* Cambridge: Cambridge University Press.
———. 1990. *The Logic of Practice.* Stanford: Stanford University Press.
Bratta, Phillip M. 2009. "Flag Display Post-9/11: A Discourse on American Nationalism." *The Journal of American Culture* 32 (3): 232–243.
Calhoun, Craig. 1993. "Habitus, Field, and Capital: The Question of Historical Specificity." In *Bourdieu: Critical Perspective*, edited by Edward LiPuma, and Moishe Postone Craig Calhoun. Cambridge: Polity Press.
Carter, Warren. 2001. *Matthew and Empire: Initial Explorations.* Harrisburg: Trinity Press International.
Casey, Maurice. 2010. *Jesus of Nazareth: An Independent Historian's Account of His Life and Teaching.* New York: T & T Clark.
Cavanaugh, William T. 2005. "Messianic Nation: A Christian Theological Critique of American Exceptionalism." *University of St. Thomas Law Journal* 3 (2): 261–280.
———. 2011. *Migrations of the Holy: God, State, and the Political Meaning of the State.* Grand Rapids: Eerdmans.
Clark, Mary. 1990. "Meaningful Social Bonding as a Universal Human Need." In *Conflict: Human Needs Theory*, edited by John W. Burton. New York: Palgrave Macmillan.

Clore, Gerald L., and Karen Gaspar. 2000. "Feeling Is Believing: Some affective." In *Emotions and Beliefs: How Feelings Influence Thoughts*, edited by Antony S.R. Manstead, and Sacha Bem Nico H. Frijda. Cambridge: Cambridge University Press.
Coakley, John. 2012. *Nationalism, Ethnicity and the State: Making and Breaking Nations*. Los Angeles: Sage.
Colborne, Nathan. 2013. "Violence and Resistance: Towards a Politics without a Scapegoat." *Toronto Journal of Theology* 29 (1): 111–124.
Constantineanu, Corneliu. 2018. "Hospitality and Welcome as Christian Imperatives." *Transformation* 335 (2): 109–116.
Cooney, John. 1984. *The American Pope: The Life and Times of Francis Cardinal Spellman*. New York: Times Books.
Cregan, Kate. 2006. *The Sociology of the Body: Mapping the Abstraction of Embodiment*. London: SAGE.
Crites, Stephen. 1971. "The Narrative Quality of Experience." *Journal of the American Academy of Religion* 39 (3): 291–311.
Csordas, Thomas J. 1990. "Embodiment as a Paradigm for Anthropology." *Ethos* 18 (1): 5–47.
Davis, Wayne A. 1984. "The Two Senses of Desire." *Philosophical Studies: An International Journal for Philosophy in the Analytic Tradition* 45 (2): 181–195.
De Tavernier, Johan. 2014. "Personalism and the Natural Roots of Morality." In *Questioning the Human: Toward a Theological Anthropology for the Twenty-First Century*, edited by Yves De Maeseneer, and Ellen Van Stichel Lieve Boeve. New York: Fordham University Press.
Decker, James M. 2004. *Ideology*. New York: Palgrave Macmillan.
Eagleton, Terry. 1991. *Ideology: An Introduction*. London: Verso.
Esler, Philip F. 2000. "Jesus and the Reduction of Intergroup Conflict: The Parable of the Good Samaritan in the Light of Social Identity Theory." *Biblical Interpretation* 8 (4).
Esler, Philip F. 2017. *The Mediterranean Context of Early Christianity*. Vol. 1, in *The Early Christian World*, edited by Philip F. Esler, 3–25. New York: Routledge.
———. 2011. *Was America Founded as a Christian Nation?* Louisville: Westminster John Knox Press.
Fletcher, Jeannine Hill. 2017. *The Sin of White Supremacy: Christianity, Racism, & Religious Diversity in America*. Maryknoll: Orbis Books.
Freeden, Michael. 2004. "Ideology, Political Theory and Political Philosophy." In *Handbook of Political Theory*, edited by Gerald F. Gaus and Chandran Kukathas. London: Sage.
———. 2003. *Ideology: A Very Short Introduction*. New York: Oxford University Press.
Freeden, Michael. 1998. "Is Nationalism a Distinct Ideology?" *Political Studies* 46 (4): 748–765. Freyne, Seán. 2004. *Jesus, a Jewish Galilean: A New Reading of the Jesus Story*. New York: T&T Clark.
Gabriel, Markus. 2017. *I am Not a Brain: Philosophy of Mind for the 21st Century*. Cambridge: Polity Press.
Gagey, Henri-Jérôme. 2014. "The Concept of Natural Law in the Postmodern Context." In *Questioning the Human: Toward a Theological Anthropology for the Twenty-First Century*, edited by Yves De Maeseneer, and Ellen Van Stichel Lieven Boeve. New York: Fordham University Press.
Geertz, Clifford. 1976. "'From the Native's Point of View': On the Native of Anthropological Understanding." In *Meaning and Anthropology*, edited by Keith H. Basso and Henry A. Selby. Albuquerque: New Mexico University Press.
Girard, René. 1965. *Deceit, Desire, and the Novel: Self and Other in Literary Structure*. Baltimore: The Johns Hopkins University Press.
———. 1996. *The Girard Reader*. Edited by James G. Williams. New York: The Crossword Publishing Co.
Girard, René, Pierpaolo Antonello, and João Cezar de Castro Rocha. 2007. *Evolution and Conversion: Dialogues on the Origins of Culture*. New York: Bloomsbury.
Goldenberg, Robert. 2007. *The Origins of Judaism: From Canaan to the Rise of Islam*. Cambridge: Cambridge University Press.

Gorski, Philip. 2009. *Conservative Protestantism in the United States: Toward a Comparative Historical Perspective.* Vol. 1, in *Evangelicals and Democracy in America,* edited by Steven Brint and Jean Schroedel. New York: Russell Sage.

Gramsci, Antonio. 2000. *The Gramsci Reader: Selected Writings, 1916–1935.* Edited by David Forgacs. New York: New York University Press.

Hagner, Donald A. 2012. *The New Testament: A Historical and Theological Introduction.* Grand Rapids: Baker Academic.

Haidt, Jonathan. 2012. *The Righteous Mind: Why Good People Are Divided by Politics and Religion.* New York: Pantheon Books.

Hamerton-Kelly, Robert. 2008. "A Theory of Religion and Violence." *Paper Presented to the UCLA Dept. of History.* Accessed May 8, 2010. http://www.hamerton-kelly.com/talks/Theory_of_Religion_and_Violence.html.

Hawkes, David. 1996. *Ideology.* Second Edition. New York: Routledge.

Hefner, Philip. 1993. *The Human Factor: Evolution, Culture, and Religion.* Minneapolis: Fortress Press.

Hilgers, Mathieu. 2009. "Habitus, Freedom, and Reflexivity." *Theory & Practice* 19 (6): 728-755.

Hultgren, Arland J. 2017. "Enlarging the Neighborhood: The Parable of the Good Samaritan." *Word and Worship* 37 (1): 71–78.

Inbody, Tyron. 2005. *The Faith of the Christian Church: An Introduction to Theology.* Grand Rapids: Wm. B. Eerdmans.

Ingham, Mary Beth. 2017. *Understanding John Duns Scotus: 'Of Reality the Rarest-Veined Unraveller'.* St. Bonaventure: Franciscan Institute Press.

Jacobs, Carly M. and Elizabeth Theiss-Morse. 2013. "Belonging in a 'Christian Nation': The Explicit and Implicit Associations between Religion and National Group Membership." *Politics and Religion* 6 (2): 373–401.

Janzen, Waldemar. 2002. "Biblical theology of hospitality." *Vision: A Journal for Church and Theology* 3 (1): 4–15.

Kassab, Hanna Samir. 2016. *The Power of Emotion in Politics, Philosophy, and Ideology.* New York: Palgrave Macmillan.

Keating, Thomas. 2012. *Invitation to Love: The Way of Christian Contemplation.* 20th Anniversary Edition. New York: Bloomsbury.

Kirwan, Michael. 2005. *Discovering Girard.* Lanham: Rowman & Littlefield.

Koyzis, David T. 2003. *Political Visions and Illusions: A Survey and Christian Critique of Contemporary Ideologies.* Downers Grove: InterVarsity Press.

Lawtoo, Nidesh. 2019. *(New) Fascism: Contagion, Community, Myth.* East Lansing: Princeton University Press.

Lechte, John. 2008. *Contemporary Thinkers: From Structuralism to Post-Humanism.* 2nd Edition. New York: Routledge.

Lints, Richard. 2015. *Identity and Idolatry: The Image of God and its inversion.* Downers Grove: InterVarsity Press.

Lossky, Vladimir. 1974. *In the Image and Likeness of God.* New York: St. Vladimir's Seminary Press.

MacKenzie, Ian. 2003. "The Idea of Ideology." In *Political Ideologies: An Introduction,* edited by Alan Finleyson, Vincent Geoghegan, Michael Kenny, Moya Lloyd, Iain MacKenzie, and Rick Walford Robert Eccleshall. New York: Routledge.

Mackie, Diane M. and Crystal L. Wright. n.d. "Social Influence in an Intergroup Context." In *Blackwell Handbook of Social Psychology: Intergroup Processes,* edited by Rupert Brown and Samuel L. Gaertner. Oxford: Blackwell Publishers.

MacLellan, David. 1996. *Ideology.* Reprint Edition. Ballmoor: Open University Press.

Malina, Bruce. 1996. *The Social World of Jesus and the Gospels.* New York: Routledge.

Maslow, Abraham. 1954. *Motivation and Personality.* New York: Harper and Row.

Maton, Karl. 2008. "Habitus." In *Pierre Bourdieu: Key Concepts,* edited by Michael Grenfell. Durham: Acumen Publishing Limited.

Matsumoto, David and Jessie Wilson. 2008. "Culture, Emotion, and Motivation." In *Handbook of Motivation and Cognition Across Cultures*, edited by Richard Sorrentino and Susumu Yamaguchi. Cambridge: Academic Press.

May, Gerald G. 1988. *Addictions and Grace: Love and Spirituality in the Healing of Addictions*. New York: HarperCollins.

Merleau-Ponty, Maurice. 1962. *Phenomenology of Perception*. London: Routledge and Kegan Paul.

Miller, David. 1977, Reprinted 1995. *On Nationality*. New York: Oxford University Press.

Moore, Sebastian. 1985. *Let This Mind Be in You: The Quest for Identity Through Oedipus and Christ*. Minneapolis: Winston Press.

Navone, John SJ. 2004. "Divine and Human Hospitality." *New Blackfriars* 85 (997): 329–340.

Neusner, Jacob. 1975. "The Idea of Purity in Ancient Judaism." *Journal of the American Academy of Religion* 43 (1): 15–26.

Newman, John Henry. 1891. *The Idea of a University*. London: Longmans, Green, and Company.

Nowak, Andrzej, Robin R. Vallacher, and Mandy E. Miller. 2003. Social Influence and Group Dynamics. Vol. 5, in *Handbook of Psychology: Personality and Social Psychology*, edited by Theodore Millon and Melvin J. Lerner. Hoboken: John Wiley and Sons.

Nudler, Oscar. 1990. "On Conflicts and Metaphors: Toward an Extended Rationality." In *Conflict: Human Needs Theory*, edited by John Burton. London: Palgrave Macmillan.

Ormerod, Neil. 2007. *Creation, Grace, and Redemption*. Maryknoll: Orbis Books.

Osborne, Kenan OFM. 2009. *A Theology of the Church for the Third Millennium*. Leiden: Brill.

Ostrow, James M. 1981. "Review: Culture as a Fundamental Dimension of Experience: A Discussion of Pierre Bourdieu's Theory of Human Habitus." *Human Studies* 4 (3): 279–297.

Oughourlian, Jean-Michel. 2010. *The Genesis of Desire*. East Lansing: Michigan State University Press.

———. 2016. *The Mimetic Brain*. East Lansing: Michigan State University.

Overing, Joanna. 1997. "The Role of Myth: An Anthropological Perspective, or: 'The Reality of the Really Made-Up'." In *Myths and Nationhood*, edited by Geoffrey Hosking and George Schöplfin. New York: Routledge.

Plessner, Helmuth. 2015. "The Conception of Ideology and Its Vicissitudes." In *Knowledge and Politics: The Sociology of Knowledge Dispute*, edited by Volker Meja and Nico Stehr. New York: Routledge.

Polotsky, Matthew. 2006. *Mimesis*. New York: Routledge.

Powell, Mark Allen. 2013. "Table Fellowship." In *Dictionary of Jesus and the Gospels: Compendium of Contemporary Biblical Scholarship*, edited by Joel B. Green. Downers Grove: IVP Academic.

Prendiville, John G. SJ. 1972. "The Development of the Idea of Habit in the Thought of Saint Augustine." *Traditio* 28: 29–99.

Radcliffe, Elizabeth S. 2008. "The Humean Theory of Motivation and Its Critics." In *A Companion to Hume*, edited by Elizabeth S. Radcliffe. Oxford: Blackwell Publishing.

Rahner, Karl. 1971. *Theological Investigations: Volume VII*. New York: Seabury.

———. 1991. *Theological Investigations: Volume XX*. New York: Crossroad.

Redekop, Vern Neufeld. 2002. *From Violence to Blessing: How an Understanding of Deep-Rooted Conflict Can Open Paths to Reconciliation*. Ottawa: Novalis.

Sanders, John. 2016. *Theology of the Flesh: How Embodiment and Culture Shape the Way We Think about Truth, Morality, and God*. Minneapolis: Fortress Press.

Saracino, Michele. 2015. *Christian Anthropology: An Introduction to the Human Person*. New York: Paulist Press.

Schnelle, Udo. 2009. *Theology of the New Testament*. Grand Rapids: Baker Academic.

Schroeder, Tim. 2017. *Desire*. Summer Edition. Accessed August 8, 2018. https://plato.stanford.edu/archives/sum2017/entries/desire/.

Sinhababu, Neil. 2017. *Humean Nature: How Desire Explains Action, Thought, and Feeling*. Oxford: Oxford University Press.

Sites, Paul. 1990. "Needs Analogues of Emotions." In *Conflict: Human Needs Theory*, edited by John Barton. Palgrave Macmillan.

Spencer, Philip and Howard Wollman. 2002. *Nationalism: A Critical Introduction.* Thousand Oaks: Sage.
Swartz, David. 1997. *Culture and Power: The Sociology of Pierre Bourdieu.* Chicago: University of Chicago Press.
Sweetman, Paul. 2003. "Twenty-first century dis-ease? Habitual reflexivity or the reflexive habitus." *Sociological Review* 51 (4): 528–549.
Taylor, Charles. 1994. "The Politics of Recognition." In *Multiculturalism: Examining the Politics of Recognition*, edited by Amy Gutman. Princeton: Princeton University Press.
Thomas, Scott M. 2014. "Culture, Religion and Violence: René Girard's Mimetic Theory." *Millennium: Journal of International Studies* 43 (1): 308–327.
Thompson, John E. 1984. *Studies in the Theories of Ideology.* Berkeley: University of California Press.
Thompson, John. 1991. *Language and Symbolic Power.* Translated by Gino Raymond and Matthew Anderson. Cambridge: Harvard University Press.
Triandis, Harry C. and David Trafinow. 2003. "Culture and Its Implications for Intergroup Behavior." In *Blackwell Handbook of Social Psychology: Intergroup Processes*, edited by Rupert Brown and Samuel L. Gaertner. Oxford: Blackwell Publishers.
Verdery, Katherine. 1993. "Whither 'Nation' and 'Nationalism'?" *Daedalus* 122 (3): 37–46.
Wharff, Jonah. 2007. "Bernard of Clairvaux and René Girard on Desire and Envy." *Cistercian Studies Quarterly* 42 (2): 183–210.
Whitehead, Andrew L., Samuel L. Perry, and Joseph O. Baker. 2018. "Make America Christian Again: Christian Nationalism and Voting for Donald Trump in the 2016 Presidential Election." *Sociology of Religion: A Quarterly Review* 79 (2): 147–171.
Wierzbicka, Anna. 2001. *What Did Jesus Mean: Explaining the Sermon on the Mount and the Parables in Simple and Universal Human Concepts.* Oxford: Oxford University Press.
Wieviorka, Michel. 2003. "An Old Theme Revisited: Sociology and Ideology." In *Sociology and Ideology*, edited by Eliezer Ben-Rafael. London: Brill.
Williams, Rowan. 2018. *Being Human: Bodies, Mind, Persons.* London: SPCK.
Winters, Michael Sean. 2016. "Happy (sort of) Fourth of July!" *National Catholic Reporter.* July 1. Accessed September 10, 2019. https://www.ncronline.org/blogs/distinctly-catholic/happy-sort-fourth-july.
Zampaglione, Geraldo. 2001. *The Idea of Peace in Antiquity.* Notre Dame: University of Notre Dame Press.

Index

Althusser, Louis, 77
appetitive, intrinsic, and instrumental desires, 41
Augustine, St., 6, 26–27, 29

Bacevich, Andrew J., 124
Bacon, Francis, 74
Barrett, Lisa Feldman, 32; emotional concept, 34; instance of emotion, 34; simulation, 33
Bar-Tal, Daniel, 79, 86, 87
Bataille, George, 128
beliefs and group influence, 86
Berger, Peter and Thomas Luckmann, 11–13
Billig, Michael, 122, 127, 151
Bourdieu, Pierre: cultural capital, 24–25; dispositions, 20–21; durable dispositions, 20; field, 21; habitus, description, 16–19; hexis, 20, 31, 58, 130; power, 24; practice, 23; socially informed body, 17; structure, 21; structuring, 21; symbolic capital, 69, 131
Bratta, Phillip M., 123

Calhoun, Craig, 24
Casey, Maurice, 102
Cavanaugh, William T., 119; exceptionalism, 125; nationalism as idolatrous, 125–126

Cervantes, Miguel, 61
Clore, Gerald and Karen Gaspar, 35; affective feelings, 35; attention hypothesis, 39; emotion categorization, 38; emotional concept, 34; feeling as evidence hypothesis, 37; moods, 36
Coakley, Paul, 119–120
Colborne, Nathan, 69
Constantineanu, Corneliu, 112–113
Cooney, John, 126
Cregan, Kate, 19; bodily hexis, 20–21
Crites, Stephen, 130

Dacatur, Stephen, 126
Damasio, Antonio and Vittorio Gallese, 59
Davis, Wayne, 41
De Tavernier, Johan, 46
Dei Verbum, 94
Delanty, Gerard and Patrick O'Mahony, 122
desire—appetitive, intrinsic, instrumental, 41
desire-belief theory of action, 42
Destutt de Tracy, Antoine, 73
dualism, 15
Duns Scotus, John, 26; *haecceity*, 25–26

Eagleton, Terry, 83; ideology and epistemology, 84
embodiment, 11
Esler, Philip F., 100, 102, 106

Falwell, Jr., Jerry, 126
Feldman Barrett, Lisa, 32–34
Ford, Christine, 87
free will, 25
Freeden, Michael: five components of nationalism, 121–122; ideology, 75, 78
Freyne, Seán, 106, 107

Gabriel, Markus, 51n60; neurocentrism, 46
Gagey, Henri-Jérôme, 46–47
Geertz, Clifford: individualism, 96
Girard, René: desire as triangular, 62; Don Quixote, 62; exterior and interior mimesis, 61; metaphysical desire, 67; mimetic desire, 60; mimetic doubles, 67; mimetic rivalry, 63, 68; original sin, 143; scapegoat mechanism, 68; surrogate victim, 69
Goldenberg, Robert, 110–111
Gorski, Philip, 128
Graham, Franklin, 126
Gramsci, Antonio: hegemony, 77; intellectuals, 78–79
groupthink, 89

Hagner, Donald A., 98
Haidt, Jonathan, 31
Hamerton-Kelly, Robert, 61
Hart, David Bentley, 5–6
Hawkes, David, 74
healing the idolatry of Christian nationalism, 149
Hefner, Philip, 48
Herod Antipas, 105–106
Hilgers, Mathieu: habitus, 25
Hill Fletcher, Jeannine, 77; white Christian supremacy, 131–134
Huckabee, Mike, 134
Huckabee-Sanders, Sarah, 134, 147
Hultgren, Arland J., 104
Humean Theory of Motivation, 41

identity needs: action, 58; connectedness, 57; control, 56; meaning, 53; recognition, 57; security, 57
ideology and power, 82
idolatry: definition, 5
imago Dei, 6, 46
Inbody, Tyron, 94–95

Ingham, Mary Beth, 26

Jacobs, Carly M. and Elizabeth Theiss-Morse, 134–136
James, William, 54
Janzen, Waldemar, 110
Jeffress, Robert, 126
Jesus: beatitudes, 105; the good Samaritan, 99; hospitality, 109; the kingdom of God, 98; sermon on the mount, 105; table fellowship, 110; tax collectors, 111

Kassab, Hanna Samir: ideology and emotions, 78
Kavanaugh, Brett, 87
Keating, Thomas: beatitudes, 150; church's mission, 8; instinctual needs, 145; kingdom of God; programs for happiness, 145; stages of consciousness, 146
Kirwan, Michael, 62
Koyzis, David: ideology and idolatry, 85–86

lack and ontological needs, 47
Lawtoo, Nidesh, 60, 128, 139–140
Le Bon, Gustave, 128
Lechte, John, 24
Lints, Richard, 6
Locke, John, 13
Lossky, Vladimir, 26
Lumen Gentium, 8

Mackie, Diane M. and Crystal L. Wright, 90
making emotions, 32
Malina, Bruce, 96, 97
Mannheim, Karl: ideology, 80
Marx, Karl: *camera obscura*, 75; false consciousness, 75; ideology, 75
Maslow, Abraham, 54–55
Maton, Karl, 21
Matsumoto, David and Jessie Wilson, 87–88
May, Gerald, 27
Meltzoff, Andrew, 60–61
Merleau-Ponty, Maurice, 15–16

Index

Miller, David, 117; elements of nationalism, 120
mirror neurons, 59, 139–140
moods, emotional feelings and beliefs, 35
Moore, Sebastian, 32, 66; desirability, 140; oedipal stage, 141; original sin, 140

Napoleon, 74
narrative and memory, 130
nationalism: American identity, 131; definition, 120, 121; exceptionalism, 118; idolatrous, 119
Navone, John, 109
Neusner, Jacob, 110
Newman, John Henry, 13
Nietzsche, Friedrich, 81–82, 84
Nowak, Andrzej Robin R. Vallacher, and Mandy E. Miller, 88–89
Nudler, Oscar, 53–54; metaphor dialogues, 56

Ormerod, Neil, 144
Osborne, Kenan, 8
Ostrow, James M., 17, 37
Oughourlian, Jean-Michel, 59–60, 63–64
Overing, Joanna, 124

Pharisees, 111, 112
Plessner, Helmuth, 80–81
Polotsky, Matthew, 60
Powell, Mark Allen, 111–112
Prendiville, John, 27
purity, impurity, and table fellowship, 110

Rahner, Karl, 107, 150
Redekop, Vern Neufeld, 58
revelation, 85, 94
Rizzolatti, Giacomo and Corrado Sinigaglia: mirror neurons, 60
Rosch, Eleanor and Carolyn B. Mervis, 135

Samaritans, 100–103
Saracino, Michele, 47
Schnelle, Udo, 98–99
Schroeder, Timothy: intrinsic desire, 42
Shimron, Yonat, 126
Sinhababu, Neil: the attentional aspect, 43–44; amplification aspect, 44–45; desire-belief theory of reasoning, 45; the hedonic aspect, 43; instrumental desire, 42; the motivation aspect, 42–43
Sites, Paul, 54
social psychology of white Christian supremacy, 134
something bigger than myself, 148
Spellman, Francis Cardinal, 126
Spencer, Philip and Howard Wollman, 119
Swartz, David: habitus, 25; symbolic capital, 131
Sweetman, Paul, 20

Talfel, Henri, 87
Tarde, Gabriel, 128
Taylor, Charles, 57; the imago Dei and morality, 46; the social and cultural world of Jesus, 96
Thomas, Scott M., 70
Thompson, John B.: ideology and power, 82–83
Triandis, Harry C. and David Trafinow, 89
Trump, Donald, 40, 126, 128

Verdery, Katherine, 120–121, 123

Watts, Craig M., 130
Wharff, Jonah, 48–49
Whitehead, Andrew L., Samuel L. Perry, and Joseph O. Baker, 128–129
Wierzbicka, Anna, 107–108
Williams, Rowan, 26, 49

Zampaglione, Geraldo, Witherspoon, John, 105

About the Author

Kyle Edward Haden, OFM, a Catholic Franciscan priest, holds a Ph.D. in Historical Theology/History of Christianity from Fordham University. Currently, he is an assistant professor of Theology and Franciscan Studies at St. Bonaventure University.

www.ingramcontent.com/pod-product-compliance
Lightning Source LLC
Chambersburg PA
CBHW050908300426
44111CB00010B/1433